Praise for

Women Confidential

"Moses . . . speaks her mind and doesn't sugarcoat the truth. And it's that same honesty, brutal or otherwise, that comes through in her new book. . . . *Women Confidential* doesn't hold back, but it also doesn't slide into a gossipy bitch fest about how women have been wronged. While the book is targeted for women in midlife, younger women, those in earlier stages of family and work lives, will find solid advice from women who have been there, done that."

—*Calgary Herald*

"Fascinating. . . . Avoiding one-size-fits-all solutions to complex issues, Dr. Moses brings together the experiences of over one thousand incredibly diverse women. . . . The cumulative effect is enormously reassuring and empowering, providing a road map for future choices based on welcome advice from a host of friends."

—*Flare.com*

"This is a thoughtful look at the needs of midlife women at work, which will be of direct interest to all women, and many men as well."

—*execuBooks.com*

"Sharing advice and experiences from real women, Dr. Moses, has compiled a guide on how to be successful and happy at work, at home and in your relationships. . . . This inspiring guide is a well organized, easy read."

—*Metro News*

"Mythbusting at midlife. . . . Work-life expert [Moses] gets hundreds of Boomer women to share the 'awful bitchy truth.'"

—*Ottawa Sun*

Author bio

Barbara Moses, PhD, is a sought-after media commentator on career management. Dr. Moses appears frequently on network and local TV and radio, and is the author of *What Next?: The Complete Guide to Taking Control of Your Working Life*; *The Good News About Careers*; and *Career Intelligence*. She is a columnist for the *Globe and Mail* and is a featured expert on various Web sites. Dr. Moses lives in Toronto. She can be found online at www.bbmcareerdev.com.

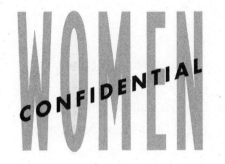

Also by Barbara Moses, PhD:

What Next?: The Complete Guide to Taking Control of Your Working Life
The Good News About Careers
Career Intelligence

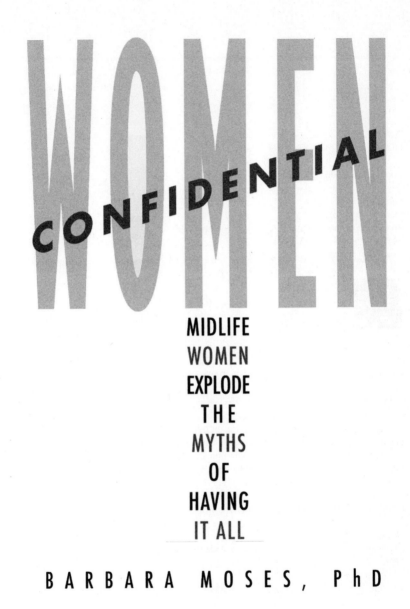

WOMEN CONFIDENTIAL

MIDLIFE
WOMEN
EXPLODE
THE
MYTHS
OF
HAVING
IT ALL

BARBARA MOSES, PhD

Marlowe & Company
New York

WOMEN CONFIDENTIAL:
Midlife Women Explode the Myths of Having It All

Copyright © 2006 by Barbara Moses, PhD

Published by
Marlowe & Company
An Imprint of Avalon Publishing Group, Incorporated
245 W. 17th Street, 11th Floor
New York, NY 10011–5300

AVALON
publishing group incorporated

Published as *DISH: Midlife Women Tell the Truth about Work, Relationships, and the Rest of Life*
by arrangement with McClelland & Stewart Ltd., Toronto, Ontario, Canada.

Library of Congress Cataloging-in-Publication Data

Moses, Barbara.
  Women Confidential: midlife women explode the myths of having it all
/ Barbara Moses
    p. cm.
1. Midle-aged women. 2. Middle-aged women--Psychology. I.Title. HQ1059.4.M677 2006
305.244'2--dc22
                              2006012055

ISBN-10: 1-56924-270-4
ISBN-13: 978-1-56924-270-4

9 8 7 6 5 4 3 2 1

Printed in the United States of America

To all the wonderful women in my life across the
generations, especially: Kristine Wookey, Lynn Moses, Sussannah Kelly,
Carolyn Clark, Iris Adler, Florence Minz, Jane Fellowes, Heather Campbell,
Alexandra Blum, Evguenia Potachenskaia, Jessie Hutcheson, Lauren Moses-
Brettler, and of course, always and forever, Tamara Weir-Bryan, and Jane
Hutcheson.

Contents

Chapter Two

The Awful Truth about Corporate Life: *Organizations*   37
Are Built by Men for Men

Chapter Three

Besieged and Restless: *The Emotional Mathematics*   65
of Contemporary Career Maladies

We Contain Multitudes:

Our Many Roles,

Many Selves

M anager, professional, mentor, mother, wife, volunteer, artist, friend, athlete. Never before have there been so many demands on women to excel in so many domains of life, so many opportunities for self-expression and success, for disappointment and frustration. Our sense of self is nuanced, intricate, and rich. We derive our feelings of satisfaction from multiple roles.

Freud famously said: "Love and work are the cornerstone of our humanness." If we augment "love" to include our friends and our passions and "work" to include paid and unpaid activity, this is all that matters. These are the issues we are particularly likely to reflect on at midlife, a time of significant opportunities and challenges when we take stock and ask, "What next?" and "How can I feel better about my life?" and reevaluate our priorities.

We have so many needs and desires. In my career/life-planning workshops with managers and professionals, I am always aware of the different ways in which men and women identify and rank their values. The most striking difference is not in the values themselves or how they are ranked, although there are differences, but in how the lists are completed. The men finish the exercise in a few minutes and move on to the next question. The women write the list. Then they erase it. Then they do it again. Disaster! Children aren't at the top of the list! Guilt! Erase! Erase!

We want it all. We need it all to have a sense of a fulfilling life.

We all have unique needs, but we also have a lot in common. Each of our roles provides opportunities for a deep sense of satisfaction that supports important values and desires. Each also opens us up to disappointment and sadness. What mother is not deeply, viscerally wounded when her child tells her she hates her? What professional is not furious when her male boss tells her she is not a good team player or that she needs to toughen up? What woman is not exasperated that she has to choose between the great career and the great family life?

We wear our hearts on our sleeves. We are tender but can be tough. We lead interior lives, always on a quest, always asking, Is this all there is, is this how life should be, am I doing this right, should I make a change, is everyone in my care happy, how do I compare with others in my situation?

We use subtle vocabulary to describe our emotions. We are explorers of an emotional terrain quite foreign to the land of doing, acting, and achieving. The one thing we can't do is segment our lives. If we are deliciously happy in one area, we are full of lightness. If we are hurt in one area, it spills over and colors everything else. A sharp word from a friend. A child's rejection or failure. A boss's criticism. A partner's ennui. Don't take it personally, we are told. But we do. We may get angry at our environment momentarily, but finally we ruminate: What did *I* do wrong? What could *I* have done differently? And we blame ourselves. "If I was smarter or tougher or a better partner or parent or professional, this wouldn't have happened, or I would be better able to cope," we tell ourselves.

Who are we? We are midlife women who have been doing what we're doing long enough to know a few things about life and work. We are experienced enough to have perspective on ourselves, our work, and our relationships. We can be bitchy. We are sick of engaging in male-pleasing behaviors. We are sick of pretending we are good girls. We are sick of putting others' needs first.

We are also nosy. Very nosy. Am I thinking and feeling similar things to other women? Are they doing something I can do? This curiosity gives us insight into our own experiences and what we can do differently. It is how women learn.

We compare ourselves to others in *all* life arenas. We used to ask: "How did you do on the test?" Now we ask: "How are you doing at work?" "How are you doing as a mother?" "How are you doing as a partner?" "How do you feel about X, Y, Z?" In this way we can answer the critical questions: "Am I doing OK?" "Are my feelings—whether positive or negative—normal?" Social psychologists call this phenomenon *social comparison*.

Women Confidential will give you the inside scoop and allow you to check your experiences and feelings against the lives of women who have grappled with the same questions, insecurities, thoughts, and challenges, and overcome them. It provides no-holds-barred career and life intelligence on what women need to know and do in order to feel good about themselves. It provides a psychological framework for women to understand and reshape their lives, make good decisions, and move forward with grace.

We are all in different places. Some of us have a degree of financial independence. Most of us do not. Some of us have a household full of kids, some are empty nesters, some are childless. While some of us are happy, many of us are struggling. We are tired, lonely, unhappy at work, irritated with our partners, worried about our kids, or disappointed with how our lives have turned out so far. As the pampered baby-boom generation, we thought we could have it all. Some of us feel that all we got were the dregs; most of us feel that what we got was something in between.

What We Want Now

The second half of our lives presents us with unique challenges and opportunities. We have been busy. By now we have fallen in and out of love, been married, had babies, been divorced, made friends, lost friends, worked for bad bosses, made career changes, suffered heartbreak, and experienced loneliness and bereavement. All of our life experiences have left their mark and shaped us. They have given us strength and perspective. They have left us asking questions. They have left some of us reeling from good fortune, others reeling from twists and turns less kind.

This is a time for asking ourselves what we really want. The answer depends on our situation, talents, and needs. Some of us want to feel contentment. Others want to ignite passion. Some of us want to test ourselves in new and inventive ways. Others want to reconnect with earlier career themes and return to the path not taken. The stories and voices in *Women Confidential* will show how others have coped with their own twists and turns.

We are each different in terms of what we need from our work, whether we are looking to contribute to something important, seeking collegiality or to hone professional skills, or simply wanting to make enough money to have a rich life outside of work. But although we are all different, at our core we are all finally looking for the same thing, and that is to be able to express ourselves in our work—paid or unpaid—and in our personal lives. Our work should make us feel good about ourselves because it is in tune with deeply held values and speaks to us at an emotional or intellectual level. And it should still allow time for a life.

In our personal lives we want to be able to express ourselves in our totality, whether by giving back to the community or by applying our creative side. We are also reevaluating our relationships, becoming more selective about our friends, and more accepting— or demanding—of our partner, if we have one.

Many of us have unfinished business. We worry that we are becoming our mothers, mothers whom in some cases we are ambivalent toward, or worse, angry at. Or we regret never having developed a closer relationship with deceased parents. Or we are trying to finally accept our parents.

It is now that we deal with unresolved issues in our work and personal lives, reclaim disowned parts of ourselves—ambitions left unfulfilled, dreams unsatisfied—and give expression to entrepreneurial or creative impulses we have too long denied. As one client, a forty-one-year-old magazine publisher, said, "I'm feverish with all the possibilities." This is also the time when we start to think about what kind of legacy we want to leave behind.

But there is also our inner bitch that yearns to be heard, silenced for many until midlife. As a forty-eight-year-old friend of mine said, or rather, ranted, "Is it too much to ask for it to be my time now? For my husband to think about what needs to be done around the house without my telling him? For my son to not act like I'm a piece of crap? For my boss to recognize I'm not his personal productivity machine? For my friends to stop being so needy?"

Another friend, a home-based consultant who describes herself as "Mary Poppins nice," complained about her husband's plans for self-employment after he lost his job at a large corporation. "I know. I know. I'm supposed to be supportive. But OK, I'm territorial, and I don't want him hanging around the house. And I'm pissed because now I have to make even more money and work even harder. Why can't he just be a normal guy and just find another job? Why should he be happy? He should just eat it like I did. I sound like a bitch. But I'm fifty and tired of being nice."

By midlife, whether we began adulthood as good or bad girls, we have become *almost* good girls. We have a polite, agreeable exterior. But we tell our friends the awful bitchy truths.

Almost Good Girls

When you were in high school and university, were you a "good" girl or a "bad" girl?

Now let's try again. Were you a "good" girl, "bad" girl, or an "almost good" girl?

My guess is that you answered "almost good" girl.

Why do I know that? Because you are restless and seeking more in some aspect of your life. You are prepared to deal with the big questions; you may even be pissed off about some things.

Let's parse it.

Good girl: In high school, she wore the kind of clothes that led your mother to ask you all the time why you didn't dress more like Susan. She consistently did the "right" thing, as defined by authority or society. She engaged in appropriate adult- and society-pleasing behaviors so that she got a good education, which enabled her to get a good job, and gave her lots of resume-enhancing experiences. Now, she lives around the corner from her parents and has them over for Sunday dinner at her perfect house. She cooks an elegant five-course meal. She also has perfect kids—or so she says. They volunteer, clean their rooms, get great marks, and are always polite. She works out, eats sensibly, doesn't drink, loves her job, and spends buckets of quality time with her family. If she's married, she describes her husband as "supportive." If she's divorced, she hung in there well beyond when she should have. There is also a good chance that she is depressed, is taking prescription drugs, and is barely holding it all together.

She may now be rebelling and becoming an almost good girl.

Bad girl: When she was younger, she made bad choices, the kind of choices that did not give her the underpinnings at midlife to see her life as full of possibility. She came to class with hickeys (when she wasn't skipping school), had a boyfriend with a motorcycle, and was notoriously "easy." Opportunities were either never available or were rejected. Authority and status quo were anathema—she would do anything to shake things up. She rebelled against everything and trusted no one.

She may have returned to school or in some way pulled her life together so she now has choices and is, in fact, an almost good girl.

Almost good girl: In high school, she got good or even great marks, was involved in extracurricular activities, was respectful (sort of) of adults, had sex (hopefully wild) in her parents' house, and generally walked close enough to the dark side to know it was dangerous. She avoided the bad boys or at least got out of bad situations fast enough to keep her self-esteem intact. She took risks, asked some penetrating questions, was irreverent, did some dumb things (though not without a safety net). She knew how to project outward conformity but never held back from telling her friends the tough truths. She still does.

She didn't fit in totally with the good girls or the bad girls but was never rejected by either. Now, she has the ability to fit in almost everywhere, if never completely. She refuses to accept received wisdom and increasingly challenges herself: Am I happy? Is there more? Can I be more? What about me?

It doesn't matter how you get to this place in your life—as a good girl rebelling, a bad girl reformed, or an almost good girl grown up. What matters is that we are reaching this point and moving on together.

Moving Forward with Grace

The challenge of the first half of our lives is to make our way in the world: to demonstrate our competence, to test ourselves against others, to get feedback from the world about what we are and are not good at. This externally driven phase often involves dealing with petty bosses, putting up with less than fully satisfying work, kowtowing to the needs of high-maintenance friends, repressing important parts of our personality, or putting our partner's needs before our own.

In the second half of life, the midlife years, we are internally driven. We should have a sense of who we are, both our strengths and our weaknesses. And yes, I'll call them weaknesses—they are a part of us; we should accept them, and refuse to think of them in silly corporate euphemisms such as "areas for development." How do we know this about ourselves? Well, for one thing, we've been through enough performance appraisals, whether literally from bosses and clients, or metaphorically from friends and family, to know what they are.

Accepting our limitations and disappointments means we don't beat ourselves up for being less than perfect. It means we can move ahead rather than endlessly revisiting the past, decrying slights and instances of injustice in an endless, negative feedback loop. We see expressing all our complex needs and desires as a right, not a privilege, or as my friend said, an "irresistible" pull. If we fail to focus on what we really want and care about now independently of the "shoulds" of the past, then we continue to play out old scripts, scripts about what we *should* do, how we *should* behave, what we *should* be happy with. Or as Carl Jung said, we walk "in shoes too small."

It is time to celebrate our achievements, which are many. We have fought the wars at work, we have raised children, and hopefully done a few interesting things in our lives. Remember, we have been very, very busy.

We Still Have a Lot to Worry About

To a large extent women have always dealt with the challenges of balancing work and family. What is new, though, is the complexity of these challenges. Parents have always become ill and needed help. But now women are caring for them while working for demanding employers, scrambling to get more business in the door, and continuing to look after the kids. And many of us are doing it alone.

As for the kids . . . either they can't wait to leave home or they've set themselves up under our roofs for what looks to be a very long stay. We worry about them working at McJobs, not being able to decide on a career, and the lifelong repercussions of making bad choices. Mothers with younger children worry about predators in the classroom, perverts in the schoolyard, and their kids getting a leg up in what they perceive as a scary and competitive world.

And then there are the secret anxieties we are too embarrassed to discuss with anyone but our closest friends. Your kid is going to become a sanitation worker. You think you're going to be fired because of your age. You think your friends are all doing better than you and what's worse (and you hate yourself for this), you privately resent them for it. You are lonely. You are bored with your life.

Finally, there are the secrets that we tell no one, because revealing them would be deeply painful to others or because they are hurts so unbearable or scary or shameful we can scarcely contemplate them. A child addicted to drugs. A violent sibling. A husband having an affair. Most of us have at least one thing in our life we don't talk to anyone about. All women have secrets.

Thinking about What Really Matters

At the same time, a significant majority of us are asking ourselves: What do I really want to do with my life? Why am I working so hard for so little emotional, intellectual, or financial gain? Is this all there is? Those working for organizations despair of the soullessness, the endless demands and personal sacrifices, the assaults on ego, the lack of harmony between their personal values and those of their employer, the inability to practice their craft in the way they want. Many of those who are self-employed are at once bored and over-worked, and are looking for more meaningful challenges. On the home front, we are asking penetrating questions about the nature of all of our relationships, coming to terms with our parents, redefining friendships, looking for more from our partners. In other words, we are deciding what really matters.

What are we optimistic about? What are our sources of sadness or regret? What kind of unfinished business do we have to address in order to move forward with grace? What can be learned, and what lessons can be passed on to our daughters? What are our challenges, and how are successful women meeting them?

This book will help the questioning, seeking woman, whether she suffers from career malaise or life malaise, or seeks confirmation of her choices. It will illuminate what we wish we had known earlier, good advice in the voice of a very smart friend whispering secrets in our ear. It will help younger women by sharing life lessons from savvy women about what they did well and what they would have done differently. And it will satisfy the prurient need we all have to snoop into each other's lives.

I hope you will consider me and the other voices in *Women Confidential* as a collective life mentor for approaching the midlife challenges of seeking to redefine work, relationships, and the rest of life. Can we have it all? How can we be authentic in male work environments? How can we parent in the way we want to and still have satisfying work?

The Voices You Will Meet

I recently read a review of a book that admonished women who want to get ahead to follow several rules. If you are a woman of a certain age, you know the drill—all those rules about what women should and shouldn't do. Don't be nice. Don't express emotion. Toughen up. I was so disgusted by the soul-crushing advice based on traditional male success models that I wrote a column for the *Globe and Mail* on why the advice was retrograde. My advice? Women should refuse to become "mini-men," wear a corporate mask, or pretend they are someone they are not. I received a record number of responses from readers agreeing with me.

Shortly after that, I wrote a column for the *Wall Street CareerJournal* on why women should fight to express their authentic selves at work. I sent the column out in a mass e-mail to my clients along with a few questions:

"Can you be authentic in a corporate environment? Are the rhythms of corporations antithetical to female rhythms? Where are women happiest? Are you going though a transition . . . If so, what? What is most important to you at this life stage? If you had one piece of advice to give to a younger woman, what would it be? Please share all the juicy details. This is confidential. All your identifying attributes will be changed."

I was deluged with replies. Women even asked if it would be okay to respond to my questions if they were not on my list (the column was forwarded extensively), and I'm still receiving comments today.

The responses were remarkable—candid, intimate, and yes, often bitchy, angry, and full of all the juicy details. Obviously this is an important subject, and women want to *share* their experiences. These women asked me, "Can I help you some more?" About half of them said something like, "Sorry for the rant, but I had to sound off. This was great therapy."

This book is populated by many voices. I have spent my career fascinated with the psychology of women, especially professional women. I have taught courses in this area, conducted research as part of my PhD, done internal corporate studies on why women aren't moving ahead and the issues they grapple with, and delivered many, many speeches and workshops.

I have also been collecting data for more than twenty years on what motivates women, most recently through my online career/life-planning resource, *Career Advisor*, which provides me with information on values, needs, challenges, and desires broken down by age and gender. To date about ten thousand people have completed assessments on *Career Advisor*.

I have spent my life counseling women, listening to women, advising women. I know what excites and inspires them. I know what derails them. So I am a key voice, an "expert" voice if you will, giving my perspective by distilling, interpreting, and providing ideas and advice based on my research and observations as a practitioner, writer, thinker, and social psychologist.

Over the past few years, I have also received close to a thousand stories from women, including those from this recent e-mail survey. I have married these thousand voices to those of thirty women, in their late-thirties to midfifties, whom I call life mentors, insightful, thoughtful, interesting women whom I have personally selected to be part of this group. (All names have been changed.)

In spite of the temptation to describe these women as successful, I call them *interesting* because they have defined success on their own terms. Like many women, I struggle with the word *successful*. I always think of those eighties women in their power suits pursuing the holy grail of their career. I don't like speakers' series in which women politicians or CEOs hold themselves up as role models or talk about their lives with the "if I can do it, so can you" or "surely you want to be like me" attitude.

Some of these women are successful in the traditional sense of the word—lawyers, owners of thriving businesses, vice presidents of major corporations. But of equal interest are those women who left prestigious jobs to do something they cared about deeply, whether to live in a cottage in the country, to volunteer, to paint, or to coach others. My group is fairly representative of the occupations of university-educated women. It includes writers and editors, human-resource professionals, a TV producer, an accountant, independent consultants, an artist, a teacher, career and life coaches. Most of the women live in major urban centers in the United States, Canada, and the United Kingdom. As in the general population, about two-thirds have children; in terms of partners and family configurations, they represent all the tangled possibilities.

Regardless of their path, the women understand the choices they have made and can reflect on what was and wasn't wise. They accept who they are instead of endlessly second-guessing decisions they have made (and if they have had bitterness in the past, they have moved on). They are excited about their futures. As the French say, they are *bien dans sa peau*, they feel good in their skin.

They are savvy about the work world, have important things to say about their personal lives, and understand the complexities we all deal with. They are generous and want to share with other women what they have observed and learned.

But don't think Pollyanna. Most of them are wry, edgy, and sometimes quite rude, in other words, *almost good girls*. Their comments are often wickedly funny and candid. They are prepared to deal with uncertainty and self-doubt; they know that life does not consist exclusively of sentiment-laden Hallmark moments, and have a sharp, critical take on corporate environments (not to mention husbands, current and former). Their insights provide important information for women seeking to understand their lives and how to move forward.

As you will read, there is good news—there are lots of inventive ways to redefine your life to give you more of what you want.

The women completed an in-depth questionnaire (see Appendix) and a follow-up interview of more questions. You may want to refer to the Discussion Guide at the end of this book when you get together with your friends to talk about each other's lives and benefit from each other's wisdom.

In this book, I show you how strong and interesting women are redefining what really matters in the areas that determine how we feel about our lives—work, partners, children, friends, and the rest. So get comfortable and get the dish.

chapter one

Almost Good Girls:

Meeting Expectations during the Approval-Seeking Years

My father died when I was twenty-three. I was a hippy and had just returned to North America from London, England. Like most of my generation, I didn't have any particular expectations or thoughts about the future. I had just started teaching psychology at a junior college, a cool job, with thirteen hours of lectures, four hours seeing students, and the chance to work with neat people. Even though my husband wasn't working, I earned enough to support both of us. As hippies, material stuff wasn't high on our list of what was important.

My parents lived fairly close by. They didn't have much money, but they lived well enough. Although I knew intellectually that there wasn't a bottomless financial well, I didn't really worry or think about money. There was always someone to take us out to dinner, or in an emergency, to bail us out.

But when my father died, I had a profound sense of having lost a buffer between me and the world. I was IT. I was no longer a child. It was not that my father had the resources to protect me, but the sense of protection was psychological—I had a tacit belief that if I screwed up or something bad happened to me, there was still someone who could make it better. My mother had never filled that role and never would.

I lost my childhood when I lost my father. I developed at my core a niggling sense of "I must be successful, I must achieve." I had no particular vision of what that success would look like, just a vague concept of being someone important. This had nothing to do with money, and everything to do with being recognized by others as a good person, a smart person, a person to be reckoned with.

As I no longer had the opportunity to elicit my father's words "I am proud of you," I internalized an abstract parent who would be proud of me. This meant a drive to succeed that could not possibly be satisfied, as there was, in the literal sense, no one to please. But I think if my father had died later in my life, when I was more fully baked, I would have felt less of a need to prove myself. As it was, I craved approval, as did most parent-pleasing women who flirted with bad behavior while managing to stay on the "good girl" side.

Where did this desire to please everyone come from? Well, most of us as children were almost good girls with the accent on the "good," socialized to internalize all the dominant messages of society: "Get good marks." "Be a well-rounded person." "Be polite to your elders." "Don't say anything that is hurtful." "Be popular." We grew up seeking approval from everyone—parents, teachers, friends. The list of adult-pleasing behaviors we were expected to demonstrate was endless.

The origins of this need for approval lie, in part, in our families:

"I'm from a large, noisy family. The only way I could get my parents' attention was by being excellent at everything."

"As a middle-class girl, by the time I was five I must have heard the words *be nice* a million times."

"My brother was killed when I was eleven. I felt I had to make up for my parents' loss. He had been the one they were most proud of, a great student and athlete. Now it was up to me. They canonized him after his death, and I could never really fill his shoes. But I kept trying."

The need for approval also comes from our culture, which largely values adolescent females in terms of their attractiveness. Girls must sacrifice parts of themselves to be protected and valued by society, say many developmental psychologists such as professor, author, and scholar Carol Gilligan, who has devoted her life to understanding female development, and has conducted seminal research in this field.

In one of her studies documented in *Meeting at the Crossroads* (1992), she and her coauthor, Lyn Mikel Brown, conducted intensive interviews with one hundred mostly upper-middle-class girls over a five-year period to answer the question "What, on the way to womanhood, does a girl give up?" They found that girls are initially more self-assured than boys, but that at adolescence, girls lose their sense of self—they stifle their creative urges and natural impulses and are boxed into the standards of "good girl" behavior. In other words, their authentic voice is driven underground. They lose self-esteem—a loss that continues to reverberate even in adulthood.

Susan, for example, recalls that as a child she was a "tomboy" and her parents thought it was "cute." But as soon as she became a teenager, "My mother was all over me in terms of how I dressed, talked, and walked. It was like I had become a different person and who I had been was no longer OK. And of course it wasn't only my parents, it was all that awful high-school girl stuff of trying to fit in and be one of the popular girls."

The impact of this adolescent need for approval continues to be felt later on, in all areas of life: women stay in bad marriages to avoid the wrath of parents, indulge the kids so they won't be angry, and make work choices that don't support personal needs because they look good on a resume.

I have known Helen, for example, for twenty years. I have seen her in about ten jobs, each progressively more senior, the past three as a vice president of human resources.

Each time she starts a new job she tells me, "This is it. I've done my research. They're great and are committed to doing the right thing." Then there is a honeymoon period. "I love it. I've finally landed." Six months later, I start to hear the first rumblings that all is not well. "I'm so tired. I seem to be fighting all the time. But you have to fight if you want to make sure the right thing is done." And nine months later, she says, "I can't take this anymore. They're [referring to the male senior management team] brutal." Then the process starts again.

Helen's father was a doctor. Like many doctor fathers of daughters, he was critical and demanding. He wanted her to follow in his footsteps. She was on a lifelong journey to win his approval, to be a success. Even though she wouldn't be a doctor, she would be a player in the high-stakes game of senior organizational life.

Helen's story, though extreme, is similar to that of many women. Why did she continue to pursue so many unsuitable jobs? To put it simply, she needed the approval of male senior managers, who were the place holders for her father. When she failed, no matter what swear words she used to describe her employers, what she really felt was unworthy. She needed to prove to them that she was okay and, in the process, prove to herself and her father that she was okay. Making it in a "status" job was a substitute for self-worth. Each time she started a job she was really saying, "I'm going to show these men that I'm worthy," and "I'm going to show my father that I am lovable and successful even if I'm not a doctor."

The expectations placed on us as children—by our parents and our culture—helped to shape an entire generation of women. So did the tremendous economic and cultural changes of the sixties.

The Other Messages We Got

Although we each have our own story, there are common themes in all of our experiences beyond just the desire for approval. We didn't know exactly what our dads did other than being told that "money doesn't grow on trees." Dads went to work and, for the most part, moms stayed home. There was little diversity in our family arrangements and little discussion of *how* parents made a living. If they were unhappy with their work, we didn't know. Work was not a subject for discussion or debate. It was not supposed to make you happy, and you weren't supposed to evaluate it in those terms.

As indulged boomer children we were the first generation to grow up with widespread abundance and a feeling of security. It was a time of North American political and economic ascendancy, and it formed the bedrock of our beliefs about what we could achieve in the world. Growing up during a time of rapid expansion, we understood, whether explicitly or not, that we would reap the rewards of economic stability and growth and that with our university educations we could be anything we wanted to be. The advent of feminism coupled with a shortage of workers translated into a great broadening of opportunities. We were the first middle-class female generation who thought we would have all the goodies society could provide—the great career, the great family, the freedom to express our glorious, uninhibited selves. We could be a sexy, powerful Katharine Hepburn in terms of independence; we could be mothers if we chose, and goddesses in the bedroom. To the extent we thought about the future at all, one thing was certain: we would not live lives of domesticated numbness and repressed resentment like our stay-at-home mothers.

There were, of course, individual expectations about university, which in part were formed by social class, in part by parental expectations. Although most of us would go to university, some would go into studies that would lead to a career in a traditionally female occupation, such as teaching or occupational therapy, while others would go into a "where-does-it-lead-to" program in the liberal arts or social sciences; a few would pursue high-level professional degrees. (Between 1970 and 1997 the proportion of degrees awarded to women soared by almost 500 percent in medicine, 800 percent in law, and 1000 percent in business.)

For me, going to university wasn't a choice. This was simply what middle-class girls did, especially if you were from a Jewish family. My father had left school in Grade 9 to help support his family. He was deeply ashamed of this. For my father, the son of a cutter working in a dress factory, a daughter in university was the ultimate achievement. Indeed, at my graduation ceremony, he said, "We all graduated today," a comment I callously thought very stupid at the time.

When I was four years old, he took me to the gates of the McGill campus in Montreal, and said, "This is where you will go to university." (The seeds for achievement motivation were sown at an early age in my family.) Like many others of my generation, I felt that university was a rite of passage, part of being "finished," not purely an instrument to a career. A university education had value over and above its long-term economic utility. I never thought about how one course of study might better prepare me for future employment than another. Its purpose was to enrich my life, to teach me how to think, to expose me to the world of ideas, and, most important, it was a chance to have fun, sex, and all the rest of it.

Our varying expectations about universities and careers were not much different from those people have today, except that now,

as tuition fees have skyrocketed, and everyone's career consciousness has grown, parents and their university-aged kids are more
anxious about the value of a degree as a professional stepping stone.

Some people, like Karen, always had a sense of their ultimate
career destination. From the time she was in Grade 8, she knew that
she wanted to be a journalist. She did her undergraduate degree in lit-
erature and worked on the student newspaper. Karen, though, was
somewhat unusual in having had a clear career concept. Many women
didn't have a specific vision of how they would participate in the
workforce and went to university through a circuitous route. Iris, for
example, recalls: "Both of my parents were university-educated so of
course I was expected to go. But I never really thought about what
university would do for me in terms of my long-term career interests.
I went into translation because I was good in languages, but quit after
a year because I hated it. As a child of the sixties, the idea of thinking about a career was distasteful, and business was boring. The idea
of money was distasteful. It connoted greed."

She took a job as the assistant to the owner of a factory. About
a month into the job her boss told her "giving him a blow job was
part of the job." She quit. When her prudish parents asked why she
quit, she says, "There was no way I could tell them what had happened. My mother thought the word *sex* was unladylike. I was
embarrassed so I just blurted out that I wanted to go back to school.
And that's why I went back." Like many women, she had a vague
sense that she would work, be independent, but the form it would
take was not articulated.

Finally, there were those who were not given a choice about
what to study. Steph's parents, for example, were prepared to help
her pay for university but only if she studied to be a teacher.
University wasn't a place to play or to be enriched. For her the cost
of education was such that it had to be a ticket to a good job; it was
an investment in financial independence. Steph, whose father
owned a small, not very profitable store, says, "I was very jealous

of my friends who could pursue a social sciences degree." It took her twenty years to get over her resentment toward her parents.

Our Concept of Success

We had a sense of entitlement even if we didn't know how it would express itself. Implicit in going to university was the notion that it would have long-term economic benefit, but we didn't think about what that would be. Nonetheless, as Hannah, the owner of a speakers' bureau, said, "It was a ticket to success that knew no boundaries."

Although our concept of what we would do was diffuse, we had some very clear expectations about what work would be like: it would be fun, provide financial independence, be glamorous, and, most importantly, be a source of *personal fulfillment*. It never occurred to us that our incomes would be important as half of a dual-career couple or as the head of a single-parent family.

The Early Trajectory

After we graduated, most of us had choices—maybe a trip to Europe to find ourselves, maybe a stay on a commune, maybe a first job.

I went to England to work after completing my undergraduate degree—it seemed as good an idea as any. As we will see later, it is this kind of apparent happenstance that guided so much of what we did as a generation, and led us to ask questions such as: *How did I get from there to here?*

When someone would ask my mother what I was doing, she would say, "She's taking a year off," a comment that deeply annoyed me. Here I was, for the first time in my overprogrammed, high achieving, parent-pleasing life, doing something not "productive." From my mother's point of view, if I was not either achieving in school—doing a master's degree—or starting a real "career," then I was taking a year off. From my point of view, I was putting a year *on*, a year into life.

Angst: Trying to Find Our Path

Like most of my "almost good" girlfriends, I spent my twenties in a *Seinfeld* kind of way, doing nothing. Or at least nothing in the sense of a clear vision of what I wanted to do with my life and how my activities would help me get there. (By the way, if you are reading this and you are in your twenties, don't worry if you are clueless about your career desires. Most twentysomethings don't have a clear career definition—finding out what you want to do with your life is a process of self-knowledge, trial and error, and reflection. I actually worry more about young people who know exactly what they want to do than about those who don't.)

That doesn't mean I was relaxed about not knowing what I wanted to do. The good girls from university all seemed to know their career destination exactly. A few went to law school; others got jobs. They seemed happy. They weren't constantly second-guessing themselves about whether this was right for them, or navel-gazing about whether they were happy. I was jealous; they seemed to have it together. (It took me many years to realize that it wasn't so much that they had their lives together, rather they were just less *leaky* about their insecurities.)

I, on the other hand, was neurotically obsessed and *very leaky* about my insecurities. While completing my PhD, I worked at an oil company in the human resources department, conducting employee research and psychological assessments. I used to ask the women I worked with, How do you know you are in the right career? How can you be *sure*? How do you know there isn't something better? They looked at me like I was asking "How do you know you are using the right toilet paper?"

There was something out there with my name on it, which was singularly suited to me, or so I believed. How to find it? Should I teach? Should I do a graduate degree? Should I become a clinician? I spent my twenties and, if the truth be known, my early thirties asking myself these questions (although I did manage to acquire two graduate degrees and work in various roles during the process).

Quite simply, as a generation, we had too many choices. And when you have a choice, you want to make the right one, especially if you have great expectations.

So we tried on many roles.

The Corporate Route

"It was a feast, but some of the food was rotten."
　—Corporate counsel

"Working for a major corporation seemed very sexy, very powerful, like the career girls in the movies."
　—Analyst

Our generation, unlike previous generations, had access to the corporate ladder beyond the usual support roles. Of course, women had gone this route before. But their numbers weren't large, and they were called "career girls." By the time we entered the workplace in the seventies and early eighties, women were being aggressively courted by organizations. This was a period of prosperity, and it seemed that the prospects were limitless. Organizations were expanding rapidly, there was a dearth of professionals, and there were more jobs than people to fill them. Feminism and the larger pool of university-educated women meant that women were an abundant source of labor.

The first wave of the feminist battles had been won. Sure there was the feeling of being different, as profiled in Rosabeth Moss Kantor's groundbreaking book *A Tale of "O": On Being Different in an Organization*, published in 1980, but the promise was there. (Moss Kantor argued that women, the Os, stand out from the male majority Xs, and that due to their scarcity they are treated differently and as tokens.) It was a heady period, and fertile ground for reinforcing expectations that we could have it all. There was a common belief that if you stayed longer than two years in your job without promotion, your career had been derailed.

There were important differences between us and the pre-boomer women, born before 1947, who paved our way into the workplace. We believed good work and opportunities were a *right*, not a privilege. As a result of the sexual revolution, we were freer and not as caught up with traditional expectations about "being a lady" as our older sisters were. As one trainer recalls, "It was 1985, and I was thirty years old. I was cofacilitating a workshop with a woman twelve years older than me. She noticed a run in my stockings, and wanted to go buy me another pair. She was horrified when I said I was fine with the run. I didn't have the heart to tell her that I had put on the stockings knowing they had a run, because I couldn't be bothered." Or as a journalist said, "We were drinking, smoking dope, sleeping around, and holding our own in the male world. Some of us were more men than the men. We were definitely not ladies . . ."

Organizations cared enough about retaining and developing female professionals that the progressive ones appointed affirmative-action officers (though being offered this job was considered the death knell of your career), conducted workshops to ensure that the most egregious expressions of gender discrimination—being called a chick, being fondled, or being exposed to sexual innuendo—were not acceptable, and encouraged female professionals to start networking groups. (If this sounds familiar, don't be surprised. As we will see in Chapter 2, while some things have changed, many haven't.) Bad behavior went on, but it was finally seen as inappropriate. Most boomer women can cite at least one example of being the victim of gender discrimination or inappropriate male advances.

What did professional women think about their careers in corporations? I worked for an oil company. It was the early eighties and management was concerned that the female professionals were not being promoted as quickly as their male counterparts. Internal surveys revealed that the women, relative to their male colleagues, were less happy and less able to see themselves as having a career in the company. (Sounds pretty quaint now, the concept of having a long-term career anywhere.) I was asked, along with organizational development consultant Tamara Weir-Bryan, who would become one of the most important people in my life and my mentor, to help identify the reasons.

Everyone's hypothesis was that the glass ceiling was to be blamed. And this was indeed part of the problem. But the reasons were more complex. The women looked at the senior managers, who were all male. And they despaired of having to become like them. Mini-men. Some chose to leave. Most were deeply ambivalent. "If that's what it takes, who needs it?" They thought "Ick. Who wants to be like them?"

"What's wrong with being feminine, expressing emotion?" they asked. "Doesn't good leadership require compassion and interpersonal sensitivity?" And most pointedly: "Why am I not valued for what is part of my DNA as a woman?" What followed for most professional women in their twenties and thirties was the struggle to fit in.

Trying to Fit In

Consulting at the oil company was pretty heady stuff for me. I was from a small-business family and had had little exposure to corporate life. All of my friends were in clinical or academic positions. How to behave? How to dress? I wanted this consulting contract to be turned into a job offer. Corporate life seemed very glamorous. Fortunately, I would be a shoo-in—or so I thought. *Everyone* in the history of the company who had held a similar position had been offered a full-time job.

There were three professional women in the human resources department who were around my age. In my mind I called them the three Christines: Christine A, Christine B, and Christine C, as there was little to distinguish them. They all wore the same regulation Career Woman boxy suit, the same polite pearl stud earrings, the same ribbon tied around their neck that made them look like prize pigs about to be entered in a 4-H contest. I studied them and tried to emulate them. (In hindsight, I realize how harsh my assessment of them was; I'm sure they had their own struggles.)

But I just couldn't get the hang of it. Or rather, some part of me wouldn't allow me to get the hang of it. I hated the sexless suits—why spend serious money on something that made you look like a guy? Or worse, *fat!*

I didn't get that job offer. They said I was too direct, too expressive, too, well, everything.

As we will see in Chapter 2, some of us were able to fit in better than others. And because so many of us tried desperately to fit in, many women such as the Christines lost their voices.

We had great expectations for ourselves, and the greater the expectations, the more room for feelings of failure. As Janice, a small-business owner, said, "As a boomer, as a woman, I could never reconcile myself to doing an average job at anything. Having all the balls in the air—kids, career, jerk of a husband (former)—was a given. But then all you could do was not make any of them work. The higher your personal expectations for success, the less successful you will feel. You're playing where the air is thin and where you always get knocked down."

The opportunities for assaults on our egos were endless—from parents, our partners, kids, and all of our own preconceived notions of what life should look like. "No matter what you did," said a career coach, "you were still screwing up in some other area."

The Schizophrenic Years

"There was a siren in my head. Go to work and force myself not to smile too much or else get beaten up by my boss for being Mary Poppins, not being tough enough. Go home, go into mommy mode, and become warm and nurturing."
—Freelance journalist

Although many women complained about the struggle and trauma of trying to have it all, many had their children in the eighties, when there was still some wiggle room for work and family life, when a workweek was forty hours long. So although some married women wrestled with whether to have children or not, most felt they were forced to choose between the "brass ring" or spending time with their family.

Flexible work options didn't exist. There were no models of women who had satisfying careers and were also able to fulfill their roles as mothers. What we knew about mothering came from our own mothers, most of whom were homemakers, often bored, depressed, or anxious and simmering with petty perceived grievances and serious resentments. We knew as a woman if you wanted to be respected, good enough would not do—you had to be spectacular. What we knew about careers were the silver-screen independent "career girls" portrayed by Lauren Bacall. In any case, there were few women in senior corporate roles, so if you did the math, you realized your chances for success were limited. Why put yourself in the game? According to Catalyst, a research and advisory organization that has been tracking the participation of women in senior roles, in 1995, the first year they collected this data, 8.7 percent of Fortune 500 corporate officer positions were held by women. In 2002, the number had increased to 15.7 percent. No one knows what the percentages were before 1995, but it is safe to assume they were very low. Also according to Catalyst, the first recorded family-friendly support systems were in 1987 for child-care initiatives.

If you wanted to have a chance at a successful career in an organization, one thing was clear: behave like a man, dress like a man. There were tons of books aimed at "ambitious" women that were full of soul-crushing advice about what you should and shouldn't do. There still are.

Behave like a man: avoid using adjectives, don't express emotion, don't say "I feel . . ." And whatever ever ever *ever* you do, do *not* cry at the office. Dress for success, in authoritative colors such as navy or black. Men's clothes sized for women, but please wear a skirt to be polite. And don't forget the stockings! (I'm embarrassed to confess I actually wrote an article in the 1980s on how to dress for success for a women's glossy. But I needed the money, so forgive me.)

As an organizational consultant in the early eighties, I gave feedback on psychological tests to young professionals for developmental purposes. Often when I told a woman about a problematic aspect of her personality, such as being overly sensitive to criticism, she would say, "That's true of me at home, but at work I'm completely different—negative feedback doesn't really bother me. It's the only way I can develop myself." At the time, I thought it was impossible for people to change their behavior when they walked through the office door, but today I realize they were telling me the truth, or at least the truth as they saw it.

Herein lay the nut of the dilemma, a dilemma that is still very much alive in today's workplace. If you are not valued for *who* you really are, then you have to engage in what psychologists call *impression management*. This means monitoring your environment and changing your behavior so you will fit in. One set of behaviors at work and another at home.

But we were in our twenties and thirties, the approval-seeking years, the time when we are still asking the world: "Am I OK?" "Do you like me?" "Do you think I am competent?" So we didn't think to challenge this. We had less confidence about who we were because we had had less experience and had received less feedback about what we were good at. And there were so many arenas in which we could be "not OK." All those insidious internalized media images of how we should behave as a good daughter, wife, or mother, the superwomen who always remembered to pick up their husband's dry cleaning and who baked cookies for the school fair instead of buying them and pretending they were homemade, women who were always charming, unflappable, and in a good mood.

Were we angry? We were resentful, certainly, but not angry the way women are today. Because unlike thirtysomething women now, who, because of all the media and corporate chatter, know there is a problem, we were oblivious. The buzz in corporate environments in the 1980s was about the glass ceiling, not about the demands of parenting, or balancing work and personal life, or about having to repress important parts of who you are in order to fit in. This was *girly* stuff, and not something to be talked about. The serious stuff was about ambition and getting ahead.

The Nineties—A Sea Change Still Reverberating Today: Work as Extreme Sport

*"If I didn't do the overnight travel or breakfast meetings,
I worried I'd be fired. If I didn't go to my kid's soccer game,
I wasn't being a good mother."*
— Director of human resources

There was a profound sea change in the 1990s, foreshadowed in the mideighties, when organizations were restructured to have fewer levels. Here was this great population bulge of baby boomers, accustomed to a feast of endless promotional prospects, competing for fewer opportunities, and having to adjust to career growth slowed to a crawl. But organizations in the eighties were at least still civil.

In the 1990s, all of this changed. The pace of business increased. Workers became disposable units of productivity. The bar for performance went into the stratosphere. Forty-hour workweeks became a quaint memory. This was the beginning of the era of work as *extreme sport*. It wasn't fun. Organizations weren't congenial places where you could actualize yourself.

Where were we? Some of us were starting families; some of us had young kids at home; some of us were beginning to feel something important was missing. We started to ask ourselves new questions: "Why am I working so hard for so little?" "What is the emotional cost to me of working?" "What is the impact on my kids?" Pandora's box had been opened—people started to *think* about work choices. If your work is relatively pleasant—a decent paycheck, interesting colleagues, challenging work that can be put to bed at the end of the day—you don't need to second-guess whether your work is meeting your needs. Of course there were sacrifices, but you could still be at home at 6 p.m. and turn into

Mommy or go for a run. But now the effort-reward equation was seriously out of whack.

The nineties heralded a new era of heightened work consciousness. With that came a whole new set of interior monologues. And as the decade drew to a close, we didn't keep them to ourselves any longer. We started to share our private concerns about the impact of intense work on our personal lives and about the choices we felt we were being forced to make.

Talking about what you were feeling was *new*—there was a crack in the corporate armor. When I started work at the oil company in the eighties, I used to watch people approach the fancy head office. As staff walked along the street together they would chat amongst themselves as casual friends do. And then something most bizarre happened, in my imagination at least, when they entered through the big glass doors.

It was as if the lobby of the head office were lined with row upon row of employee lockers, each identified with an employee number, under a gallery of oil portraits of pale male faces. There people would go to their locker and hang up everything that was important to them or that characterized who they were as human beings. Into their locker would go their personalities, their sexuality, their concerns about their kids, their irritations with their partners, their politics. And out they would come—dressed in corporate mask, ready to meet the day head-on.

But as people's work consciousness awakened they started to demand *more* from work. If they were going to have to make serious sacrifices in their personal lives in order to work, then their work should meet deep personal needs. One should not only be satisfied by one's job, but *passionate* about it. And if you weren't passionate about your work, there was something wrong with you. This set the foundation for the career angst we see today.

From the Late Nineties Until Today

"To be honest, I was secretly pissed off when my company introduced flextime. It wasn't bad enough that I was killing myself. Now I had a choice over how I wanted to kill myself."
—Director of public relations

"I was so sick of hearing about all those choices. What choices did most of us really have? It's not like I woke up every morning and said, 'Today I want to go to work and kill myself.' When you are a single parent on a limited income, where's the choice?"
—Librarian

Panic in HR. Women were starting to leave organizations. They'd had enough already. They were screaming, "I can't take this anymore." It was a media fest. As one career writer recalls, all you read about were "stories about people who chucked it all in, who chucked it all on, or quite simply just chucked it all over the place."

If you could believe what the media were saying, the choices for women were endless. They could quit and move to the country. They could find work about which they were passionate. They could homeschool their kids. They could work full-throttle, 24/7, or they could calibrate how they wanted to design their lives. Part-time work, telecommuting, portfolio careers—the choices were breath-taking. They were also overwhelming, and made many women feel even worse.

Here's what it all added up to: more thinking, more guilt. More agonizing over choices we did or didn't make or never considered. Call it choice fatigue. And if you chose just not to think about the choices, then you were left feeling somehow wanting, that you weren't in charge of your life.

As one freelance marketing consultant, then a manager of marketing in the financial services sector, said, "I felt inadequate because now, whatever I did, it was a choice. Like somehow every time I went to work, I had made a decision to go into work and prove myself at the expense of my kids. Like there was someone up there screaming, 'Hey, get with the program. You've got choices now.'"

Another assault on the ego, another opportunity to feel one had failed. But were there really any more choices to be made? Although many organizations were offering work-life balance programming, such as flexible hours and telecommuting, in practice many of these policies existed—and exist—more on company's intranets than in the lives of their staff. And women knew that even if they could take advantage of them, they would do so at the cost of their careers. Another set of choices: Career or family? Passion or contentment? And of course, there was the ever-present "money issue," since it seemed—and still seems—to many women that deep pockets were required to take advantage of these choices. For most women, the choice to give up their income was about more than giving up a Caribbean vacation or club membership. Their incomes were essential.

Lives Bursting at the Seams

"When my husband was looking after the kids, he described it as babysitting."
　　—Interior designer

"My brain used to actually hurt. I would think, 'It's going to explode if I have to remember one more thing.'"
　　—Curriculum designer

Busy, busy, busy. We were so busy keeping our shows on the road—worrying about our kids, looking after our parents, being a partner, seeking a partner, getting divorced, remarrying, facing death and health scares—we had no time to reflect. We juggled it all, doing, acting, achieving, and looking after others.

And truth be told, we kind of liked it, or at least a lot of women did. We wore our busyness like a badge of honor—"I'm so busy. I must be important." It was the era of the cult of busyness. "I stopped asking people 'How are you?'" one woman explained. "I was so sick of hearing their busyness mantra. They weren't really complaining; they were *boasting*."

Yes, we had men in our lives, but they could be as demanding as our kids. Worse, according to many women, they had "small" brains when it came to thinking about any problem outside their work and their hobbies.

I have developed an instrument that measures, among other attributes, people's preference for having many things on the go versus working on a few things at once, completing them before going on to a few more things. The dimension is called Pacing. Every time I conduct a career/life-planning workshop, I am asked the same question by the women in the group: "Do men score lower on Pacing than do women?" Because, they say (often in an exasperated chorus), "Men can't multitask." In fact, I have not found any differences in the scores of men and women.

The fissure between men and women is not in their ability to think about and do several things at once, but in their willingness to think about and do several unpleasant or *boring* things at once.

And the thinking is as important as the doing. As an independent consultant, then a trainer working in IT, said, "It wasn't enough that I had to get my kids to school, prepare their dinners, and book their appointments. I had to think about all this stuff, as well as all the stuff related to my work, as well as all the boring stuff my husband didn't want to think about, such as his parents' birthdays and remembering to pick up his dry cleaning. Like I somehow found this interesting because I was a woman."

And what do the men notice in relation to their kids' well-being? Not much, I hear over and over. Says Sandra: "My kid had a teacher when he was in Grade 3 who had the IQ of a pine cone. He told us on parent-teacher day not to feel bad about his low marks, because he was good in gym, and personal training was a hot profession. When I freaked out later, my husband said I was overreacting. 'OK, so the teacher's a jerk,' he said. 'But everyone has teachers who are jerks.'"

I have heard hundreds of similar stories. You probably have a hundred of your own to add.

Demands on all fronts. And we people-pleasing women had to make sure that we did it all, that no one's needs would be overlooked.

But it wasn't all bad. I did some of the most exciting things in my career in my thirties. And as we will see, many women had their greatest achievements, at home or at work, during this life chapter.

chapter two

The Awful Truth about Corporate Life:

Organizations Are Built by Men for Men

- *"I lost myself, my sense of being because I had to conform to an alpha-male world. You have to become one of them, because if you don't, they cut you out. Twenty years of trying to fit in, to be accepted. You have to become a sycophant, to nod and yield. I would come out of meetings sick to my stomach not because of what had happened in the meeting, but because of what had happened to me."*

- *"I actually can't point to one egregious thing. It's the subtle things, the ones that seem to say, 'You're not welcome here. You're too emotional, not tough enough, you don't fit in.'"*

"The business world is a hotbed of politics and unethical behavior. I was the starry-eyed young woman who thought it would be civil."

"Management says, We want and value women. But then if you do what women do—express your feelings, talk about values like they really matter and are more than lip service, you are seen as soft and touchy-feely."

"The only place where you can be really authentic is running your own business and creating a culture sympathetic to your needs and values."

"In a word, most organizations are alienating."

"There are great employers out there, if few and far between. But you have to be aggressive in knowing what you want, being clear about priorities and refusing to compromise your values. You also have to be aggressive in searching out those great employers and communicating what you need."
    —Midlife women discussing whether organizations are hospitable to their needs

A s every professional woman in the Western world knows, if you get a group of women together talking about their jobs, there will be instant rapport as they share war stories, especially if they work in male-dominated environments.

Huge numbers of women continue to feel alienated from the testosterone-fueled corporate culture—the spinning, the gap between espoused and practiced values, the politics and chasing of power, the bravado. These hurt women more than men as they tend to be more credulous and have a greater belief in the goodness of others.

When I taught introductory psychology, I had an exercise for the first day of class. I would write on the blackboard: "People are born basically _____." The men completed the sentence with expressions like: empty; needing to be socialized; potentially bad. The women completed the sentence with such sentiments as: good; kind; caring.

Tamara Weir-Bryan, who has seen many women in her counseling practice, says women have higher expectations of the trustworthiness of management. "They want to trust and believe in the organization, then their trust is 'disabused.' They buy into the values, like the importance of people, then see it's just something said to gain employee commitment, but it's not actually practiced. So they become disappointed and angry."

As Marie, a project manager, said, "The environment is about productivity and the bottom line. Who cares whether the customer is satisfied, people are broken, true value is created, quality is produced, the environment is destroyed? The worst part is that people have resigned themselves to this outrageous dehumanizing process. Then management says, 'People are our most important resource.' Yeah, right."

In my survey to the midlife women whose experiences are recounted in this book, I asked whether they felt they could be authentic in an organization and whether organizations welcomed their needs and style. If I had to summarize the key theme that emerged from the near four hundred responses I received to this question, it would be this: *Most organizations are built by men for men.* And it doesn't appear to be any different in the public sector than in the private sector. Although this is my take on the issues raised, several women actually used this expression. This is not male-bashing. It is clear that the dominant cultural values of organizations are still male and that the rhythms of organizational life run counter to women's needs and interpersonal style. How?

Live-and-Die-by-the-Numbers Culture

"The business world has become more hostile, not less hostile, to the female side with economic conditions which favor cutting costs to the marrow, extracting every last ounce of productivity out of everyone, and assessing talent in a fiendishly Darwinian manner."
    —Self-described recovering MBA

Harder, faster, leaner, meaner. These have become the mantras of contemporary organizational life. As management professors Jeffrey Pfeffer and Robert Sutton say, "The leadership model is based on a competitive dynamic that emphasizes winning as contest in which one person's success requires the failure of another." This toughness and live-and-die-by-the-numbers, only-results-matter culture is abhorrent to many women, an affront to our rhythms, language, and what we feel is acceptable behavior.

As one writer said, "Think about those best-selling titles by CEOs, like *Straight from the Gut* and *Only the Paranoid Survive.* Reading (former General Electric CEO) Welch's revisionist history is like being the lone woman trapped in a smelly locker room with a bunch of good old boys and a coach who keeps slapping you on the back while he tells you how great he is. Welch considered his greatest purpose in life was to increase GE's stock prices, and for his self-serving methods I hope he will be remembered, not as the greatest CEO who ever lived, but as the world's greatest stocksucker."

Other women said the values—lean and mean—are out of whack. "The atmosphere in most organizations is Darwinian, and the intense competitiveness runs counter to female personalities," said one corporate refugee. "When I was a VP of human resources, all I saw was the compromise of values to get results. What kind of results are you getting when abuses are overlooked, and people are completely demoralized? These guys are tough and mean," she said, referring to her former male senior management team members. And she added: "I have spent my career watching how people behave at work. This is what I know to be true: men fight to win, women fight to survive."

What do most women want? They want kinder, more caring work environments. They also detest being seen as a "unit of productivity" rather than as a human being. And don't think of these women as soft and mushy emotional types. Many of them hold senior jobs in the public and private sectors, are results-oriented, understand contemporary business realities, and are abundantly accomplished.

Nevertheless, women are essentially relational beings, wanting to connect with others on an emotional level and to develop caring relationships. As one marketing manager said, "I want to relate to my colleagues as people. I am as interested in what happens to an individual as I am in the company's welfare." But because of intense productivity pressures, there isn't time to get to know or value colleagues on a personal level. Certainly there is that contemporary business saw about the importance of teamwork, but in many cases, teamwork could be rephrased as: "Wham, bam, thank-you, Ma'am."

In a hit-the-ground-running business culture, there is no longer an opportunity for the casual banter before the meeting, the daily give-and-take conversations that cement interpersonal relationships. As Sean Elder, an author who specializes in men's issues, observes, the skills needed to be successful in organizations at senior levels "are antithetical to the caring-sharing sort. Success and even heroism are still measured by a man's ability to compartmentalize, desensitize . . ."

"We work in teams but it's in name only. You come together, do your thing, then move on to the next project," said one marketing specialist. Women want to have a relationship beyond the strictly task-focused. They care about getting results, but they care just as much about *how* the work gets done as what gets done.

And they want their contributions recognized.

Not Being Seen as a Serious Player

> *"There was growing dissatisfaction in my company from the professional women. I was asked to do a survey to determine the sources. (I didn't need to. I already knew them . . .) The findings were that the hard-driving Type-A environment made it very hard for women to be themselves. Intuition, soft skills, and people management were less appreciated compared to fact-based research, toughness, and competitiveness. The women also said that despite great remuneration and working conditions, they would all leave if the culture didn't change. Why? Because they weren't valued for who they are. Three years later, all these women were gone for promotions to other companies."*
> —Human resources director, financial services

There are thousands upon thousands of studies, research papers, testimonials, anecdotes, conferences, books, columns, and articles with titles such as "Women still face challenges in the modern workplace," testifying to the fact that it's hard for a woman to be seen as a serious player, especially in male-dominated work environments. If you don't believe me, google "career advancement of women" or "glass ceiling for women" and what you will find is that whether you are talking about the career experiences of MBAs, academics, artists, human resource specialists, IT workers, lawyers, high-wire walkers (okay, I made that up), or just about any other profession, discrimination still exists. But please don't print out the references unless you want to be personally responsible for the destruction of the rain forest. Indeed, a recent survey of women's business "clout" detected slowdowns between 2004 and 2005. The surveyors concluded that "women's influence is creeping slowly . . . and probably won't equal men's during this decade or the next." (To give you a brief taste of the percentage of women holding senior roles: 17.1% of partners in law firms in 2004; 15.7% of Fortune 500 corporate officer positions in 2002; 11.2 % of Financial Post 500 corporate board seats in 2003; 21.1% of college professors in 2002.)

Women need to work harder, take more risks, and be more exceptional if they want to have their work taken seriously. The glass ceiling is cracked, not broken. This comment from a public relations specialist was typical of the responses to my survey: "It's not one big thing where you have to prove yourself. It's in everything you do from the big to the small. If you are working in a mostly male environment, you have to be always out there, always outperforming everyone else." Many of the women who responded to my survey couldn't point to one particular instance of discrimination, but at the same time virtually all of them felt some kind of strain.

Madeline Heilman, a professor of psychology at New York University, has conducted important and interesting research into sex biases in work settings. She argues that women are scarce in senior positions due to stereotypical ideas about what women are like and misconceptions about what they *should* be like. Traditional stereotypes attributed to women, such as being co-operative, kind, and understanding, are considered oppositional to traditional male stereotypes of being aggressive, independent, and decisive.

Now your blood will boil: The problem is that senior positions are thought to require attributes associated with men. So much for emotional intelligence being a desirable attribute in leadership. Heilman's data indicates that when women are obviously competent they are described as "untrustworthy" or "conniving"—what she defines as the bitchiness cluster of traits, because, in sum, they are seen as awful. And women and men shared the same stereotypes, so women may be directing these stereotypes at themselves.

The result is that women are penalized when their success defies gender expectations. Dammed if you do, and dammed if you don't. If you are not successful, you are assumed to be incompetent. If you are successful, you are assumed to be unlikeable. As a career coach said: "We have to work harder to be seen as competent, but then when we get results we are accused of being a perfectionist or a control freak."

A man can be mean 364 1/4 days a year, until one day he does something humane and the staff response is "He seems tough, but he's really a nice guy inside." A woman can be great 364 1/4 days a year, but one day gets frustrated and lashes out and the staff says, "Sure she seems nice, but watch out 'cause she can be a real bitch."

But it's not all about discrimination. Many women have decided enough is enough. As we will see in Chapter 4, many women are pushing back and saying, "That's it. I'm out of here."

They flee to female-friendly organizations or set up their own businesses. This phenomenon is not new. In the late 1980s, the challenge in organizations was creating a level playing field to promote women into senior positions. Since the late 1990s, the challenge has been to keep women. "I grew tired of being a stranger in a strange land," said a former recruiter. "I left corporate life to pursue an entirely different career as a teacher." Her comment about alienation is typical of most of the women who responded to my survey. Unfortunately, if they quit at midcareer, they also reduce the pool of senior women in organizations. The result is that organizations will become even more masculinized, putting yet more strain on younger women.

Yes, there are many more women in senior positions today than there were ten years ago. But they are stressed and feel that they are under tremendous pressure to do everything right. But because "right" is often defined by men, many women feel they will never succeed.

Women want to be valued for who they are. They want to express their feminine voices, not engage in role playing, and still be seen as an important contributor. In other words, they want to be authentic.

On Being Authentic

"Sometime in my forties, I realized how important it was to be one whole, integrated person. I did not want to work in an environment where I would have to segregate a work persona and a personal persona."
—Writer

Can you be authentic in organizations? About 80 percent of the midlife women answered "no" to this question. (This was not a scientific survey, and many of the respondents were corporate refugees, so the real percentage would probably be lower.) But my research and observations over many years of counseling women show the answer is more complicated than that: it depends on the organizations, the number of women in the senior ranks, your position in the company, the individual's personality, and whether the match between the individual and the corporate personality is a good one.

For example, women in senior roles who are closer to where decisions are made, and consequently more aware of the compromises, are more likely to say you can't be authentic. Similarly, women in male-dominated organizations are more likely to despair of the lack of female role models who would feminize the culture. And some women, as we will see, are more capable of fitting into organizations, reflecting both a greater adaptability on their part and an organization that welcomes their style.

But the opportunity to be authentic is the critical quest. If I had to name the number-one issue that drives women, it would be that we want to express our authentic selves in our work. We don't want to repress important aspects of our personality, particularly the feminine voice that is supposed to be key in emotionally intelligent leadership, and is, ironically, the voice that many women say is more difficult to express than ever before.

But although being authentic was at the top of everyone's career wish list, it's not always easy. "It's a constant struggle" said a book publicist. "You need to make a conscious decision not to overlook who you are for the pursuit of your career. Being authentic is different from being comfortable. You are comfortable in your own skin but have to have the courage to be bold and express what may not be palatable."

What does it mean to be authentic? The women's answers are as individual as they are. For some it meant expressing their values. For others it meant being "real." As one independent marketing consultant explained it, "Authenticity means being your true self. Not what others want you to be."

Being authentic means not thinking about how you are perceived, talking about what you want, expressing personal views, behaving in a way consistent with values, not changing your behavior from one situation to another, and having a personal style that is readily communicated. As we will see later in this chapter, some of us are simply more capable than others at being able to express our authentic selves in corporate environments.

What is clear to me from my own experience working with women and looking at the wealth of responses to my survey questions is that, as one woman put it, "authenticity is as essential as breathing." The cost of not being authentic is losing one's self and ultimately becoming depressed or anxious. The other aspect of authenticity is that it's harder to be authentic when you are younger and still trying to win approval. As a marketing manager in a professional services firm said, "Early in my career I tried to emulate my male colleagues. It took me two decades to realize that I don't need to copy anyone's style. I can be silly and giggle, or hug my colleagues, and still be recognized for my contributions." I've heard similar comments numerous times.

The good news is that although many of the younger women I work with today report similar anxieties about trying to fit in, the opportunity to be authentic is a central part of their career vocabulary. Moreover because they are more often reporting to senior women who value self-expression, they are less likely to feel the need to repress their personalities at work. It will be interesting to see how they fare once they rise to more senior positions.

It is also possible that midlife women are simply better at picking up on B.S. In a study comparing older and younger women and men in their ability to detect lying, researchers found that older women soared above the other groups in decoding whether they were being presented with truth or lies.

Dissembling, or the Art of Fitting into a Square Hole

> *"I was one of those eighties girls, trying to be a mini-man, walking the threshold of being true to natural strengths, and at the same time disguising them so they didn't call attention as being too feminine. It was hard work and resulted in a gut-wrenching feeling that I had compromised myself. This went on for two decades. Many of my colleagues and friends know the pain and disappointments that we all went through during this time. The tragedy is that I don't think it's changed. I have yet to feel a celebration of effective women in the workplace. We continue to fight the battles men don't fight. It's akin to a low-grade infectious disease, which depletes energy, passion, comfort, and engagement."*
> —Manager in government

Catalyst surveyed women executives from Fortune 1000 companies to learn what strategies they employ in order to succeed. Forty-seven percent said they have developed a style with which male managers are comfortable. Can you imagine about half of men saying they attribute their success to a working style with which women feel comfortable?

This is where women pay the biggest price—in needing to fit in, in modifying their personalities to be "appropriate." They constantly struggle to be seen as feminine but not soft, decisive but not aggressive or bitchy. Apparently not much has changed since the early eighties. Women still engage in impression management, wondering, How will I be seen? This places a huge strain on them, and they resent it.

A vice president of human resources put it this way: "I want to exercise leadership and do it in a nurturing, caring way. And then I know someone is going to trash me for being too touchy-feely. So I'm always thinking, 'How will this be perceived?'"

Career coach Tamara Weir-Bryan concurs. "The major issue for women is having to hide their emotional selves, walking a tightrope between displaying behavior that men think is strong, but not too strong." In other words, desired behaviors—the gold standard of what is effective—are male. But as we've already seen, women are penalized for demonstrating these behaviors.

Okay. I know men will also say that they, too, want to be authentic, that organizations make demands on them in terms of how they express themselves. And it is true that some men also experience the strains of trying to fit in. But think of it this way: Have you ever heard of a man attending a workshop that teaches him how to use his voice, how to dress, or how to use his hands where the female style is held up as the example? Have emotion in your voice! Show your curves! Use your hands to emphasize a point! Can you imagine a man reading a book with a title like *Why Boring Men Don't Get the Corner Office: 50 Ways You Can Shine Like a Woman in the Boardroom and Still Win Like a Man at Home?*

Given the role prescriptions for women, it is not surprising that women who are relatively successful in corporate environments tend to fall into some recognizable "types."

Five Archetypes of Midlife Women Who Populate Organizations

"Calling someone corporate is the gravest insult I could level against a person . . . it implies all manner of perversity."
    —Novelist

Here are five archetypes of women in the middle and senior ranks in organizations. Of course no one is purely one thing or another—most of us are a blend of behaviors. That said, although these are caricatures, I believe you will recognize yourself, and your colleagues, bosses, clients, and friends, in these women in a less extreme form.

Siren: She is sharp, sexy, and tough. She wears European, usually French, designer clothing, prefers skirts to pants and can walk with a degree of grace in high-heeled shoes. She loves Manolos and Jimmy Choos; if she can't afford them, she buys the knock-offs from Zara. Everything she wears is sharp: knifelike creases, stilettos, angular lapels, long collars that end in points.

Her taste in jewelry—she *loves* jewelry—leans toward diamonds (big) and gold (chunky). Some might say it flirts with the vulgar.

She spends serious money on maintenance—weekly manicures (acrylic nails), regular pedicures, and facials. The telephone numbers of her "service providers" are on her BlackBerry—she scares them. She also has had a number of cosmetic surgical interventions. She belongs to an expensive gym that caters to CEOs and investment banker types (great for networking), runs five days a week, and does Pilates. Right now she is on the South Beach diet, but who knows what will be fashionable tomorrow?

Her skills in creating the right alliances at work are finely honed. She knows who's "in," and who's on the way out—usually before they do. She is highly strategic in her relationships, including those with her staff. She has pets, whom she keeps anxiously dancing on a string. They know they can be dumped at any moment in favor of someone who can make her look even better. She enjoys keeping them "interested" and plays them off each other. Everyone understands she is dangerous and can't be trusted. Her staff despises her.

No one can quite figure out how she's gotten as far as she has—despite brilliant networking skills, she's often not very smart. People gossip about her. It is rumored that she is having an affair with the CEO, although some say she's having an affair with a company director. They also speculate, unkindly, about her background: "I heard she started as a secretary," they whisper. She can turn any guy she works with into a sniveling marshmallow. Her reaches into the senior echelons are legendary.

She is "pronoid," suffering from delusions of admiration. A narcissist, she has a bottomless need for adulation and never-ending feedback about how great she is, what an unusual person she is, how "out there" she is.

Her favorite word is *strategic*. The Siren is usually found in the middle or senior management ranks in a knowledge work sector, such as investment banking or a pharmaceutical. It was tough to get ahead in the 1970s and 1980s in these cultures. She may not have started out as a Siren, but she learned that using her sexuality gave her an edge in these competitive, male-dominated environments.

Supermom: She is warm, nurturing, and caring. Everyone likes and trusts her. She is an extrovert; people describe her personality as "bubbly." She takes a keen interest in you, especially your personal life. She not only remembers your wedding anniversary, she knows what grades your kids are in and their birthdays. When you went through a difficult patch, she gave you the telephone number of a therapist (although she made it clear that she has personally never needed to see a counselor).

While she may wear inexpensive "career girl" suits if she has to look corporate, she really prefers "comfy" clothes. She has a large wardrobe of holiday-themed jewelry and sweaters. She's been to a day spa a few times—a gift from her husband. But under normal circumstances, she would never spend "this kind of money" on herself.

In her office cubicle, you will find many photos of her family and the dogs. She has a poster with an affirming message, such as: "Soften your heart—heal the world"; her coffee cup also has an affirming message. She signs her e-mails with smiley faces and makes liberal use of CAPS!!!!!!, a mannerism she picked up from her eight-year-old daughter.

She brings brownies to the office, organizes all the office parties, and does more than her share of kitchen detail. She *loves* all the holidays and decorates the office accordingly. She wears a costume on Halloween.

She is inclusive and likes everyone. Her motto: if you find someone boring, it's because you are not looking at how they are *not* boring. As a manager, she is supportive and nurturing, and she has trouble giving negative feedback (she doesn't want to hurt your feelings). She is undemanding and easy to please.

She cares about the people she works with, not about whether an assignment is strategic or good for her career, which is why she never reaches the senior ranks. She will happily take on low-profile tasks if it will please her boss or her colleagues. An ambitious man in her department once called her the "office garbage can."

The Supermom is happily ensconced in the middle-management ranks and is probably in a department with more women than men, such as human resources or public affairs.

Suit: She is an ambitious, no-nonsense "mini-man" striver. Her career is what is most important to her. She lives in the suburbs and resents the time the commute digs into her work.

She wears two-inch regulation heels, "good quality" navy or black suits (she read a book that told her this would make her look authoritative), and running shoes for the train commute to the office (she walks whenever she can, being a strong believer in never missing any opportunity for self-improvement and making the best use of time).

She hates shopping. If she is in a senior role, she has a personal shopper at Holt's who calls her twice a year to tell her she has put aside a "nice" selection of business clothes for her. She wears polite pearl or gold earrings and a small gold necklace. She does, however, permit herself one indulgence—her weekly manicure. This is "my personal time," she says. This is one of the areas in which she shows her femininity—long, acrylic nails polished in orange or an "off" color of red.

She is highly strategic in how she manages her career. She has a nose for high-profile assignments. She doesn't pay attention to projects with a lower visibility. Like the Siren, she cultivates alliances with powerful people who can help her further her career. Many people call her a bitch.

She is politically correct, to the point you often don't know what she is saying. She rarely uses emotive adjectives such as *fabulous*, nor does she use emotionally loaded words like *love*, as in "I loved that idea." Her favorite expression is "strategic partnership." At the end of the year she often has unused vacation days.

As a manager, like the Siren, she has pets, favoring staff who will make her look good. She can be quite mean to average- and low-performing staff. They don't like her; in fact, they call her "the boss from Hell."

Although she is generally reserved and discusses little about her personal life (it is rumored that she doesn't have one), in a weak moment she has confided to one of her pets that she wears La Senza lingerie and has a tattoo at the base of her spine, hinting that she is a tiger in the bedroom. Needless to say, the pet, although sworn to secrecy, told everyone.

She strongly believes that nice girls don't get the corner office.

The Suit can be found in the middle or senior ranks of most organizations, although most often in traditionally male environments, such as technology, manufacturing, and investment banking. At midlife, she sometimes changes her behavioral style. As a result of psychological growth or a personal trauma, her values may lead her to want different things from life beyond a career.

Saint: She is a long-suffering victim of what she sees as bad management behavior. She spends a lot of time fighting to do the right things for her staff, clients, and customers. She feels overworked and underappreciated and constantly lets you know this.

She is not particularly interested in fashion. She favors either comfortable clothes or those with an ethnic feel. She loves silver, hates gold and any stone that shines. When she travels, which is frequently, she picks up "interesting" artifacts made by local craftsmen.

She is often well educated. She uses the word *values* a lot. She feels that values are woefully lacking in the business world, and she is bitter about this. She has high professional standards and complains that the workload is such that it is impossible to do the work to the desired professional level. Sometimes she's also a whiner. Moving to gorgeous new offices? She complains about changing her telephone number. Going to a conference? She complains about the food.

She is honest, sometimes to a fault. As a manager, she tells her staff about all the things that have been done wrong by senior management. This can poison and demoralize staff. Some Saints, however, will go to bat for their own staff, to protect them from the "bullies."

She may also micromanage her staff because she wants to make sure that any work coming out of her shop is perfect. She uses the "F" word a lot, especially when talking about bosses and colleagues. Her staff usually doesn't like her. There is high turnover in her department.

She takes every vacation and personal day available. If she has the opportunity, she will buy additional vacation days. She has visited many "off the beaten path" destinations. She loves yoga retreats.

The Saint can be found in the middle ranks of most types of organizations that are not heavily populated by men. Ultimately, she is often happiest in self-employment or playing a role in a not-for-profit. If she moves into a job that is a great match for her in terms of its values, she may become a Seeker.

Seeker: She is direct, honest, and expressive. People call her a straight arrow, as she will always tell you what she is thinking. She tells people the truth, and she expects the truth from others. She refuses to sell her soul to her employer or play a "role" in the corporate environment in order to fit in. She is a career activist seeking opportunities for deep satisfaction from her work, regularly reflecting on how and whether her work is meeting her needs. If she is unhappy, she usually quits. If she can't, she is miserable. (And she may become a Saint.)

Like the Saint, she is driven strongly by values. As a manager, she has created an environment consistent with these values. Her staff are encouraged to express themselves. She has had many male staff members cry in her office. Her staff adores her and is intensely loyal to her. She is a great champion of their work. She wants them to be happy and effective. She is not a political animal, but she can be very strategic in the work she takes on and in the alliances she makes to support the work of her department.

She dresses in a way that is expressive of who she is, anything from Armani to jeans, designer jewelry to multiple piercings, depending on her personality and the organization. She has her own personal style, and is not drawn to trends. She is the new female role model.

She can be effusive. She doesn't believe in impression management. Unlike the Suit, she does not hesitate to use words like *fabulous* or to tell people she "loves" the work they did. She has been known to use obscene language in senior management environments if that is appropriate to the issue at hand. She doesn't care about being seen as a people-pleaser.

The Seeker can be found anywhere in middle and senior management ranks, most often in female-friendly organizations, NGOs, or government. She despairs of the fact that there are few organizations that offer a good fit for her. She believes almost good girls can get the corner office, but her definition of success usually doesn't involve the corner office.

She may not always have been a Seeker but at midlife she feels good about who she is and refuses to compromise.

Who Fits In and Who Flees?

"I've never really struggled with fitting in. I enjoy corporate environments . . . this is where I do my best work.
I 'get' the rhythms and the expectations."
   —Market researcher

"I've always been Sandra . . . a bit loud, a bit pointed,
a bit aggressive."
   —Management consultant

I spent my early working life trying to fit into corporate environments. I failed, but it wasn't for lack of trying. Some people are simply more capable of fitting into the corporate world than others.

We are not talking about being authentic here, because many women who are happily employed in corporate environments are honest and expressive. In fact, I would describe them as Seekers. But they don't experience corporate environments as being hostile or impossible. They worked hard to find a place for themselves and were very picky about fit, but through trial and error, finally found it.

They have a number of characteristics in common, which I would describe as *interpersonal flexibility*.

Allysia, for example, a much-respected VP of learning for a bank, has been known to swear, wear leather pants in the board-room, and cry at the office. She is clear about who she is, and she is not a caricature of a career girl. But she is also one of the most adaptable people I know. In any given situation, she has the emotional discipline to step back and ask herself what she wants to accomplish and how it will affect others. Does she want to compromise or fight? One of her favorite expressions is "You can be right. But dead right. You have to know what battles to pick." Her ego needs are modest. She's by no means a doormat, but she also doesn't need to be the star all the time.

She quickly establishes relationships with others. She can work with people she doesn't care for, although she would prefer not to. She can use charm when necessary to influence others, but she isn't manipulative; she is for the most part even-tempered, and doesn't get annoyed by small things. "In the big picture, who cares about this stuff?" she says. She is a moderate extrovert. She enjoys talking to people and being part of something bigger than herself. But she also needs her downtime. She says her mother used to describe her as a chameleon. She is easygoing, sociable, and affable.

In contrast, the women who said they could never fit in or had difficulty fitting in were either "larger than life" extroverts like Sheilagh, formerly a training manager, now a recruiter, or "opinionated, self-conscious" introverts. In other words, they had more extreme personalities.

The range of acceptable behaviors for a woman is narrower than that for a man. None of the women mentioned above, who experienced difficulty fitting in, conform to the stereotypes of how corporate women should behave. Sheilagh, for example, is so ebullient and naturally expressive that many people describe her as "over the top." She always has several storylines going on at once in a conversation, so that by the end of five minutes I have to ask her to tell me the end of each of the stories. "If it's in my mind, it's out my mouth," she says. She has what she describes as big Ohio hair. (She's from Ohio. Now that I think of it, my Ohio-born mother also had big hair.) She is always dripping in costume jewelry. If there is a part of her body or clothing that can be adorned, it is. Too much! Too much! I always tell her. I describe her personality as Technicolor. She agrees.

The self-conscious introverts faced similar challenges. Cheryl, for example, says she is "incapable of dissembling. . . . Either I was too direct and abrupt and people said I was pushy, or I didn't say anything and people said I was not a team player." She says she was never able to mold herself to fit into an environment and that she always lacked "the social graces, tact and diplomacy." She spent much of her corporate career being criticized for being too opinionated. I don't think it was expressing her opinions that was the problem, rather *how* she expressed them, a problem I can personally relate to. Remember why I didn't get the job offer at the oil company.

Women who fail to fit in are often self-conscious and spend their life feeling different. They describe early experiences of being an outsider. Take Sarah, for example, who went to a private school where her mother was a teacher. "I was the Jewish girl with the dark curly hair in a sea of small-boned Wasp princesses. But my sense of being different went deeper. I didn't share my classmates' interests. I was intensely studious and worried obsessively about my shortcomings. When I was nineteen, I wished I was just a normal blond, a vivacious, light-hearted, extroverted woman who got lots of dates and knew how to giggle at the right time."

Alita reports feeling the same way as an adolescent. "In high school, I faked disdain for the popular group. Called them 'typical.' It was a defense because I couldn't fit in. But I secretly longed to be anointed into the inner sanctum."

Both Sarah and Alita never quite made it in the corporate world. Their checkered career histories reveal a series of jobs from which they were fired, several contract positions, and long periods of unemployment. Both sought the help of therapists. With time and much personal work they are no longer trying to change themselves in order to fit in, but have carved paths that allow them to be themselves. Sarah became a writer. Alita went back to school and did a master's degree in counseling. She now has a successful clinical practice, specializing in women.

There is no one reason some women simply can't make it in a corporate environment. Some are too sensitive and experience every assault on their ego—and, as we have seen, there are many in corporate life—as a deep personal wound. These wounds fester, resulting in depression or anxiety. Bosses and colleagues tell them to toughen up and not to be so thin-skinned. They hear a lot of comments such as "You shouldn't take it so personally."

Others have personalities too big to be contained—they have never been capable of the give-and-take of corporate life, which sometimes requires dissembling, not expressing personal opinions, while being able to deal with the salad of personalities you encounter in a team environment.

If I had to name one quality this group of women shares, it would be *directness*. (My clients and friends would probably put me into this category.) In contrast to those who succeed, they are also more intolerant—they don't suffer fools gladly. They have more difficulty getting along with people who don't interest them. I call it the "piss off" factor: they piss off more people, and it's easier for them to become pissed off.

For example, I once listened to my friend talking to one of her staff while we were on vacation together. Hearing her end of the conversation, it was pretty easy to get the gist. After five minutes of what I experienced as one of the most excruciating conversations since the earth cooled, and I exaggerate only slightly, I imagined what I would have said to her staff member: "I'm on vacation for heaven's sake. You're a professional. You don't need me to bless every e-mail you send or conversation you have by the coffee machine." Dana, on the other hand, spent just under two hours on the phone, acting like it was one of the most important conversations she had ever had.

When she hung up, she said, "I wish it was legal to murder your staff." Okay, so she shared the awful bitchy truth, but the point is she was capable of *acting* like a caring, compassionate manager.

The Work-Life Juggernaut

"Our CEO goes around promoting work-life balance. But when I asked him about why he hired his new CFO, what qualities did she have? He said, 'She BlackBerried me back the answers to my interview questions until one minute before she gave birth.'"
—Recruiter, human resources

"My boss, the VP of HR, said, 'We really need to promote work-life balance in the company. Let's have a meeting Monday morning at seven-thirty to discuss it.'"
—Human resources manager

"The VP wanted to hire me. She said, 'Two things are important to us – work-life balance, and passion. We can meet your needs as a single parent. I can tell you are a passionate person, just like me. So I may call you sometimes at two in the morning, because I've had a great idea and want to discuss it with you. And I know you will feel the same passion as I do.'"
—Marketing professional

Big announcement. A prominent woman leaves her financial service-sector job. It's a major headline in the business section. "Executive chooses family over career." Much babble around the water cooler that week. "Didjahear . . . ?" I receive four calls and seven e-mails. I don't know why anyone thought I would be surprised. To be honest, I sometimes wonder why we don't see articles with headlines such as "Executive came to work today despite the fact that she has three kids at home, a sick parent, and went to bed at 3 a.m., after completing her business reading."

A week or so later, a column appeared in the paper about a CEO who planned to take "six to eight months to reconnect with his wife and teenagers." Women *choose* one thing and in the process give up something else. Men *reconnect.*

The choices women make can also be practical. In a recent study conducted by the Families and Work Institute, the researchers found that 34 percent of female executives downsized their career aspirations in light of family and personal commitments.

Now you may be thinking: Who cares about women in senior positions downsizing their career desires? They make more money, so they have more wiggle room in terms of the choices they can make. But women at all levels are making these kinds of choices, choosing to work part-time or simply opting out. And some resent having to. Many of the younger women despair of the work-family juggernaut. For example, only 60 percent of business-school graduates are working outside the home five years after graduation. They look down the road and see an impossible path.

Torn. Always torn. Do work at the desired level of quality and sacrifice other commitments, or satisfy personal commitments and compromise the work. As one management trainer said, "I have this constant shouting match in my head . . . work . . . family . . . work . . . family. I know it sounds trite, like I'm just spouting out the Careers page of the paper, but it tears me apart."

Of course, men also complain about a lack of work-life balance and care about spending quality time with their families. But I have never had a man ask me, as women frequently do, "How did you manage to have a career *and* a family?"

The obvious reason is that women are still the primary care-givers. The less obvious reason is that women think and care about a host of more subtle things related to others' welfare, and when there is a problem in one area of life, it spills into other areas.

I personally have never heard a man say, "Sorry, my mind just drifted off. I'm a bit depressed today because my daughter is having trouble with her teacher." Nor do men deal as often with the gut-wrenching decision: great career or time for my family. Certainly they feel the conflicts and younger men are increasingly putting work-life balance on the table as key to their career satisfaction, but they don't have the same ongoing interior monologues about guilt and choices.

The problem is simple: *there is a lack of will to actually practice espoused beliefs and policy.* Sure, organizations boast about their work-life programming, but how many women do you see in senior positions working part-time? I'll tell you a secret, and remember I have been a consultant in this field to organizations for many years: there is an almost inverse relationship between the amounts of propaganda an employer has on its "best of class" work-life balance policies and the degree to which they are actu-ally implemented.

One woman, for example, who works for a bank celebrated in the media for its family-friendly practices, tells the following story: "I report to the director of work-life policies. I told my boss that on my son's first day of school I would telecommute so that I could pick him up for lunch. She said, 'I'm paying you to work, not to have lunch with your son.'"

I think I have written something like the following sentence a thousand times over the past ten years so please forgive me if I sound crabby: although managers may talk about respecting and promoting work-life balance, it is not practiced in most organizations.

Extreme Work Hurts

Who pays the price for work overload? Everyone, including our children. (And by the way, so do organizations in terms of lost productivity, but that's beside the point here.) When we come home tired and grumpy, we are not effective parents. Many of the women described situations when they were physically in the same space as their kids, but mentally miles away while they worried about work-related issues. Children are not programmed to share what's important to them when it's convenient for their parents. We want to be there for our kids—physically, which in itself is a significant challenge—but emotionally as well. If there is one thing I have worried about for the past decade, it is this: What is the long-term impact of the spillover of work demands into family time on the healthy development of children? (Acclaimed child psychiatrist and advocate Dr. Paul Steinhauer first raised this question in the early 1990s, when he worried about parents' time-poverty undermining children's wellness.)

Let me remind you of my summary statement about corporate life: Most organizations are built by men for men. Implication: the rhythms of corporate life are contrary not only to our own needs, but also to those of our children. I have heard the following statement several times over the past few years: "Organizations have made their productivity gains on the backs of our children."

What We Want from Our Work

Work is one of the most important sources of life satisfaction. Great work inspires us and brings out the best in us. Bad work destroys us. When we are depressed with our work, it affects how we carry out all our life roles as partner, friend, or parent. Although work is not the centerpiece of our identity, it is a key contributor to our sense of well-being.

We work for many reasons—money, collegiality, to make a difference, to perform our craft, to be stretched professionally. But at the core we all want the same thing: *to be able to express ourselves in our work and to still have time for a life.*

Given the challenges so many of us are experiencing at work, it is not surprising how many people today are singing the new career blues. But lest you commit suicide over your cubicle wall, for now let me say that in later chapters we will see how midlife women are pushing back and finding and designing work that meets their needs, seeking out female-friendly employers or setting up their own businesses. They know what is important to them and refuse to compromise their values.

chapter three

Besieged and Restless:

The Emotional Mathematics of Contemporary Career Maladies

"Every professional breath I take is a gasp."

"It was the values which were off, doing the same thing over and over, not any one thing in particular, but a whole bunch of things which together made my work life intolerable."

"When you are going through a career crisis, you become your own worst enemy. You're too depressed to do anything which would change your situation."

"Do I like my work? How would I know? I have no time to think about it. I'm always just in reacting mode."

"I have nothing left over for myself. I'm completely empty."

*"I don't hate what I'm doing. But it gives me no satisfaction.
There is nothing I do that allows me to say at the end of the
day, 'I'm proud of what I've accomplished.'"*
    —Midlife women discussing how they feel about their work

Almost every day I receive a call from a female client or friend that goes something like this: "I can't do this anymore. I'm running on *empty*. I'm stretched to the max and holding on by my fingernails. My kids, my husband, my work . . . it's just too much."

My client Alison, for example, is a forty-three-year-old training manager for a school board. "I leave work at six-thirty and rush home," she says. "When I get there, my kids are pissy because they're hungry and had to wait for me to have dinner. My husband is pissed because he has to cook every night. And my boss is pissed because I'm late on a project. So here I am trying to meet everyone's needs, failing them all, everyone's annoyed with me, and I'm not even having any fun. And if I complain about this, I sound like a whiny bitch because at least I have a husband to cook for me. But the truth is I'm not sure I can sustain this any longer."

When we think about a career crisis, we tend to think of an apocalyptic moment when something dramatic happens, leading to a radical and sudden life transformation. The media is full of these kinds of stories: "CEO quits her job to move to the country and make jam after health scare."

Certainly this is sometimes the case. A career crisis can be triggered by an unexpected or disturbing event—the death of a friend, a sudden job loss, the breakup of a marriage—that leads to a significant rethinking of how we are living and what we want and need from our work. One woman, for example, after experiencing a near plane crash, quit her new job and had a "meltdown" that lasted several months.

Sometimes a crisis is triggered by what can best be described as a *career-defining moment*. A former family doctor who made a dramatic move into a new clinical specialty says that when she received notification for the renewal of her lease, she thought: "Is this what I really want to do with the next ten years of my life? Am I doing this only because I am owned by some real estate and a legal agreement?" (Lease renewals are a common catalyst for career-defining moments for independent health practitioners.)

A journalist's moment of truth came from a dream. "I went to my boss with a Styrofoam cup half full of my blood. 'This is all I have left for you,' I said."

But for most, crisis is the result of a long accumulation of stressful factors rather than one single event, coupled with the psychological turbulence that often occurs at midlife. As one woman said: "How long does midlife last? I'm not sure I can take much more of this. After working for a bank for many years and living through several stressful downsizings, and after a failed marriage due to money and other sordid details in which my ex disappeared and was not paying child support, I took a course in body work. I tried to make it in this field but couldn't make enough money, so here I am again—needing to keep the family afloat, wanting to do something creative and interesting, and trying to find my way."

Often, it is only in retrospect that we can understand the stimulus and underlying issues, and often the issues are more complex than they appear at first blush. Identifying the real cause of career distress can sometimes take years; you don't go to bed happy one night and wake up the next day realizing you are living a lie and are, in fact, miserable.

Sandi, a forty-two-year-old banker, never really thought about whether she was happy in her work. If she had been asked about her feelings, she says, she probably would have said something like "I like my colleagues and the work is interesting." But when her sixty-five-year-old father, with whom she was very close, died suddenly, she went into a depression that lasted two years. "I thought I was experiencing a very long period of mourning," she says. It was only when she finally consulted a therapist that she realized that she was replaying her father's safe but unsatisfying career path. She had felt that by questioning her work she would be questioning her father's life choices, and so she had repressed any dissatisfaction with her work.

"He hated his government job. He had always wanted to write. But he stuck to it because it was safe and he had a family to look after. I had always wanted to be a chef, but I was scared about the insecurity. But more importantly, I felt if I changed paths I would somehow be *repudiating* him—all the goodness and love I had for him—because basically I'd be saying that how he'd lived was wrong." She realized she could still love her father and what he stood for but take a different life path. She is now working as a Pilates instructor.

More often, a career crisis isn't triggered by a single, apocalyptic event. We *drift* into career distress. This is why most people are slow to recognize the warning signs.

Consider forty-eight-year-old Faye, a director of public affairs for a media marketing firm. Her Eastern European–born parents had always bickered and, as the oldest first-generation American-born daughter, her role in the family had always been to soothe tensions and help her parents navigate in a world they often found perplexing. As her parents aged, however, their bickering escalated into nasty fights that stopped just short of physical abuse. They depended increasingly on her. The police would be called. She finally had to fetch her mother from three hundred miles away to give her parents a break from each other.

During this period, she started to notice that her fifteen-year-old daughter was becoming more sullen and having difficulty with her homework and class exams. To add to this ripe stew, she had a new boss as a result of restructuring, who she felt didn't like or respect her.

Still, it took Faye more than a year to realize she had a problem, much less to put a name on it. "I became depressed, although I didn't realize it then. I was going through a bad time with my daughter. She kept on yelling, 'Mom, check your hormones.' I was so tired just trying to keep everything together, I didn't really think about my life. In fact, I did everything possible to *not* think about my life. If I thought about it at all, I started to think it was my hormones and that I was just this crazy premenopausal witch."

Two things occurred almost simultaneously that led to the final meltdown. At a dinner party, people started to play the "What is most important to you?" game. She automatically blurted out: "To make a difference in people's lives."

And the next day, she went to a stress-management workshop, which everyone in her department was required to attend. "There was this boring instructor. I wasn't really paying attention; I was fascinated by how his teeth were the same color as the walls. Then all of a sudden, after he had been incanting symptoms of stress, I ran out of the room and started to bawl."

Faye took a medical leave for nine weeks. She read about aging and learned what she could do to help her parents and what was beyond her control. She took her daughter to a child psychologist, who identified a learning disability. She also went with her daughter on a weeklong vacation, where they reestablished some of the intimacy they had lost. And she gave serious thought to her work and what she wanted and needed from it. She realized that even if she could be effective, she really didn't care about making a difference in a marketing organization.

When she returned to work, she confronted her boss, saying, "You don't like me or trust me so basically I'm useless in this role." He agreed to give her a package. Five months later, she started a job—which she loves—with an NGO.

These days, it's very easy to drift into career distress. After all, who has the time, much less the energy, to even *think* about whether they are happy?

What happens is this: You have a mild feeling of discontent, but you repress it, telling yourself, "Things will get better" or "Toughen up, you can take it" or "Don't be so indulgent." A few months later, you again experience this discomfort and tell yourself something like "It'll get better when I finish this project/go on vacation/stop this traveling." Or "It's not the right timing to do something." And so it goes until one day you wake up and, like Faye, you are no longer experiencing a low-grade type of career malaise. You are facing a full-blown crisis.

In her book *The Breaking Point: How Female Midlife Crisis Is Transforming Today's Women* (2005), Sue Schellenbarger says that more women than men experience the psychological turbulence known as midlife crisis. Sometimes it presents itself as a creeping discomfort, other times it's a seismic shift in perspective that takes family, friends, and career down with it. At its core, midlife crisis is a yearning to speak the truth—and to live it.

There Is Nothing Wrong with You

I have been collecting data for the past twenty years on how people feel about their work. In speeches and workshops I routinely ask questions such as:

- Would you quit your job tomorrow if you could find another job with the same pay?
- If you had the financial resources, would you continue in your current work?
- Does the thought of another workday make you feel slightly depressed, especially on Sunday evenings?

- Do you look forward to going to work each day?
- When you reflect on your accomplishments, do you have a sense of pride?

My findings are that career distress is at an epidemic level today.

Why are so many women suffering from career ennui? In Chapter 2, we saw how women are struggling to find their place in organizations, and how the rhythms of organizations run counter to female rhythms. But obviously there is more—not all the challenges are related to women's needs and relational style.

But before I describe these new career blues, I must tell you one thing: if you are experiencing these types of career distress, THERE IS NOTHING WRONG WITH YOU! (And if you've been blaming yourself, you might be wise to say out loud, "There is nothing wrong with me.")

The most common comment I receive when I write a column or give a speech describing how, to paraphrase Henry David Thoreau, most people lead work lives of quiet desperation is "I thought there was something wrong with me. Everyone else seems to have it so together. Why don't I?"

First, they don't have it more together: many are experiencing similar strains. This is where women's heightened tendencies for social comparison hurts us. We look at others for clues to understand our own experience and misinterpret what we see. Or rather, what we see or focus on are the cues that tell us how well everyone else is doing, and thus, in comparison, we assume we are sadly wanting.

What we don't see are their interior monologues, which are very similar to our own. And because we tend to be competitive with each other, we "present well" as clinical psychologists say.

Let me give you an example. You know how sometimes it seems that every woman you talk to has a kid who gets straight A's, volunteers, works part-time, does brilliant artwork, helps out at home, and runs their own entrepreneurial business, and oh yeah, they really *like* their parents, and then you think, "OK, I went to school. I know about the normal curve, I know SOMEONE out there has to be flunking or getting D's and in general screwing up their life." Well, the same principle applies to work. Those people you are eyeing enviously are definitely not living a straight "A" work life—they just don't talk about it unless, that is, they are your friends.

Women are experts at *blaming* themselves, attributing their difficulties to personal deficiencies rather than external sources, which only adds to feelings of personal inadequacy. In other words, we are kinder than we should be in evaluating others' competence, and harsher than we should be in evaluating our own. So I don't know whether this is good news or bad news, but the bottom line is that either everyone else is as miserable as you, or you're not more miserable than anyone else!

The Acid Test: Are You Suffering from Career Malaise?

- You are no longer engaged by your work.
- Things you used to care about no longer elicit any emotion.
- You frequently find yourself saying "whatever" and giving up on issues that once would have concerned you or led you to lobby for change.
- You are not interested in or proud of what you do.
- You flirt with the idea of quitting but think "Better the devil you know" or "It will be too much work to find something else."

Common Career Maladies

The emotional mathematics of our era can be briefly summarized as follows: Intense productivity pressures lead us to question the effort-reward equation, which leads us to ask: "What do I really want to do with my life?" and "How is my work contributing to my sense of well-being?" The struggle many women face to fit in with what they experience as inhospitable corporate environments only exacerbates this restlessness. This is part of the reason so many are singing the new career blues.

As we will see in the following chapters, normal midlife developmental changes also contribute to this turbulence, since this is the time when we start to think about our mortality, priorities, and what kind of legacy we want to leave.

All of the women I have interviewed have grappled with one or more of these challenges. Of course, these challenges are not unique to women.

Values Angst

"I need to derive a sense of purpose from my work and feel I'm part of something good and important, not something ugly for which I get a six-figure paycheck to satisfy the needs of greedy people whose values I detest."
—TV producer

"Organizations say they value people and that people are our most important resource, but when push comes to shove, the only things valued are the results on the performance numbers, budget, and deliverables, with no regard for human toil."
—Middle manager, government

As we have seen, one of the principal sources of distress for women who work for organizations is the clash between their personal and professional values, and those of their employer. We've looked at these tensions and their sources—intense productivity pressures, obsessive focus on results, and lack of time to develop and nurture caring relations or to carry out work to the desired standard.

Many professionals and managers feel they are constantly going cup in hand to get the resources they need to do the job they are being paid for. This ultimately takes its toll on their self-esteem and sense of competence.

"They hired me to develop a recruitment strategy to attract younger workers, and told me this was a priority," said a human resources manager. "But this takes more than just being creative. . . . I needed money and other resources. I kept on lobbying and they kept on saying, 'Be creative.' Eventually, I felt like I wasn't contributing and started to feel I was doing something wrong. I completely lost my sense of confidence." I've heard this story a thousand times. Chances are you've been there.

But of course values angst is about a lot more than broken promises and lack of necessary resources. Madeleine's story is typical. A self-described Type-A personality, she quit a high-powered, professionally challenging job in a communications company because of the "lack of values and ethics in the organization and the varmintlike integrity of the management group."

As vice president of human resources, she says she "watched stock options being thrown at incompetent managers who sucked up to the CEO while underpaid junior staff were regaled by bosses who boasted about their five-star vacations and their expensive new midlife crisis cars."

But Madeleine is not yet ready to abandon work. She is hungry to leave a legacy. In fact, this is all she talks about. As we will see, there are many women like Madeleine who are designing interesting and challenging new career chapters.

Many women believe that the cost of doing business, in terms of what the organization really cares about, is too high—the cost to the environment, staff, service delivery, and personal emotional well-being. At midlife, many of us are ambitious but still want to leave a legacy and do work in tune with deeply held values, whether that is contributing to the environment, an important cause, or the community.

Ambition: A Dirty Word?

"It embarrasses me to say I'm ambitious. There is something nasty about this word. To me it implies that you would stomp over others to get what you want. But if you take the idea of being greedy, of obsessive focus on career goals in order to get ahead out of the equation . . . yes, I am ambitious. I want to be in the vanguard, but not at the expense of anyone else, including my family."
—Psychologist

Psychiatrist Anna Fels, in her groundbreaking book *Necessary Dreams* (2004), shows how ambition is often fraught with painful conflict for women but not for men. As a result of their conflicts about femininity and competitiveness, many women chose to nurture and defer rather than to compete with men.

Ambition, Fels argues, rests on two pillars: recognition and mastery. To maintain their dreams, women need not only the opportunity to gather skills and experience, but also to have their accomplishments recognized. As women are less likely than their male colleagues to have their competence acknowledged, their ambitions are eroded. The result is that they appear less committed, which undermines their career progress, which in turn further erodes their aspirations.

In a study of 421 women at the middle- and senior-management levels conducted by the Simmons School of Management and Hewlett-Packard, 80% of respondents said they were comfortable with power and what they could accomplish with it. But the majority of women were not pursuing power out of personal gain or self-interest: 70% wanted power to make positive changes in their organization; 84% said it was to ensure their business operations were socially responsible, while only 45% said they wanted to move up the organizational ladder.

There has been considerable research on whether women are as ambitious as men. This research reveals that the underpinnings of ambition, the nature of the goals, and how ambition is shaped and expressed are different between men and women. The results of one survey of 2,443 highly accomplished women and 653 highly qualified men from across the United States found that, while almost half of the men describe themselves as very or extremely ambitious, only about a third of the women do. The women's wish list differed significantly from that of the men, with the desire to have "a powerful position" ranking lowest. This is consistent with my findings from *Career Advisor*—women are less interested in building a career to satisfy needs for status or prestige.

What is also clear is that many women are ambivalent about being ambitious because the word is so emotionally loaded. When someone at a social event told me "You must be ambitious to have accomplished what you have," I wanted to go through the floor. What I heard was this: "You are a scheming, ruthless, avaricious shark who will do anything to get ahead. Your work is the centerpiece of your identity. You put your career above all else, you disgusting unevolved bottom-feeder." In other words, "You are a bad, bad person."

In fact, like many of the women I have spoken with, I *am* ambitious, if this means *wanting to excel* or be the best, as it does for me. We have already seen the psychological origins of some of our ambitions, including that pesky desire for approval.

Being brutally honest with myself, I need to be seen as a player in my field, but it embarrasses me to say this. Why? Because in my mind, being ambitious is synonymous with being competitive and ruthless. It means being the career-driven Suit we met in the last chapter. It means Condoleezza Rice and those sexless eighties women in their power suits. But take the neurotic chatter out of the word, and quite simply ambition means *desire*.

At mid- or late career, many women have a desire to accomplish something important. The majority of those working for a long time with the same employer feel they could not do it with that employer. They are frustrated with and feel stymied by all the constraints of male-dominated work environments discussed in Chapter 2.

But the self-employed can also experience the strains of thwarted ambition. Take real-estate agent Carolyn, who at forty-six left a large agency because she was sick of the vicious back-stabbing and competitiveness. "I always wanted to make money but it had to be part of something bigger and better. Money was no longer enough." She established an eponymous agency that caters to the needs of first-time home buyers; her business model rewards cooperation, and she donates a percentage of profits to the community. She sees this as a way to leave her mark.

There are also many women who are only too happy to park their ambitions. Given a choice between career advancement and time for self and family, many will choose the latter, which is why so many women are fleeing corporate life.

One woman comments on why she quit her job as a director of marketing for a health-care organization: "Be careful what you wish for. I got the BIG promotion I had always thought I wanted, and then I realized the job was simply too big for me." She simplified her life and is now a stay-at-home mom doing occasional contracts. "Not all the money in the world would get me back on the corporate path again," she says. "I'm happy. I have my kids, my volunteer work, my music and books, and my freelance gigs for money and professional stimulation."

Vertigo: "How Did I Get (from There to) Here?"

*"I'm from a family of doctors. Everyone thought I would also
be a doctor. And sometimes in the middle of the night I wake
up and ask myself, 'How the hell did I end up working for
an organization? And, for that matter, how the hell did I end
up married to this man beside me?'"*
  —Vice president, finance

In my workshops, I often ask: "How did you end up doing the
kind of work you are doing? Did you have a game plan?" About 70
percent of participants respond with something like "I just fell into
this" or "It was just an accident . . . I didn't know what I wanted
to do. A friend got me a job, and I guess things just went on from
there."

Forty-five-year-old Robin, for example, never thought that she
would become a journalist. She had a way with words, had studied
history, and, in fourth-year university, a professor suggested she go
into journalism. "I didn't really know what I wanted to do so it
seemed like as good an idea as any at the time. But I never really
chose it." Now she wonders. "It seems like it was just arbitrary. What
if I didn't have that professor . . . maybe I would have ended up
doing something completely different. So how do I know I wouldn't
be happier doing something else? What if I made a twenty-year
career mistake?"

In fact, it's very rare these days for people to make a twenty-year
career mistake. It's true that it's easy to "fall into" something—but if
it doesn't work for us, we will eventually get the message. We tend
to move away from careers for which we are fundamentally ill-suited
because doing them makes us feel bad about ourselves. That's the
pleasure principle at work.

If it feels really awful, and one has any options at all, one moves
on, unless, of course, one is truly a masochist. Through a process

of successive approximations, we move toward that which we are good at—because we feel good doing it and are reinforced for those behaviors—and away from those activities that we aren't cut out for. But even if we try to pursue the latter, it's highly unlikely we'll be successful. Even if we try to hang in there, with today's performance bar set so high, we'll probably screw up and ultimately get fired.

Still, even if one's work is a relatively good match, and not completely an accident, it doesn't mean that there isn't something better out there—another type of work that would be more satisfying.

Then there are those of us who made choices early on. Sylvia had always known what she wanted to do. "From my earliest memories I had this Florence Nightingale–type fantasy of being a nurse, caring for people and helping them deal with their pain." As a skillful young nurse adept with patients, her people skills were recognized with a promotion to unit manager. That led to another series of promotions, until one day she realized that she had ended up far removed from what had originally drawn her to her profession—nurturing people in need. We will see in Chapter 6 how underlying career themes provide important clues to deciding: "What next?"

Nothing Left to Give: 24-7'd to Distraction

"I feel like the end of a tube of toothpaste—there is nothing more to squeeze out."
—Head nurse

In the past decade, millions of words in columns, articles, and books have been devoted to the impact of our "work as extreme sport" era. You know the problem: you feel overwhelmed, you can't do your work to the standard you want to do it, you never develop a sense of satisfaction from what you do, you feel depressed because you lack a sense of accomplishment. All this makes you more incapable of doing what you need to do to not feel depressed.

In my speeches, I like to ask the audience: "Put up your hand if you have completed at least 50 percent of your projects this past year in the way you wanted to." Maybe a quarter of them raise their hands. When I increase the bar to "over 75 percent of projects satisfactorily completed," only a handful respond. And there is no difference between the public and private sector.

A forty-seven-year-old family lawyer explaining her decision to quit her job put it this way: "I love my craft and being able to help women in very difficult situations. But there was so much pressure on me for billable hours that I constantly had to make professional compromises. The result was a never-ending succession of files, none of which could I attend to in the right way. My clients got second-rate work, and I constantly felt inadequate." She made a career shift and now consults on a freelance basis to organizations dealing with family issues.

People who get their emotional and intellectual satisfaction from their profession find it deeply disturbing to compromise professional standards. Some, like the lawyer, may simply shift away from the work altogether if they can't determine how they can do their job without compromising professional standards.

Welcome to the era of the half-assed job, where work is completed below par and where there is no time to think about what one has accomplished—and being able to *think* about one's accomplishments is as important as the accomplishment itself. I say this because many people tell me they are not accomplishing anything. But when I ask them to take some time to reflect, they realize they do indeed have accomplishments—they have just been too busy to recognize them.

This sense of not achieving anything may lead to depression. For our purposes, let's say that depression can be defined as a mental state characterized by feelings of inadequacy, sadness, and discouragement. People feel helpless to control events, and believe there is no relationship between what they do and what happens to them. When people are depressed, they lack a sense of accomplishment. Depression has also been defined as "anger turned inward." Many women say that their response to unreasonable work demands is to get angry with themselves for not being able to figure out how to manage the overload, or they tell themselves, "If I was a strong person, I wouldn't put up with this." As we have already seen, women are very quick to beat themselves up. Now put these two qualities—a perceived lack of accomplishments and self-blame—together. What you get is a recipe for the new career blues.

Do I think we have a clinically depressed workforce today? Not literally. But I think if we consider the opposite of depression—optimism, a sense of accomplishment—depression is a good metaphor for describing the epidemic malaise.

I once read an interview with a psychologist who said that the human body is designed to work at 50 percent efficiency on a routine basis so that during times of major stress, such as the death of a loved one, we have resources left over to deal with these significant events. Now we are constantly working at 110 percent. The result is that we are all becoming empty shells with no energy to respond to the hurly-burly demands of the day, much less to emotionally taxing circumstances.

Been There, Done That: Overworked and Understimulated

"You start your career conveying small residential properties. Twenty years later, you're still doing the same thing in terms of the skills you're using, but now you're conveying multimillion-dollar properties. The consequences of screwing up are much

greater, but the subject of what you're doing hasn't changed. Sometimes I feel like that T. S. Eliot poem, measuring out my days in coffee spoons."
    —Lawyer

With so much overwork, is it possible to be bored? Yes, as boredom isn't only caused by a *lack* of things to do; the content of the work and the degree of intellectual challenge it provides are equally important. So many people today are simultaneously bored and overworked. In fact, boredom is one of the most common complaints of professionals such as lawyers, accountants, trainers, teachers, and journalists—people who spend their days exercising a craft or solving technical or professional problems (as opposed to management problems).

For many professionals, career progression is simply a question of increasing the arena of influence, but the technical skills being used are the same. So, for many midcareer women (and men), the prospect of spending the next fifteen years doing essentially the same type of work is about as exciting as watching paint dry.

My research shows that the vast majority of professionals falls into the motivational type that I have labeled "Self-developers." (You will meet them in the next chapter.) In order to be happy, they need to be stretched professionally and constantly learning. In the contemporary workscape, however, people are rewarded for what they can do—their ability to hit the ground running—not what they have the *potential* to do. This means that if you are good at your craft, and unless you choose to make a career shift, you are expected to continue to apply that craft. Additionally, most organizations have truncated career ladders for professionals, so beyond a particular point it's hard to grow.

By the time these people hit forty, many have gone as far as they want in their area of expertise. Looking at another twenty years of more of the same can be very depressing. But leaving is not always an option. As one woman commented: "I would love to do something completely different because I'm burnt out in the HR field. But I don't have the luxury of not making a decent income, so stepping out into something completely different would require a pretty big investment in starting from scratch, and I'm not prepared to make that kind of investment. And it would also require me to invest time—but as well as being bored, I also want to have more time with my family. And finally, as my reputation is in the HR field, I wouldn't be able to leverage that in a new line of work."

Self-employment is also not necessarily a salve to boredom and predictability. I have been self-employed as a career/life-management consultant for most of my working life; my being hired by organizations rests on the fact that I'm an expert in my area. No one would hire me (not that I would want them to) to do work outside what I am known for. So it follows that if you are good at what you do and have been doing it for some time, there is very little that someone can ask you to do that you haven't been asked to do a thousand times before. As one self-employed management trainer said: "Although I care about my work, there are times when I think if I have to deliver the same leadership or team-building program one more time and hear the same predictable questions and comments, I will scream."

At midlife many women feel a desire to do something different. A comment I heard often was "It's my time now." A key component is a desire to live more on the edge and to take risks, a common motivation in the second half of life. But there is a conundrum: you want to have a sense of exhilaration, which means taking risks, but you are very good at what you do—it's safe and it pays the bills. (As we will see, this push-pull between excitement and safety also keeps many people in less than satisfying personal relationships.)

Our Deepest Fear: Old, Ugly, and Fired

"Gray-haired men are considered distinguished, seasoned, and experienced. Gray-haired women are seen as old, tired, and not 'with it.'"
   —Recruiter

"I was fired at forty-five because of my age. My male coanchor was much older than me, but an on-air older man is thought to be trustworthy. I did the rounds of all the networks and, after a year, concluded that was it for me in terms of my on-air career."
   —Former TV presenter

In our youth-obsessed culture, despite much touted skills shortages, age discrimination—the gray ceiling as my friend calls it—is still rampant, particularly in such youth-oriented sectors as entertainment, sales and marketing, and hi-tech. (The good news is that as employers wake up to the realities of the impending shortages, ageism should decrease. Or at least that's the oft-repeated theory.) Younger workers are seen as being more malleable, more professionally current, more energetic, as having less "baggage," as well as being cheaper.

Exec-U-Net, a networking organization for senior managers and professionals, tracks hiring trends on an annual basis. President David Opton says age discrimination in hiring starts as early as age forty. Many search specialists and executives I know have told me that they believe age discrimination is on the rise.

"Old, ugly, and fired" ran the *Salon* magazine headline. In 2005, that's right, 2005, UBS, a major European bank on Wall Street, was found guilty of sexual discrimination against a forty-four-year-old former saleswoman. Her lawyers claimed that a male executive told her she was "old and ugly" and could not do the job. She was fired after she made a complaint.

Although gray hair is common among male CEOs, how many gray-haired female senior managers do you know? Professional reasons now edge out personal ones for plastic surgery. As one fifty-year-old woman who had an eye lift put it: "Elective surgery was a career move no different than attending leadership training seminars. Men with gray are considered attractive and so it is an asset, while we need to go to great lengths to look young to be viable in the market. What pisses me off is that women often hit their stride after they've attended to family matters, in other words, in their fifties."

The psychological impact of ageism on women is significant. It's easier to get people to talk about their sex lives than their age anxieties, which run deep and are rooted in our ideas about attractiveness and desirability. For many women, the thinking process goes something like this: "My kids are leaving home so I'm about to be fired from my role as mother. No one needs me—neither my kids, nor my employer. Employers want youth—young, attractive, slim people. I am no longer considered attractive. I am no longer considered vibrant. What I bring to the table—wisdom, experience, and emotional smarts—is not needed or valued. I therefore am disposable."

These anxieties can also lead to irrational thinking. Take Diane, a forty-eight-year-old nursing director who has spent her entire career at the same hospital. When I mentioned that I had had lunch with the head of staffing for her hospital and that her name came up, her first comment was "You didn't tell her how old I am, did you?" I pointed out that the director, much like every other long-time employee, would probably have a pretty good idea, and it wasn't a big deal to anyone, but no, her age did not come up. She said, with some hysteria in her voice, "Barbara, you have to promise to never, ever tell anyone how old I am."

Concerns about age discrimination kick in early. I do not have one client over forty who has been in career exploration mode who hasn't told me something such as "Whatever I do at this stage, it's got to be the right move, because there is no going back. I want to be firmly ensconced before my age becomes a serious issue." Indeed, many of my employed clients start expressing such concerns in their mid- to late-thirties (as they should, by the way, especially if they have been employed by only one organization). Older clients say, "Although I know I have great experience and the right education, I'm concerned no one will take me on because of my age."

A career counselor who sees many older women in her practice says, "The midlife women become anxious when they go out for job interviews. All older people worry about age discrimination but with the women there is something else, self-consciousness about how they look and whether they'll be perceived as attractive. They'll ask me, 'What do you think of my hair or my makeup? Do I look old in this outfit? Do you think these are old-lady shoes?' Outside the workplace, they feel good about themselves. But as soon as they approach an employer, there is this huge loss of self-esteem."

This loss of self-esteem and increased self-consciousness about age is also a source of embarrassment and anger. Unemployed women who are looking for work feel humiliated to be having an "audition" with someone young enough to be their child and having to, as they say, "suck up" to them. As a friend confided after a job interview: "Here I am, at a time in my life when I should feel good about myself. Instead, I'm putting on this show for a kid just a few years older than my daughter, this smug little kid who is poking and prodding the merchandise. And I felt like I was back in my twenties trying to win the approval of some older male boss, or like I was back in high school with all the same insecurities. And I'm worrying all the time: Do I look fresh? Am I hip enough for you? It's very upside down in terms of how it's supposed to work." She was ashamed of herself for saying this. I have found that when midlife women have their job security threatened they often feel they have been thrown back into their "approval-seeking" years.

But even the happily employed can feel a degree of self-consciousness. A wickedly funny friend who loves her job and is appreciated for her unconventional style says, "Sometimes I worry that as I get older in this job what in the past they would have considered charmingly idiosyncratic will just seem *annoying*."

Feeling Stuck

"I'm unhappy and want to do something different. But every time I start to think about what's next, I hit a psychological wall because I can't figure out what I really want to do. And then I go back to not thinking about it until I get really miserable again and the process starts all over. So I guess that basically, I'm stuck."
—High-school teacher

This teacher has spent the last ten years complaining off and on about how much she hates teaching. Every time she has one of her moments of "I can't stand doing this anymore," she makes an aborted attempt to think about other professional possibilities. She has considered designing gardens, importing jewelry from Europe, making greeting cards, becoming a writer. But she never follows through and after yet another sabbatical always returns to teaching.

Feeling stuck is one of the most pervasive types of contemporary career maladies. You feel flat. You feel restless. You are confused. All you see is a mess. You think all of your friends have glorious careers, and what's wrong with you? You ask yourself "what now?" You lose your joy and vitality. You stop liking yourself. You just can't seem to detangle yourself from your bad work situation and develop a clear and compelling vision of doing something else.

Novelist Ann-Marie MacDonald in *The Way the Crow Flies* describes this state beautifully. "You want to go forward. But something is stopping you. You feel like you should know what it is, but you can't make it out. It's like trying to identify an elephant when all you can see is one-quarter inch of it." What keeps us in our rut?

Obviously, there are many factors but one of the most common is a lack of vision of what else we could be doing. We experience a kind of low-grade career malaise, flirt with the idea of doing something else, but can't see a clear course, so end up doing nothing. And we worry "what if I decide to quit this job/go back to school/set up my own business/do something different, and it's not any better?"

The most significant challenge is that in many instances of career paralysis while there's nothing really wrong, there's just nothing really *right*. There is no push—a truly hideous work environment; and no pull—a compelling vision of something fabulous. The most significant impediment to change is fear of the unknown. Some of us, as we will see in Chapter 5, simply have a greater appetite for dealing with uncertainty.

We can also get attached to work we dislike by ties, some obvious—such as the golden handcuffs of salary, stock options, and pensions, and some not so obvious—such as status, prestige, and other qualities that flatter our egos. These attachments may go unacknowledged. One publisher acquaintance, for example, hates her work—both what she does as well as where she does it. But despite all her protestations to the contrary, the truth of the matter is that she can't look at alternatives because she loves the fact that she has an important-sounding job, schmoozes with the A-list, and all her friends think her work is glamorous. As we will see later, these attachments can also be very powerful impediments to moving on.

People may also avoid making moves in their life because they are concerned about how others will see them. If they were to radically alter their lives and go back to school to pursue a career path for less money, will their spouses, family, or friends think less of them? "Is it selfish to put my family through this turmoil? What if I fail after all this? What if my partner disapproves?" (Oh, that pesky need for approval.)

Sometimes those fears are misplaced, and people find that their families are supportive. Indeed, a supportive life partner was often cited as one of the most significant contributors to making effective transitions. But often there are serious conflicts.

My friend Cheryl, for example, who had always been the high-wage earner in the couple, wanted to quit her senior government mandarin job. She had nursed a dream for many years about starting her own communications business focusing on NGOs. She had done her homework and was confident about the need for her service, but as with any start-up it would be slightly risky: in order to accomplish her goals, she would have to downsize.

Her status-hungry husband objected vehemently. "Why can't you just like your job like any other normal person?" he would complain. He was attached to the perks of her job—meeting important people in the media and other intelligentsia, photos on the society pages, and most of all their upper-middle-class lifestyle. He didn't want to scale down into a smaller house in a less prestigious neighborhood. In the end, despite several months of marital counseling, she left him and went the self-employment route. Their aspirations were worlds apart.

Restoring Equilibrium

These challenges take a huge emotional toll on our sense of well-being. And when we feel depressed or anxious in one area of our life, it colors all of our life experiences. We all have a simple goal: to feel good about ourselves . . . whatever that means and whatever that constitutes. And for those of us who are still interested in making our mark or leaving a legacy in the professional world, who are excited about all the possibilities ahead, even if they are not clearly defined, even if they cause anxieties, we all have the ability to rise to the challenge of creating and designing meaningful next-work chapters.

When we make a change as a result of being unhappy, or because we feel an irresistible desire to throw ourselves into a new arena and explore uncharted parts of ourselves, it's the ultimate expression of our needs and desires. We haven't been fired, we're not doing it to be a better breadwinner for the family—we're doing it because we *want* to. There are no guarantees of success, and we will be held accountable for the outcomes. But how many people do you know who spend their lives ruminating over missed opportunities or paths not taken?

The psychological challenges, character, and opportunities of the first half of life are distinctly different from those of the second half. Moving forward with grace means, as psychoanalysts say, finishing the work of the first half so that one can embrace the opportunities of this special life phase.

chapter four

Moving Forward with Grace:

Who You Are and
What You Need
in This Life Chapter

* *"I didn't so much have a midlife crisis, the way the books*
* *describe it, as a gradual shift or transformation in what*
* *was important."*
*

"I feel like everything is bubbling to the surface. Although I don't know what my 'what next' is, I have a palpable sense that it's almost around the corner."

"I used to get really worked up about things like others getting credit for work I did, or someone introducing an idea I had proposed six months ago. Now I just find it amusing, disappointing, but in the scheme of things, think 'who cares?'"

"My life started to feel too small for me. I needed more . . . intellectually, emotionally, spiritually, something which counted."

"It was a gradual drift over a couple of years—moving slowly, imperceptibly into new territory."

"My partner got sick. My world came crashing down. Nothing that used to resonate was important. I felt a yawning ache for something more."

"I have a 'now or never' sense of urgency. What will my legacy be?"

"The first half of your life you please everyone else. In the second half every day you make decisions just for yourself."
   —Women describing their psychological changes at midlife

When I look at the women I know, I am struck by how some seem to move seamlessly through different life chapters, while others seem to be stuck in a continuous feedback loop; even if I don't speak to them for months, even years, their issues and stories stay the same.

We have already met some of these women—the doctor's daughter who continually goes after jobs in which she is destined to fail, in a desperate search for her father's approval; the lawyer who continues in a job she hates because of the money and status.

Take Nina, for example, an abundantly talented sales and marketing specialist. At fifty, she still encounters the same difficulties that have plagued her for as long as I have known her. In the twelve years prior to going out on her own, she held three positions in tough, male project-management environments. After the honeymoon period in each of her work situations, I heard the same, "I'm such a good person, look what I put up with" story. I call it work-victim pornography.

"Barbara, you just won't believe what it's like here," she would complain, followed by a description of several horrible incidences of managers behaving very badly. "But it's OK, I know what I'm doing is important and my staff needs me," she would conclude. Now that she is a self-employed consultant I hear a similar description of her crazy, unprofessional clients, concluding with "I'm here to serve them. I'll meet their needs."

According to Nina, the problem is that all these people are jerks. Whether or not this is true, the underlying issue is Nina's overwhelming desire to be liked and to be seen as a good person meeting others' needs before her own. Indeed, when she tells me her stories, I can't help but think she is actually *boasting*: "See what a good, self-sacrificing, accommodating person I am." And so an intelligent, accomplished woman with some degree of self-knowledge continues to put up with unacceptable behavior, and to be secretly proud of herself for being a martyr.

I know many Ninas who in mid- and late career still suffer from a need for approval. Midcareer men can be similarly trapped, but they are more likely to get stuck on issues related to achievement, recognition, and status rather than likeability. How many men do you know who still measure themselves by the number of stock options they hold, their titles, who they network with, or the size of their budget?

Our careers have many chapters, each posing unique challenges. Managing your career with grace means facing up to those challenges, riding them through, assimilating what you've learned, and moving on. People get stuck when they cannot make effective transitions from one chapter to another, or when they move on without resolving business from earlier life stages, as we have seen in Chapter 3.

Over the course of a full career we make a number of transitions. In our twenties we are still finding out who we are and where we thrive, because our experience of the world is limited. The challenge is to test ourselves in various roles and environments and ask: How do I choose the work that's best for me? How can I put off making a commitment to anything? How do others see me? Where can I find work that doesn't suck? What should I do with my life?

By the time we are in our midthirties, we have been exposed to an array of experiences and have received feedback from the world about what we are good and not good at. We should have a deeper understanding of ourselves. Although we are still acquiring new skills, we are also refining existing ones, and learning how to leverage our special talents while starting to accept our limitations.

For some people there is smooth and continuous progress along a path chosen in their late twenties or early thirties. More commonly, there are bumps in the road—moments of panics or crises where we think: "I hate this work. I need to find my fit." "What should I do with my life?" "How can I have fulfilling work and still have time for a life?" Such moments can lead to significant rethinking of career direction.

The challenge in this first part of our life is to make our way in the world: to demonstrate our competence, find the best work fit, test ourselves against others, and understand what we are capable of and what is important to us. In essence we are *proving to ourselves* and others that we are capable and are evaluating our successes against the milestones of our peers and colleagues.

Finding Your Truth in the Second Half

In the second half of life, we should be able to transcend these earlier preoccupations. Instead of being externally driven, constantly striving to prove ourselves worthy and acquire the trappings to demonstrate it, we should become *internally driven*, allowing us to make choices independently of others' views. These latter career chapters should be marked by excitement, anticipation, and adventurousness—they are a chance to test parts of ourselves previously untried. (And it's not only in our work. As we will see later we may reappraise our relationships with our children and what we want from our partners, if indeed we want a partner.)

We should feel good about our achievements and accept our limitations and disappointments, moving ahead rather than endlessly revisiting the past and decrying slights and instances of injustice. ("I should have gotten that job . . ." "I was the victim of office politics . . ." "I was hung out to dry . . ." "I shouldn't have been fired . . .") But if we fail to make that transition, it is at midcareer that it takes its most dramatic toll.

Regina, for example, had been a high-profile producer on network TV when she was in her twenties and early thirties. When she had children, she downsized her ambitions, and found less demanding part-time work writing employee communications in a marketing department for a public accounting firm. Now at fifty she is still second-guessing whether she made the right career decision fifteen years earlier.

"I give myself endless shit about whether I did the right thing. My friends say, 'You're starting to bore me. Just get over it. It's done.' But I keep thinking I would have had a great career now if I hadn't chucked it. And I lie awake at night thinking about this," she says.

She is now starting a new business with an almost neurotic sense of urgency. I wonder if she might take greater pleasure in her startup if she wasn't so determined to make up for what she sees as lost time. When she talks, I get the sense that somehow she sees her new business as a vindication of her earlier life choices. Some women engage in that useless "beat yourself up" game for decisions made long ago. Others are still stuck on scripts from earlier life stages related to winning approval and being seen to be successful.

Midcareer is a time for stock-taking, for asking: What do I really need in my life to feel good about myself? What is important to me now? Even people who enjoy their work often feel a yearning for something more. Our values change, our circumstances change, but often we fail to play catch-up. Things we used to think were important, such as getting promoted, or making more money, are no longer so important—and yet we fail to recognize this because we haven't revised our underlying preconceptions. "Be careful what you wish for" is a comment I have heard frequently from women who had single-mindedly pursued goals only to achieve them and realize they no longer appealed.

Many women are surprised by this. As one retailer said, "My peak career-defining moment was admitting that my love of my work now paled next to my love of family, friends, and a thriving relationship where I wanted to be available rather than wreck it."

The second half of life provides significant opportunities for discovery, exploration, and engagement. Many women discover new skills and interests or reconnect with earlier career themes that they had abandoned. Many, for example, who had shown earlier promise and interest in the arts but who ended up in the business arena, found at midlife that they wanted to explore that part of themselves that they had drifted away from, such as painting or writing or gardening.

As a child I dreamed of being a famous author. In my twenties, when I lived in England, at the encouragement of my writer boy-friend (who subsequently became my husband), I wrote for some women's magazines. I soon drifted away from journalistic writing; after that the only writing I did was of a technical nature.

In my midforties, I had a career crisis: I was deeply, viscerally bored doing the same thing over and over again. My husband and my literary agent friend said, "Why don't you write a book?" I didn't think I could do it. And throughout the entire writing process I thought I was *faking* it. In fact it's taken me four published books and numerous columns to realize that I can write and that I'm not faking it. Nine years of hearing comments such as "You're a good writer" and I'm still surprised.

If we move forward with grace, the question we consider is "Do I want to continue leading the life I am living for the next twenty years and say this is who I am, this is what I did?" We all want our lives to have counted for something, maybe even something that will live on after we are gone. We reevaluate our scripts about money and ask ourselves "What really matters to me?"

But if you're feeling crappy because you aren't this perfect person, relax. I know few people who have completely risen above envy or completely ceased to measure themselves and their achievements against those of others. But this is the ideal. And our challenge. We shift toward it, but not completely, not in all domains. And sometimes we may even struggle with the loss of parts of ourselves we used to care about when moving forward.

When I turned thirty-seven, an older friend said to me: "Soon you will be in your 'F– You' years." I was puzzled by her comment at the time. Shortly after that a major client whom I disliked intensely asked me to deliver some speeches at his company. Intellectually, rationally, I wanted to do the work. It was lucrative and easy. But I just couldn't bring myself to do it. Having to work with the guy just wasn't worth it. I declined, saying I had a time conflict.

But here's the thing: I felt, and sometimes still feel, a longing to be more malleable, more excited by the things that used to excite me. Old Barbara was saying, "Do this. It's not a big deal. So he's a jerk. Get over it." New Barbara was saying, "You'll die. You can't do this." She was feeling nauseous. And new Barbara longed to be old Barbara. Quite simply, I was *pining* for my old self. I sometimes still do. I want to *care*, to get that adrenaline high when I am given a big project. But because my priorities have changed, basically I just can't be bothered.

Early civil-rights leader Charles DuBose put it well when he said that it takes courage to "sacrifice at any moment what we are for who we could become." And you may as well be honest with yourself. Most of us do have some lingering issues. On the other hand, if we didn't, what would we talk about with our friends?

Everyone's Truth Is Different

"The last time I made a move it was out of desperation. This time it will be my own reasoned choice, based on good stuff, not bad—what's best for Camille, what I want now, not what's best for others. I want to change the shape of my work, and grow, but at this point I don't know what that will look like. That's OK, because it's about the journey, not the end point."
—Former director of communications

What do we want now? We are all in different places. Some of us have a clear vision of how we want to spend our next life chapter; some of us are struggling to define it. Some of us can reflect with a degree of satisfaction on career experiences to date, others feel remorse and disappointment. Some of us have a modicum of financial independence while others were rudely laid off ten years before retirement plans kicked in. Some of us are bored or tired or restless or just feel flat. What none of us wants, however, is to compromise our values or repress our individual voices.

However we all have a different vision of what we want from our work. Some women want to be contented in their work, looking to their personal lives to derive satisfaction. For them, the path to renewal involves stretching themselves, whether that means traveling and being open to new adventures, or taking acting classes and performing in an amateur production.

Others want to be deeply engaged, challenged, and excited in their professional lives, what some might call feeling "passionate" about their work. "I want to rise above the homogenized stew," explained one woman. "I have gifts and talents that are uniquely mine. I want to express my authentic self in a way in which I am totally *absorbed.*"

For women at midcareer this often involves the expression of a deeply held desire to do important work and make a contribution to others and society. But not everyone wants to be passionate or needs to be passionate in their work, regardless of their life stage. Women often ask me: "Is there something wrong with me? I feel good about my life, but I'm not passionate about my work; I like it, but I'm not passionate. Should I be?" They feel almost ashamed because of all the media hype about passion and worry they may be dull, uninteresting, or selling themselves short. Passion or contentment: you decide.

Often what we want to achieve and do in mid- and later life is a function of how we have spent our early adulthood. Many of the women who put family before career are now searching for professional challenge and growth. Melanie, a fifty-year-old financial planner, says, "I dropped out of the workforce for almost a decade for family reasons. I'm just ramping up now. I'm just hitting my stride." Similarly, Tina, who was a part-time artist but was too busy struggling to earn a living to develop her art, is now determined to become a serious artist and exhibit and sell her work.

Many of the women who had successful careers in the traditional sense, however, would now like to express a different side of themselves. While virtually all of the women said they need to work for financial, intellectual, and emotional reasons, some still want one more kick at the can in terms of unrealized ambitions. Others feel that work is no longer a proving ground. They are looking for *contentment*, not passion. They are satisfied with their lives; they like their work and have no repressed yearning to do something different.

One woman, for example, a laid-off middle manager in government who grew up in a blue-collar town with a millworker father said, "I sound like my father, but right now all I care about is that it pays the bills, and as my father used to say, I can do my time easy, low stress, the people I work with are OK." As we will see, these motivations are critical in determining how we shape the next phase of our lives.

Our desires will also be influenced by what else we have going on. An acquaintance, a single mother of forty-nine who has spent the last ten years looking for a partner, made this comment after a long bitch session about small slights from her boss and staff, "I wouldn't get so worked up about petty things at the office or even care so much about my job if I was in a relationship."

We also have different emotional reactions to this work chapter. Some, like one friend, feel an irresistible urge, although to do what she doesn't know. "I have a huge sense of possibility and discovery, like that of a child," she says.

Some of the women have or had a sense of urgency. They make comments such as "I only have a limited time left on the planet. I can't afford to be frivolous in how I spend it." But many women at midlife are optimistic that they will figure it out, even if they don't know what the "it" is yet. They are in no hurry; maybe they feel as Gertrude Stein said, "There is no there there."

But others are frightened in the face of change, worried whether they will make it. "I feel so lost," said one woman who was struggling with the "we-need-my-income-because-I'm-a-single-parent-but-I'm-at-the-breaking-point-in-this-job-and-need-more-time-flexibility-in-order-to-do-what-I-want-and-have-to-do-as-a-parent-and-my-mother-is-sick-but-in-any-case-I-don't-really-know-what-I-want-to-do" conundrum. And "nervous" because she didn't think she would ever find a solution.

Another said, "I'm in turmoil. Everything that I thought important is no longer. I don't know what I want or care about."

Knowing What You Need

What do you want to accomplish in this next stage? What do you care about? When do you feel great, and when do you feel awful?

We each have different needs, values, and desires. As we have seen, some of us are embarking on new career paths, while others are looking to their personal life for deep fulfillment.

My research indicates that people are driven by eight distinct work motivations. Here I describe the implications for midlife women. As you read this consider which two motivational types you identify with the most.

Authenticity-seekers

"I refuse to hang up my personality at the door of my client or employer. I am who I am, and I refuse to play-act or pretend I'm someone different. What I need in my work is the opportunity to express who I am."

These people are often told "You're so natural" because they don't change how they behave from one situation to another and are incapable of dissembling. Many of the women I described in Chapter 2 who at midlife find themselves incapable of fitting into corporate environments fall into this motivational type.

There are two kinds of Authenticity-seekers. Some are values-driven such as the many midlife women who now want to leave a legacy, set up their own business, or are fleeing the "for profit" sector to NGOs. For others, it's just their nature. What both types have in common is a need to express who they are. They refuse to compromise their values or "style," or repress important parts of themselves. They strongly identify with statements such as "I will not change my 'style' to please an employer" or "My values must be expressed in my work."

At midlife these women are very clear about what they will and will not do and what they need to be happy, even if they do not know exactly how that desire will be expressed. They fall into the Saint or the Seeker types we met earlier. They are found in NGOs, environments that reward people for their individuality, or are self-employed.

Sociability-seekers

"I get my energy from the people I work with. I can't stand what has happened to organizations over the last ten years, because now it's all about the numbers, and nothing about the people. What makes me happiest? The connections I make with my team members."

Sociability-seeking women find contemporary, results-obsessed business environments challenging. They miss earlier work environments where connections could be made between colleagues. Consider this comment from a collegiality-seeking banker: "We say teamwork is important, but it's really teamwork in name only. We come together, do our thing, then move on. I used to know all kinds of things about my colleagues, such as their kids' birthdays. I liked being part of their lives, and them being part of mine. I miss those days." This woman complained about the demise of the company Christmas party. Other than Security-seekers (see below), no other type would be motivated by these kinds of corporate social events or feel sad about their demise.

The major challenge for midcareer Sociability-seekers is coming to terms with work environments they describe as "ruthless," "cold," and "not fun." Going out on their own is usually not an option: they miss the watercooler banter.

Sociability-seekers tend to work in more female types of occupations, for large organizations such as government, banks, and telcos.

Security-seekers

"I enjoy being part of something bigger than myself, having a sense of belonging. And being completely honest with myself, I don't like change."

Security-seekers, like Sociability-seekers, are mostly found in large, relatively stable organizations such as banks. They account for about 25 percent of midlife women.

When I ask women in my workshops to identify themselves in terms of which type they belong to with a "hands up," few will identify themselves as a Security-seeker. When the survey is confidential and on paper, the numbers increase significantly. Everyone knows today that to admit to wanting security is like admitting to longing for the 1950s.

Security-seekers do not like change or surprises. At midlife they can often experience serious conflicts as they reflect on their life choices. Could I have done something braver or more interesting? they ask. As all women have more than one significant motivator, Security-seekers often find themselves torn between the desire for something new, and that which is secure.

Novelty-seekers

"My friends say I have a short attention span. If I'm not constantly moving into new territory, I get bored. I was at my peak last year when I started a new job, dumped my boyfriend, and bought a new house."

Novelty-seekers often have resumes that look like Swiss cheese because they change their work so often. Some change where they work; others change what they do. Often these women are talented and have many interests, but have never really sunk their teeth into anything. This leads them to wonder whether they lack depth and are simply dilettantes. They may also suffer from imposter syndrome, worrying "they will be caught out."

They may also have had very exciting careers. "I wish I had done half the things you've done" is a comment a Novelty-seeker friend of mine who has worked in media, government, consulting, and now runs her own company hears frequently.

At midlife many Novelty-seekers want to commit to something at a deeper or more sustainable level but they worry about becoming bored, and the path they are *not* taking. Novelty-seekers can be found in every sector. A significant psychological challenge they need to overcome is the idea that they are "settling" if they make a work choice commitment. Novelty-seekers are a minority of the female midlife population. Although we tend to think of men as being adventurers and women as nest-keepers, I have not found differences in the number of male and female Novelty-seekers.

Career-builders

"I'm ambitious. I want to have one last shot at the brass ring. I want to be a player and be seen as a player."

Career-builders are most often found in senior roles in large public- and private-sector organizations or running their own companies. They are motivated by money, prestige, power, and public recognition. Most of the Sirens or the Suits we met in Chapter 2 fall into this motivational type. The numbers of midlife women who own up to being Career-builders (even in confidence) is likely lower than the actual number because of women's ambivalence and discomfort about what it means to be ambitious.

That said, this motivational type still accounts for a relatively small percentage of the female professional and managerial population. In fact, at midlife, many former Career-builders move into new motivational arenas. But some women who have set aside their ambitions in favor of raising a family say, "This is my time now," and become intensely career- and goal-focused.

Career-building women at midlife who have not reached the level they had hoped may struggle to come to terms with what they have in fact achieved. Sometimes they are bitter and frustrated. If they work for an organization, they worry about the effect of their age on future career progress.

Many career-building women at this stage want to build an entrepreneurial business that has profit potential. This is their last chance, they say. And some are prepared to take significant financial risks to achieve their goals.

Autonomy-seekers

"I need to do my own thing. I can't stand being told what to do or being forced to conform to others' expectations."

Being independent is my second significant motivator. People have always said that I "march to my own drummer." When I first developed my *Career Planning Workbook* in the mid-1980s, all my clients said how original the packaging was. In those days, all training materials were presented in a three-hole binder with an ugly cover. My *Workbook* was cerloxed with a beautiful graphic on the cover. My point: it didn't occur to me that someone would want to lug around a heavy, ugly binder.

There are two kinds of autonomy-seekers. People like me often think outside the box. In fact, we often just don't see the box, or know how things are *supposed* to be done. At midcareer

Autonomy-seekers are often described as creative and inventive. Many of them run their own businesses.

The second type of Autonomy-seeker is one who has a gut reaction to being told what to do. Many midcareer women who are leaving the corporate world fall into this type: they are sick of the politics, the endless meetings, the spinning, the hierarchy. "I'm always putting my foot in my mouth, or saying the unpopular thing that really pisses people off" is a comment typical of many of my autonomy-seeking clients.

Now they want to do their own thing, free of corporate cultural expectations about how to behave. They are definitely *not* good girls.

Self-developers

"When I'm not learning or being stretched, I feel dead. I need to be taking risks and be outside my comfort zone, because that's when I'm most alive."

About 70 percent of restless midlife women describe the need to grow as their top, or next-to-top motivator. They put doing challenging work at the top of their wish list, despair of compromising professional standards, feel most alive when they are taking professional risks, and react strongly to being bored.

Some Self-developers decide to go out on their own to practice their profession in the way they want to. Others say, "I've taken everything I can out of this profession: I've learned what I wanted to, now I'm bored." They consider a shift into a new professional arena to become reengaged. Others like organizational life but are tired of begging to get the resources they need to do their work; they find an organization that provides a happier fit for them.

Fifty-year-old management trainer Lynn is typical. She worked at a consulting firm in her forties for several years and quit when she got bored of doing the same types of assignments over and over. She went out on her own, but was lonely and missed being able to connect with colleagues (sociability-seeking is her third top motivator). Now she is happily ensconced as head of management development for a young media company that places a high value on people development. She describes the work she is doing as "constantly challenging" and "leading edge."

Lifestylers

> *"I wouldn't like to be unhappy in my work, but my work isn't the most important thing to me. I define myself outside my job. What I care about lies in my personal life."*

Along with the Self-developer, the Lifestyler is the first or second most common motivational type at midlife. Some women respond to excessive work demands by saying, "That's it. I'm out of here." They set up their own consulting business, look for part-time work, or find a female-friendly employer. Often their goal is to have more time for their family.

Women in their late forties and beyond whose kids have left the nest are often looking for time for community work, or personal passions such as painting or riding. Many of these women describe earlier life chapters in which they did not take time for themselves, having put the company's or family needs before their own. Others in this age group are also often struggling with elder-care responsibilities.

Lifestylers not only crave time for meeting personal interests and responsibilities, they also are prepared to *act* on their desires. One forty-five-year-old woman, a CEO of a cultural institution, actually had written into her contract "family first in the event of any time conflict." A common statement Lifestylers make is "I work to live, not live to work." Who they are and what they do are not the same thing.

Resolving Conflicting Needs

Now here's where many women get into a knot. They are Lifestylers who crave time for family, but they are also Self-developers craving professional growth. Or they are ambitious Career-builders who also want to travel and pursue personal interests. Or, and this is a very common combination, they are Self-developers who thrive on risk, but they are also Stability-seekers who need to protect their incomes.

One of the reasons so many women at midlife are restless, if not unhappy, is that they are yearning to fulfill all their needs and play out all of these roles. This is easier for those few women who are childless, or have adult children, no elder-care responsibilities, and a degree of financial freedom. For the rest, trying to juggle work and family or to save for retirement is an endless struggle.

You can't have it all, at least not all at the same time. You need to be ruthless in identifying what you absolutely *must* have to feel happy. You have many chapters left. Each one can deeply satisfy one need. What is your priority for this stage?

The good news is that when I ask women in career/life-planning workshops to get rid of the "but I want it all" chatter, they can drill down to what is *essential* to them at this life stage. Then they are free to make interesting and creative moves to meet those needs or to continue growing in ways that reignite, reclaim, or redefine their work lives. If they are moving forward with grace, they can embrace the opportunities and challenges of the second half of life.

But it's easier said than done: we all have our inner demons to slay.

chapter five

Facing the Inner Demons:

The Anatomy

of Moving On

- *"I was a wimp—I was unfulfilled in my work, but I didn't*
- *want to give up my income because I like my comforts.*
- *I finally took the move—it was the bravest and most impor-*
- *tant move of my life."*

"After a tortuous route and a lot of work on myself,
I found a place where I could be authentic."

"I left the corporate world to pursue my dream of
becoming a writer. It took me ten years to put my dream
into action—go back to school, pay off my mortgage."

"My desire for interesting work over worrying whether
[my company] gains two-point market share made me
realize that I wanted my life to have counted for more."

"You dig down. You wrestle with your fear demons. You tell yourself you can do it. You deserve more."

"You can't keep telling yourself there will be a miraculous right time in the future, because, when that future comes, it never happens."

—Women describing their decision to move forward

Marina, an attractive, straight-shooting forty-eight-year-old director of human resources, had just gone to her third round of interviews, with a communications company that had a great reputation. The work interested her, the money was good, and the workplace was close to home. But, she said, halfway through the interview, "I felt like I was going to throw up. Instead of seeing the actual people all I saw was the façade—the self-importance, the women dressed like men, and that stupid male bullshit jocularity." They offered her the job. She declined, despite the fact that she had been unemployed for seven months. "I'm so sick of putting on a false front, that passive-aggressive corporate role-playing and that pretend, bland pleasantness," she said.

Now you are probably thinking she must have had savings, or a partner with a good income. In fact, she was a single parent with a daughter in university, few savings, and no income other than that from unemployment insurance.

I expressed surprise when she told me she had turned down the offer. She had always struck me as a career-oriented type of woman, not as someone who would particularly value being authentic. But then she said, "This is exactly the kind of job I would have jumped at even five years ago and that's exactly the kind of job I used to have. But I'm too old for this nonsense; I'm too old to have to play the corporado role."

In the light of her financial situation and obligations, Marina's decision was bold. But she trusted that she would find a better fit.

Three months later she did, in an organization in which, as she described it, "the values breathe."

Accepting Uncertainty

"There are no guarantees in life. I got my ducks in order, made a plan, and then just went for it. The worst thing that could happen is that it wouldn't work out. I could live with that more easily than never having tried."
  —Former government manager

I have always been fascinated with why some women will take risks, can live with uncertainty, why some of us, like Marina, can choose a difficult path, turning down a job because "it just doesn't feel right."

I don't mean to suggest that you *should* take risks, embrace the uncertainty, test yourself. Or that if you can't, there is something "not very of this decade's zeitgeist where we are all supposed to find our passion, insecurity be damned!" about you. Actually I hate this kind of glib coach talk (not that all coaches talk this way, but many do). When was the last time you saw someone change just because they were exhorted to do so?

The truth is that most of us are ill-prepared to deal with uncertainty. As children we are protected from the vagaries of an uncertain world. During school our parents tried to assuage our anxiety about test performance with platitudes such as "I'm sure you did well," or "As long as you tried your best."

Our educational process also reinforced the idea that uncertainty could be minimized—it had as its bedrock philosophy the analyzing and solving of problems. We learned that rational people believe in the scientific method, making predictions of probable outcomes to different behavioral scenarios. "If I study hard, I will get into a good university." "If I get a good university education, I will get a good job." In this way, we developed an expectation that we could predict and control our lives.

We aren't, however, taught to deal with uncertainty. As a result, most of us experience some degree of anxiety and respond poorly to an uncertain future.

Remember when you were in high school? As an "almost good girl," I would hazard a guess that after every exam you told your friends, "I really did badly on that," and then got an A or a B. Most of us imagine the worst to protect ourselves from the anxieties of uncertain outcomes.

Dealing with uncertainty is probably the greatest challenge we face when considering work alternatives: What happens if I can't think of anything else I really want to do? What happens if I try something and I fail? How do I know I'll be happier doing something else?

Susan Jeffries, in *Embracing Uncertainty: Breakthrough Methods for Achieving Peace of Mind When Facing the Unknown* (2003), says we should create a "wondering life" instead of a "hoping life." "Hoping" can lead to a state of unhappiness if those hopes are dashed, while "wondering" creates no expectations to be shattered. Consider the difference between "I hope I get that job" and "I wonder if I will get that job."

Still, some of us simply do not have an appetite for risk. "Help! I'm desperate," an event planner acquaintance e-mailed me. "I hate this job. The values in this company suck, I can't stand the people I work with. . . ." This was not a new feeling. In fact, she had been complaining about her work for several years. Single at forty-one, with no debt and no kids, I found it puzzling why she'd done so little to address her unhappiness. When I asked her, all she said was "I've just never been good at taking risks. It's a problem I have, and I know it, but that's the way I am."

Consider, in contrast, another woman who at the age of fifty had been in the throes of a career crisis when her husband died. While she mourned, she put her career woes aside. But when she recovered some of her emotional strength, she realized she couldn't continue in her job. "I had two children to support and little in the way of financial resources," she said. "I made a plan that involved selling my house so that I could go back to school and get a diploma in mediation."

Obviously, money plays a role in readiness to make work changes. But we all know people with huge financial resources who stay in a job they hate because they are making such good money that they feel they have no choice but to stick around. And we also all know people with no financial cushion who will jump ship if they are unhappy. As these two tales show, money certainly doesn't tell the whole story. But as we will see later the money issue is nevertheless an important and complicating factor.

The Anatomy of Moving On

Flashback: I'm thirty-three years old. It's the mid-eighties. I have a six-month-old son. My husband is a freelance magazine journalist writing what he describes as "stuff between the ads." There is a recession. (Translation: fewer ads equals less stuff between the ads.) We have a very large mortgage, and no financial safety net.

I am working for a management consulting firm. There are three partners, two of whom are psychologists, male of course: Dr. Lunatic (nice guy but completely nuts, so I forgive him his rages because I know he's crazy, not mean), C-Squared (cruel plus cold), and the Mengelian Dr. Evil PhD. You get the picture: I'm depressed, second-guessing myself, taking lots and lots of baths (they don't help), crying frequently, and after a six-month nightmare, I quit (quite gloriously, I might add, even getting to use the "F" word as I swung out the door).

Now this was a marquee, five-star, hideous career experience that I wouldn't wish on my worst enemy, and yes, having a PhD.

did put me in a privileged position, but remember this was during a recession. "You just quit without having another job lined up?" and "You know, Barbara, telling your employer to commit a sexual act on themselves does not as a general rule lead to a great reference" were my friends' incredulous responses.

But I knew anything, absolutely anything, including poverty, selling our house, moving to a one-bedroom apartment, and making my own face mask out of egg whites was better than working there. And I also knew, at my core, that I would find other work. (I did. I started consulting on my own.) Like many women who have made these kinds of risky career decisions, I told myself: "I can always get a job as a waitress."

Was this simply high self-esteem? Possibly, but I was also the insecure mess I described earlier. Indeed, my husband used to jokingly describe me as having "high self-confidence, low self-esteem." My decision was probably the result of a number of factors, but certainly feelings of self-worth and expectations about work do play a role.

You Deserve to Feel Good about Your Work

"I wouldn't allow myself to be in a bad or abusive personal relationship. Work is also a relationship. If it's bad or feels abusive, it has the same impact on your sense of self."
  —IT professional

If you suffer from low self-esteem or are going through a bad personal situation, you are more likely to tolerate a bad work situation because you don't believe you deserve anything better. Take, for example, fifty-two-year-old professor Julia's story.

"I had started hating my job to the point that just thinking about going to work made me ill. I was also going through a difficult time at home. I found out my husband had been having an affair for more than a year, and then he left me. My daughter said this was somehow my fault. So, in terms of work, I just told myself: 'This is as good as I'm going to get.'" Through psychotherapy Julia recognized that she had been allowing herself to be treated as everyone's doormat—neither her students, nor her colleagues, husband, or her daughter respected her. She also began to understand *why*: she had been modeling her meek, long-suffering mother, who had repressed her own desires in favor of her family's. And she learned she had a right to be happy in her work—that this did not make her self-indulgent. She left academia to write a book and consult.

For some women, especially those still acting out a people-pleasing life script more appropriate to an earlier career stage, acting on unhappy feelings seems indulgent. A writer who had complained bitterly about how miserable she was justified her decision to stay in her current job rather than look for different work thus: "You're not supposed to like everything you do. You are making a living and have financial responsibilities. To me it seems indulgent to be acting on how you *feel*."

Fortunately, most women at midlife are refusing to put their desires on the back burner.

One woman, in discussing what is important to her in life, says that other than ill health among family members, the worst thing she can imagine dealing with is "bad work." She famously quit a job that she had taken with a consulting firm after only one week because, she said, "I realized my boss was insane and that I could never deliver what was expected." A journalist concurs: "Good work is as vital as oxygen."

The major source of regret amongst the women I worked with is that they repressed their needs for good work or stayed in a bad work situation too long. "I should have listened sooner, way sooner, to that inner niggling voice that kept telling me *you deserve more*," one woman explained.

Recognizing and Wrestling with Feelings

*"I can do a job and focus on the job, but not the emotional
stuff. I've never been comfortable with that or in my work roles
had to deal with that."*
    —Former director of finance turned fashion-boutique owner

People vary in their sensitivity to unpleasant work situations. Some
of us are simply more attuned to whether we feel good in our work:
we are quicker to recognize the signs of distress, where others repress
these bad feelings. Psychologists call this *self-monitoring*.

I have a quick "I can't stand this" radar: I have a very low tolerance for working with people I don't care for. Try as I might, I find
it difficult to discipline myself to do what is required to carry out
work in this situation. I also have difficulty thinking about professional content that doesn't interest me.

Here's why I'm lucky. If you experienced unpleasant work interactions as almost nauseating, would you continue in bad work? Of
course not. But with all our busyness, most of us don't have time to
think about whether we are happy. As we've seen, most of us *drift*
into career distress, which often means that we don't take action
until we are in a truly unhealthy situation.

One head of learning for a bank provides a regular check and
balance for herself. She makes a "date" with herself at the end of
every workweek. She reflects on the week past and asks herself
questions like: Is this work meeting my needs? Did I do anything
significant this week? Did I have fun? Did I feel good? And then she
thinks about the coming weeks and what she hopes to accomplish.

But being happy is about more than being attuned to your feelings. You also have to be willing to wrestle with, rather than
repress, unpleasant emotions, something most of us do. A thirty-
eight-year-old marketing specialist with a prestigious degree in
public policy working in an investment bank put it this way: "I start

to get pissed off because the guys with the MBAs get paid much more and these MBA dealers treat us, the women, like we're their court jesters. Then we, the women, either just get together and commiserate, and that way get it out of our system; or else I just eat it and forget about it."

Many of the women I have met will let something slip that tells me that they are unhappy—a bitter description of their job, for example—before they backtrack and deny these feelings by going into "male jocular" mode: "We all have our cross to bear. Ha, ha, ha." "It pays the bills. Ha, ha, ha."

True enough, men are more likely to do this than are women, but women, especially those who are more career-focused or who like to play "martyr," do this as well. They believe it is a sign of weakness to admit distress, that it means they are not tough enough.

In fact, the opposite is true. It takes a strong, optimistic person to say "I'm unhappy. I will identify what I need to be happy." It requires dealing with the unpleasant emotional state associated with uncertainty while one digs down to find the answer to "what will make me happy?"

All transitions take time and work, but as one woman commented: "When you are in the unknowing state of mind, this is when you are most open to wonderment, exploration, and discovery." To paraphrase Bertrand Russell, ambiguity and uncertainty lead "to the only state in which new discoveries are made." The ability to deal with ambiguity and stay the course is the foundation to creating and designing a work life that will satisfy us and allow us to move forward with grace.

There is no bromide. It takes time to digest the issues, identify what we do and do not want, and explore new options. The media and the passion-pushing coaching industry have fed us a steady diet of feel-good "if you can dream it, you can do it" mantras. We may live in a quick-fix society, but there is no quick fix to dealing with life's important questions.

Seeing Yourself as Competent

Believing that you have the capacity to find a better work fit has as much to do with how you feel about your skills as the quality of your skills. Clearly, having in-demand skills and rich work experiences that you can readily reconfigure or sell to someone else puts you at an advantage. But the problem many women face is that they underestimate their talents. I have seen many female professionals who don't see themselves as capable, but I have rarely met one who isn't. They've worked in environments or professions in which their competence is not recognized so they don't appreciate or understand their own abilities. Or they've been so busy keeping all the balls in the air that they've never actually taken the time to think about their accomplishments.

As often as not, it's the *sense* of competence as much as the actual competencies that influences readiness to contemplate transitions, and, as we have seen, the effect of today's extreme-work tenor is to erode people's sense of their competence. I have counseled many women who tell me that they have no particular accomplishments or skills. Interestingly, it often takes an accomplishment in their personal life before they start to recognize accomplishments and special talents in their professional life.

A psychologist client, for example, wanted to leave her hospital employer; she hated the assessment work she was doing and thought her boss was an "idiot." She had taken the job twelve years earlier, after completing her PhD, because it was part-time and allowed her to be with her children.

She insisted that she had no accomplishments: How could she possibly sell herself to an employer? she asked. Soon we started to talk about her personal life and how and why she had decided to leave her husband. She came to realize that her decision to leave her husband was a very powerful assertion of her belief in herself and her vision of a better life. She said: "Leaving my husband was the first time I had chosen to be more than a mother, a daughter, and a wife." As we discussed the characteristics of her decision—being independent, being bold, and having a vision for the future—she realized that she had many work accomplishments that spoke to the same attributes.

In my career/life-planning workshops, many of the midlife women, especially those who have been employed by the same organization for a long time, have difficulty identifying their accomplishments. They confide—yes, even today—that it feels boastful, immodest, and therefore unfeminine. That women have more difficulty recognizing, much less discussing, their accomplishments has been well documented. Quite simply, when I look at these abundantly talented women who have fought many battles, stood up to bullies, raised great children and stepchildren, acted as mentors and managers, and divorced incompatible men, and listen to them decry their lack of accomplishments, it breaks my heart.

For many of these women it is a question of coaching them in identifying their accomplishments and helping them reappraise socialized beliefs about modesty. But sometimes it takes more. We develop our sense of competence through our childhood experiences and adult interactions with the world, and we lose our sense of competence through similarly complex avenues. One way to restore a sense of competence, which is so intimately tied to a sense of self, is often psychotherapy. No quick feel-good fixes, just lots of hard work.

Many of the women I talked to had either been socialized to believe they weren't competent or had experienced one or more significant events in their lives, such as a husband's affair, a bad choice of partner, or several job terminations that led to an erosion of their sense of competence. The good news is that they all reached a good place in their lives, some with the help of therapists.

Take this manager's comment: "I feel good about myself and my work, but it took me a long time to feel this way. For years I went through my professional life feeling I didn't deserve to be where I was, I wasn't as smart as everyone else. I started to recognize what I had achieved only within the past five years. I'm from a working-class family, and the message I always got was that I wouldn't amount to much and that I shouldn't dream above my station in life."

I can't say that all the women I spoke to have wrestled their inner demons to the ground. What is important is that they feel good about their lives, most of the time.

Slaying the Fear Reptile

"I was dying. Year in, year out. Same content, just different faces. I liked that I was doing something important, but was nauseated by the sameness. I went on stress leave. I took a six-month job outside the educational sector. But I always returned to teaching. It was as if my pension was always the other person in the conversation. If I didn't have a pension, might I become a bag lady?"

"I stayed in jobs I hated, which meant nothing to me other than the money I made. This translated into many wasted prime years and the possibility that I let my life pass by without thinking about how I wanted to spend it, just out of fear."

"You have to listen to that inner voice, which tells you, 'You have to move on.' It's not going to get any better, it's just going to get worse."
   —Women commenting on the fear of change

Many talented, confident people are nonetheless held back by fear. An independent communications specialist described it as "The fear reptile. And when it rules, you get stuck."

Uncertainty and unpredictability are deeply disturbing to these talented women—it undermines their sense of self and place in the world. Even if they despise their work, they choose apparent security over the risk of testing themselves in an unfamiliar world. And if they lose their jobs, they will take the first job that comes along. "At least I will have a job," they say.

Many women at midlife can recognize that their fears about security are at odds with their sense that there is something better out there for them. Often they are, or were, "good girls" who feel dissatisfaction with their work lives but are scared to look at other options. As one woman said, "What if I start to look at my life and see there is a lot of shit that's not working. It's like Pandora's box: you don't know what you'll find."

In other words, what if, in thinking about their lives, they end up turning them upside down, needing to redefine *all* their relationships? They fear they will crack the façade and lose the comforts they have enjoyed. And they fear failure.

Often, successful managers and professionals who have gone from strength to strength throughout their careers are the ones who have the most difficulty dealing with uncertainty. They are not accustomed to the possibility of failure. Nor are they accustomed to ambiguity, as they have been rewarded throughout their careers for their ability to define a problem, develop a strategy, and act on it.

One of the key ingredients in making successful life transitions is the ability to stay the course, to cope with uncertainties, and to live with the doubts that you will ever reach your new goal. Take a TV producer of nineteen years who said she plans on moving to a new city with her partner. "I don't yet know exactly where or what I'll be doing to make a living. The one thing I know is that it will be completely different."

As the communications specialist who worried about her "fear reptile" pointed out, "The reptile isn't all bad. It's there to help us survive. When it rules, you need to acknowledge it and negotiate with it. Your bargaining tools are your sense of competence, clarity of vision, and tenacity. Then it will lie down and let the hope and courage enter the room."

In order to do that you have to analyze your interior monologues.

Identifying the Stuff That Holds You Back

"Timing is important, but you can't let timing, as in 'The timing's not right now,' become your excuse for doing nothing. The right time, at least to start to put things in motion, is when you first feel that nagging malaise which says, 'This doesn't feel good.'"
—Career counselor

There is no shortage of the sort of negative statements we make about ourselves that shut down our aspirations:

- I might try something and fail.
- My partner/friends will disapprove of me.
- I'll look silly.
- My kids will think I'm an idiot.
- I can't afford this.

The origins of these statements are often from our younger selves and unless we identify and confront them, the fear reptile will continue to control us and interfere with our ability to move forward.

One woman who was embarking on a new career path said: "My parents always told me I was ordinary, nothing special, and that people should know their place in the world. I had this little siren song in my head about all the awful things that could happen and how they were probably right, but then I told myself, 'Of course you might fail. There are no guarantees, but how will you feel about yourself if you don't try?'"

She wrote down each thought that was going through her head. Then she asked herself: Is this true? How do I know this is true? Why do I believe this? What would happen if I didn't try? Will I be able to survive if things don't turn out the way I want?

Sometimes our worries are unfounded. For example, some women say their partner wouldn't support the kind of move they want to make because of the financial sacrifices involved. It later transpires they haven't even discussed the issue with their partner.

We may be dishonest with ourselves. We may be uncomfortable with our ambitions and desires, especially if the motivation isn't very ennobling, or the desires are associated with making a lot of money. One woman, for example, who started an entrepreneurial business said: "I made this move ten years too late. I wanted to make pots of money to prove to my partner that I was as important and successful as him, but I was too embarrassed to even acknowledge this to myself. It made me feel that I was a bad person."

But you need to dig down and be brutally honest with yourself. Are the statements you are making self-serving? One woman told me that she would love to leave her corporate job in sales and marketing and go freelance. She said she couldn't, however, because she would feel "guilty" about reducing her family's income. This was her script: "I don't like my job. I could go out on my own. But a good mother puts her children's needs first. I am therefore a good person." The truth? She liked the security of her job and enjoyed corporate life. But she liked the idea of flirting with alternatives because it made her feel more alive. More importantly she *liked* the idea of making sacrifices and being a martyr.

I have met a lot of women who have more fun *talking* about making a change than actually making one. They think it makes them interesting. They like playing the "I think I'd like to become a

travel writer/open a boutique/go back to school to become a therapist" game. The game is usually played in a bitch session with
friends during which everyone complains about how much they
hate their jobs or what a jerk their boss or client is. There's nothing
wrong with the game. In fact, it's a lot of fun, and I've played it
several times myself. But that's all it is: a game.

An acquaintance of mine has been in career exploration mode
for ten years. One year she wants to write a book. The next she
wants to open an interior design business. Now whenever she tells
me her plans, I think to myself "We all have a story we tell ourselves
about who we are. Whatever story you need to tell yourself is fine
with me." I think she likes the *idea* of being a person who explores
career options, but lacks the drive and ability to tolerate the discomfort of making a change. Every time she reaches the point where
she would have to do hard work she either says: "I can't be bothered" or "I have a new idea about what I want to do."

So often the game players don't make a move because thinking
about options is enough to enable them to have an image of themselves as being "edgy," even if they lack true motivation, vision, and
self-discipline. Or it is because they are intimidated by the sacrifices
they would have to make.

On the other hand, sometimes you really do need to make
sacrifices. This is what one woman who left the corporate world
said in response to the question: "What was holding you back from
making this transition earlier?" "My husband. Lo! I sacrificed the
self-serving, money-grubbing bastard." Many women who made
successful transitions made comments such as this: "I could not
have made a transition without a very patient and supportive
partner. I have friends who also tried to make a change whose partners were constantly saying, 'So when are you going to make some
real money?'"

Of course, money is one of the chief reasons people cite when
asked why they don't make a change.

Not Being Owned by Money

*"We compare ourselves with others and what they have.
So we want more and that means more money. Instead we
should accept less money and a lot more happiness because
we know what we really need."*
—Former banker

A woman I know hated her job so much that she was living on anti-depressants. But she would not contemplate quitting because, she said, "We need my income." Her husband, the publisher of a magazine facing declining advertising revenue, was worried about being fired. Nevertheless, they were about to undertake a major renovation of their kitchen. "We have to do it. It's ugly, and it depresses me," she explained.

It sounds crazy. But every career practitioner hears stories like this from clients unable to make effective career choices because of dysfunctional financial decisions. Note the language Linda used: "We *have* to do it." She was incapable of distinguishing between what she wanted and what she actually *needed*.

I talk to many women who are victims of their own lifestyle. No matter how unhappy they are, they say: "I can't quit this job/go out on my own/work part-time because we need the money." When asked why they need the money, they invoke such luxuries as a Caribbean spring break, two cars, private school, club memberships, and so on. They talk as if they had no choice in the matter, as if they were only passengers in their own lives. Telling themselves these things are life imperatives, they feel deprived if they don't have them, and threatened by the thought of losing them.

Yet at the same time, there is often a competing undercurrent in their thinking: they have a desire for work that is meaningful, speaks to their most important values, and still allows them time for a life. This inability to reconcile these ideas leads to conflict and unhappiness, which they then try to resolve by renovating their kitchen or taking an even more expensive vacation.

The truth is, we cannot make healthy and effective career decisions when our thinking is distorted by our relationship with money. Unfortunately, many of us do allow our lives to get bent out of shape, tying wealth to hefty psychological anchors.

One reason why so many managers and professionals today overemphasize their need for money is because they feel so overworked and underappreciated. As one forty-year-old IT director commented, after she accepted a job for which she knew she was ill-suited: "If I'm going to go to the wall, I may as well do it for a whack of money." While some midlife women have moved beyond their preoccupation with money as a means of keeping score, many have not.

We use money as a substitute for many things: to satisfy feelings of status and self-worth ("I must be important if I'm earning a lot of money"); to fill in for feelings of emotional deprivation ("If I can't be happy, at least I can buy stuff"); to feel like good providers ("If I can't spend more time with my kids, at least I can send them to private school"); to feel independent and safe ("I don't need to rely on anyone; I can look after myself").

A friend who was significantly in debt was so unhappy in her job that she bought a mink coat, which she kept hidden from her husband in the trunk of her car. When I asked her why she had bought it, she said she felt "deprived." Many of the women I know who are in debt got there by consuming stuff that, by their own admission, added little in terms of real joy to their lives.

As my friend said about her mink coat, the pleasure was in the buying, not in the wearing. This is a common comment from women who buy stuff to make themselves feel better about other troubling aspects of their lives. Although most midlife women don't rank money at the top of their list of what is important to them, I see many still acting out earlier scripts about the importance of money: they use money as an emotional substitute, a measure of their success in relation to others, and have a knee-jerk response about its necessity.

Consider forty-nine-year-old Anna, who was in a training job she loved, with a satisfying lifestyle and little debt. Then she was offered a new job as a human resources manager at a much higher salary, doing work that had much less appeal. The offer triggered a career crisis, which she ultimately resolved by asking herself two key questions: How will that additional income enhance my life? What would I be giving up in terms of doing work that engages me? She decided to stay put.

In talking to artists I am often struck by how they can design a life that feels "rich" to them despite continual financial challenges. "I never feel deprived," one actress said. "I may not have what some of my friends have, but when I look around my apartment, I see great vintage clothing and great old furniture finds. And if I want to indulge myself, I can always buy some expensive nail polish."

Nonetheless, money is an important determinant of later life choices. About 75 percent of the women said they did not have the financial security that they had expected at this life stage—they didn't want a lot, just some latitude or a safety net for taking risks. Virtually all of them said one of their major life regrets was "buying too much crap and not starting to save earlier."

So how much money do you really need? The money-happiness equation has been the subject of extensive investigation in recent years. What researchers have found is that if you are poor, money does make a difference. But beyond a minimum threshold of sufficient income to look after basic needs, more money will not make you happier.

If you are reevaluating how you are living, here are some ways to bring your life back into greater harmony with your most important values:

- Ensure that your finances are in order so that you can make career decisions based on your needs and desires rather than financial fears.

- Carefully review your personal values. Know what is really important to you. Ask yourself: What do I really care about?

- If you are making significant personal sacrifices to maintain your lifestyle, consider "downshifting." Be ruthless in evaluating how your current lifestyle meets your real needs for a satisfied life. When making a purchase, ask yourself: "Will I feel better about myself or will my life be richer if I do this? What need will this purchase satisfy? Am I trying to satisfy an emotional need for status, or affection? Can I satisfy this need in another way?"

Answer these questions honestly: What is the cost to me in living the way I am living? What am I giving up to maintain this lifestyle?

Take a cue from people who are able to rise above envy, acquisitiveness, and status-seeking and maintain an independent stance in thinking about money. It's as if they have an internal compass that tells them what's important. They don't use money as a substitute for happiness. They think about what they have, rather than what they don't have. As they say: "Happiness isn't getting what you want, it's wanting what you have."

They are driven by a desire to feel good about their lives. When faced with any decision that has financial implications, they ask themselves: "How will this contribute to my overall life satisfaction?" They know what they care about and what they need.

Focusing on What Really Matters

"Every life chapter provides an opportunity to do something you care about. I focused on what that chapter's theme was instead

of trying to do it all. When I look back on my life, I have a
sense of contentment. And I still have lots more chapters left."
—Sixty-five-year-old psychologist

When my son was three years old, I was invited to do an international speaking tour of New Zealand—pretty heady stuff for someone whose most exciting prior speaking engagements were in towns with unpronounceable names two plane flights from nowhere. I turned it down within a nanosecond. Why? Because my son would never be three again, but New Zealand would always be there. I had a visceral sense of what was important to me.

Can you have it all? Yes, but not all at once. In fact, not one of the approximately four hundred working women who answered this question said "yes." So if we are looking to have it all—in effect, work-life balance—maybe we need to rethink the concept; it obscures what we're really looking for, namely, the opportunity to feel good about our lives and to have a sense of accomplishment.

The problem with the term "work-life balance" is that it assumes we all have a caloric budget for meeting a prescribed set of needs— time for family, friends, and children, aesthetic pursuits, spiritual nourishment, and intellectual engagement—choosing just the right amount of each as if they were major food groups. But there is no Food Guide to tell us how to live our lives.

The truth is, we all have different needs, and those needs are constantly changing. When we have children, loved ones get sick, we land or lose a job, we develop an entirely new set of priorities. These life events force us to focus on whatever is most important to us at a particular moment. And no matter how hard we strive to achieve "balance," there will inevitably be tensions between competing needs: between the need for spiritual nourishment and the need to make money, or between the desire for personal and family time and the yearning for career advancement. These conflicts are not necessarily bad: they are what makes us grow as human beings.

What we idealize as "balance" is really a kind of throwback to a fifties idea of the good life, to a sunny but bland world with everything in moderation, where everyone read *Reader's Digest* and ate bran cereal. When we feel great about something we're doing, or passionate about a particular pursuit, then almost by definition other important aspects of our lives will get less of our attention, and may be neglected entirely. It's unlikely, for example, that many great pieces of work were produced by artists who pursued a state of balance.

Of course some people do lead lives that are wildly unbalanced, focusing obsessively on work and ignoring everything else with serious consequences for their health, relationships, and family. But when that happens, their life isn't simply out of balance, it's out of control. What we call workaholism, for example, doesn't emerge from a failure to balance work and a personal life: it's the result of deeper psychological issues, such as an inability to develop an identity separate from one's work. Such issues cannot be addressed, or redressed, through the search for the grail of perfect balance.

The real questions should be: Do we feel good about how we're spending our life? and, Are we aware of the choices we've made? Are we nourishing what is important to us? If we are making sacrifices in some areas of our life, are we doing so in a conscious way as part of a larger plan of how we want to live and work in the future?

It's not reasonable to expect our lives to be in perfect balance. Our lives are made up of chapters, and in one we may have to sacrifice some needs that can be met in a later chapter in favor of others. Giving something up now doesn't mean giving it up forever.

We worry that if we say no to something now we are saying no to it forever. But this is not so. In one chapter our personal life may take priority, in another chapter career aspirations. Over time, a kind of balance emerges.

If instead we doggedly pursue that elusive state that is work-life balance, trying to have a measured ration of everything we want at any given time, we end up feeling chronically dissatisfied, living in a kind of gray zone, where none of our needs are really being met. Life is not some gigantic mechanical scale on which you can put all the pieces of your life and weigh them up, adding and taking away bits until they come out in a state of perfect homeostasis.

Navigating the Rocky Road to Moving Forward

"I went to university in my early forties, divorced, started a new relationship, ended said relationship, got a new job, quit said job. But I rebuilt my life and confidence. Then last year I went solo and survived! But before I did, I spent many wee hours of the night wondering what the heck I was going to do with my life. I still get the wobblies."
  —Career coach

"After two decades of floundering, which even included a brief stay in a mental institution, I have finally found the work I was meant to do."
  —Writer

Some of the women who contributed to this book said they had a meltdown every five to ten years when they thought about life chapters to come or dealt with boredom. Some did crazy things—like Kristine, who had a very public affair with her boss and then took a job for which she was completely ill-suited, primarily *because* everyone told her she was completely ill-suited for the position. She said, "It pissed me off to be told I couldn't do something, that something was unwise. I didn't want to live in a world where you made decisions because they were sensible. That made me feel dead and middle-aged."

In the next chapter, we will look at the moves people made. They were ultimately gratifying, but many took a circuitous route. Career books and media are full of inspiring stories and make it sound easy.

Although most of the women eventually had a soft landing, the path to renewal was not necessarily smooth.

It takes time to identify the next steps. It takes time to identify what we want, and the shape that work will take. Sometimes this means waiting it out and trusting you will get there. As Virginia Woolf wrote in *A Room of One's Own*, "It is in our idleness, in our dreams, that the submerged truth sometimes comes to the top." Unfortunately, we are so accustomed to doing, acting, and achieving, so busy living in multiple moments, that taking a pause can make us feel as though we don't exist.

Some of us need a vision. One woman trusted a vision would come to her. It did, but it took several years. "I knew I was ready for something that felt like it was just over the horizon. But I couldn't give it a name. I just knew it was my next step, and that it would show itself to me. For the most part I trusted my inner voice—but sometimes it felt like hell waiting for it to reveal itself . . . I thought long and hard, I wasn't passive, but just couldn't figure out what the 'it' was." (She ultimately found her path running a trekking business focused on women.)

One woman who was fired from her senior management job said, "At first I thought, This is great. Time for myself, yoga, and spas—all on my odious former employer's dime. But then I realized so much of my life had been defined by my corporate role—I didn't really have a 'non-executive me.' I drifted for a year. I was offered another job. I took it, and then quit a month later. But that was the move I needed to make, because I realized that 'corporate me' was no longer. I went back to school at the age of forty-seven." She is now a high-school teacher.

We fall into two camps when it comes to setting goals. Some women aggressively and routinely identify goals. A financial planner said that if she didn't have a goal, she wouldn't have a reason to get out of bed in the morning. "I need goals to motivate me; otherwise I would drift and achieve nothing." She fears that without rigorous self-policing her "inner slacker will take command."

But others, like me, are almost allergic to setting goals. As one woman said, "If I make a goal, it will end up owning me, and I will be its servant. I will lose the spontaneous moments where opportunity usually lies. I have something in me that gives me a sense of what I want, but it's not specific—it's more like a vision. It gives me a more relaxed feeling as I don't feel as though I'm being dictated to by my goals."

Another concurred. "When the right opportunity presents itself, you need to recognize it, but you can't necessarily plan for it. None of my moves were planned, and it's been a successful strategy so far. I know some people who have five- and ten-year plans, and I think, How boring is that? Who wants to plan with absolute certainty the specifics of your life or your career? I think that's insane. And insanely boring."

As John Lennon once said, "Life is what happens when you are making other plans." While it is true that you can't get there if you don't know where you are going, you may find that adhering rigidly to a preconceived plan means that you arrive somewhere you actually don't want to be.

For goals to be meaningful, like our lives, they must be dynamic and changeable. Do you see yourself as being on a journey, or are you on a fixed path to a predetermined destination? Many women in midlife see themselves as moving toward a *state*, such as being debt-free, or leaving a legacy, but their goals are implicit, not explicit. They trust they will get there.

Our Wish List

Not all of us look to our work as an important or principal source of happiness. But all of us pay a price when our work makes us feel like less than ourselves.

Regardless of what motivates us—and all the women in this

book have a different vision of what constitutes what they want from work—in essence our wish lists are very similar. At the core, we all want the same thing—work that we care about, whether professional or unpaid, which plays to our strengths, while still allowing time for a life, in environments where we can be true to ourselves with impunity.

Dismiss List – What We Don't Want in Work:

- Values compromised
- Having to do crappy work (compromising standards, work that isn't satisfying, and yes, the dead-end suffocatingly boring and oppressive work that many women are tragically forced to endure, without choices)
- Self-satisfied people in the environment
- Ditto boring and humorless people
- Participating in the cult of business
- Engaging in male-pleasing behaviors
- Repressing important parts of ourselves
- Supporting the singular pursuit of money or production of useless products

Wish List – What We Do Want in Work:

- Important values satisfied
- Signature strengths used
- Interesting people in the environment
- Appreciation from those we work with or serve
- Opportunity to connect in a meaningful way with others
- To be authentic
- To give something back
- To create or deliver something of value

chapter six

Women in Motion:

The Paths to

Midlife Renewal

"I got off the career path to raise three beautiful children. I'm now back at fifty trying to establish a business. I worry about how much time I have left and whether I will be the best-kept secret in this city. But I don't regret for a second the decisions I've made."

"It's great to be in that sweet spot where you are absolutely clear about who you are and what you are good at. For me this is about leading others and making a difference."

"I own my work, my choices, my life. . . . Since I left corporate life I have a sense of freedom and purpose I haven't had for decades. I got my soul back."

"I'm working my way down the Maslow hierarchy. What I want now is security, a predictable paycheck,

and to catch up on building some kind of nest egg. At fifty-five, I just went back to the corporate world after ten years of being an independent—being self-actualized doesn't pay. The job is pleasant, which is enough for me."

"I have a business idea. It's so good, I can't tell you what it is. But I've devoted the last year to researching it and I'm desperate to make it happen."

"I just said screw it and I quit my fancy corporate job to become an inner-city teacher. It was a radical move—I had to go back to school, and downsize absolutely everything. But life is too short to be doing work that you don't care about and you're not proud of."

"I took everything I've learned throughout my career and put it all together. Same skills but applied in a new way. There was and is huge risk, but I've never felt so alive. Like this is my song."

"Right now, all I care about is leaving a legacy."

"I left the consulting world to take a leadership job well below what I was being paid. This is my swan song. I have influence and the capacity to make a difference in a way I never did before. In part I think it's because I'm doing this for me and what I believe in as opposed to trying to please others. But it's also because my skills have come together in a way they never did before, and I found the environment in which I could make it happen."

—Women describing their midcareer plans and moves

Russian-born Sarah moved to North America when she was ten years old. She was a strong student who excelled in writing, painting, performing—one of those artistic, introverted types who receive modest attention for poetry and drawings in the school yearbook. Her father was Russian, her mother French, and she was fluent in both languages. When it was time for her to go to university, her father said, "I'll pay your tuition if you go into a program that leads to a profession." She put her creativity, as she said, in "the creativity box and filed it away."

She studied languages and eventually became a translator. At thirty-five she married a professor turned entrepreneur. Sarah quit her government translation job and devoted the next ten years to being "her husband's best friend," traveling with him on business and for pleasure, arranging musical soirees, and preparing gourmet meals. They did not want children. "We had a rich and playful life. We felt complete," she said. One day a friend, after listening to her recount her father's experience of the Holocaust, said, "You have to tell that story. You should write an article and submit it to a magazine." She wrote the article, and it was published. She received many comments about what a powerful writer she was.

It was as if someone had lit a fuse and apparently out of nowhere all these creative sparks ignited. Within two years she had written and illustrated a book and had mounted an exhibition of her photo-collages. She is one of the most multitalented women I know—she continues to produce words and images at an almost alarming rate.

There are many women like Sarah who at midlife find their creative juices welling. As Sue Shellenbarger says in *The Breaking Point: How Female Midlife Crisis Is Transforming Today's Women* (2005), "The vital juices of joy, sexuality, and self-discovery are bubbling within, more powerfully and compellingly than ever" during this life phase.

F. Scott Fitzgerald famously said, "There are no second acts in American life." Today many of us envisage second, third, and fourth acts—one act in our late thirties and early forties, another in our fifties, and, sometimes, another in our sixties.

Whether or not we envisage a new act, or continue to grow along already established paths, ideally we now engage in a way that is different from when we were younger. We now have the mature vision the second half of life affords us—we know who we are, have an honest understanding of our strengths, and are able to park our ego. But not all of us manage the transition to the second half with grace. Some women simply flame out.

Take Dana, for example, who had worked her way up the government ladder to a high-profile role as a policy analyst and was frequently being quoted in the media. She lost her job at forty-eight when there was a change of government. She told me she wanted to reinvent herself as the head of a think-tank or a university department.

Dana is smart and knows her way around government and lobbyists, but she lacks interpersonal skills. She is variously described by her acquaintances as "arrogant," a "professional social climber," "tactless," and "clueless when it comes to making other people feel good about themselves."

When she told me her career aspirations, I told her the unvarnished truth—that she had had no prior management experience, would be competing against people who had significant experience, and that she wasn't known for her interpersonal finesse. She was offended by my assessment of her suitability. She also told me many people had told her to pursue this particular career direction. (Note to reader: If you tell acquaintances in your network, especially women, that you want to do something for which you are clearly unsuited, they will often be polite, even encouraging, so as not to hurt you.)

It took Dana more than a year of applying unsuccessfully for big management jobs before she accepted the reality. She is now working for a consulting firm as a lobbyist; I can't say, as I would like to, that she has benefited from this experience and has developed new insights. She is bitter and thinks the people who didn't hire her were narrow-minded and unfair; she continues to send in her resume for executive roles. Dana, like many women whose attempt to change direction at midlife fails miserably, had no insight into her strengths and weaknesses.

Some women flame out even more spectacularly, especially women who decide to set up entrepreneurial businesses with a large bank loan but little research, awareness of their strengths, or ability to seek and accept feedback.

Michele, for example, had been making an adequate income as a landscape designer but at forty-seven wanted, as she said, "to do something big." I think she was being competitive with her successful investment banker partner, who she felt belittled her service business. She wanted to prove to him that she was as successful as he was, and in order to succeed she needed to make serious money.

After considering various business options—all of which involved a significant financial investment—she decided to open a nursery, reasoning that she had been sourcing garden ornaments and plant materials for many years and knew what people wanted to buy.

She had no retail experience, no hard business knowledge, and had never managed a payroll. A close friend of hers who had some knowledge of the business told her she was getting in way over her head; but rather than testing the waters and starting small, as her friend encouraged her to, she leased a large lot in a pricey neighborhood, took out a huge loan, and found investors. She declared bankruptcy twenty-four months later. She might in fact have made it in her business if she had heeded her friend's advice. (If you think this is unusual, right now I can think of thirteen other women who made or are in the process of making exactly the same mistake. Eavesdrop on what people are talking about the next time you are at the hairdresser—you will hear at least one similar story.)

There are, of course, many success stories of women who start an independent business at midlife. Indeed women are more likely than men this age to carry off this transition, because they are more cautious, more capable of asking for and listening to advice, and more aware of their strengths and weaknesses. But some women, like Michele, try to follow the traditional male model: make it big, borrow big, overestimate your abilities.

Whether they are changing jobs or setting up a business, what these women who flame out have in common is hubris: arrogance about their abilities, issues about status, and obliviousness to the market for their talents. Dare I say it: they have a more "masculine" style.

Can You Reinvent Yourself?

Both of these women were trying to, in their words, "reinvent" themselves. The idea of reinvention is very seductive and resonates with the North American zeitgeist. Throw away the old, embrace the new, completely reinvent yourself. If you watch TV, you can see boring "befores" and great "afters" in virtually every aspect of life. We imagine completely new and improved selves living fulfilling new and improved lives.

I have a deep distaste for the expression "reinvent myself." I routinely get calls from women asking to do just that. The concept of branding has become so entrenched in our culture that we think of ourselves as products constantly needing to be rebranded and repackaged.

My difficulty with the concept of reinvention is philosophical: how do you reinvent the "self"? Who you are—your personality, your values, how you look—is not plastic, capable of being molded into whatever the *self du jour* happens to be. In other words, one can never really reinvent oneself. (We are told that "in the future we will all have six careers" and many women are discomfited by the idea. They think that means they will have no identity or center, nothing to count on that makes them unique, that they will be constantly reshaping themselves—today a government manager, tomorrow a masseuse, the next day a flight attendant!)

I think of a person's skills and attributes as being like a Lego vehicle: the vehicle can be turned into a family car, an ambulance, or a spaceship, but it is still a vehicle. At base we all have singular attributes that make up who we are. We should celebrate them, rather than throwing them away.

The truth is that if you have never done something before or shown the remotest inclination or talent for a particular skill, it is rare at midlife for it to suddenly become part of who you are. (Women such as Sarah, whom we met earlier in the chapter, are the exception.) The policy wonk was destined to fail: her personality simply did not lend itself to a management role. The failed entre-preneur might have made it if she had not taken such a dramatic route of going from small service provider to entrepreneur playing in the big leagues overnight.

The women who make successful moves to reignite tired work lives have usually thought deeply about what they want to accomplish and what matters most at this life stage. This involves isolating key motivators and values, as well as signature talents. Making interesting moves is not easy: it involves overcoming fears about uncertainty, facing financial risk, asserting a right to have meaningful work, and believing in oneself.

But one of the pleasures of midlife is that sometimes these interests just bubble to the surface without deep reflection. I recently received an e-mail from a business owner who has never expressed any interest in writing. She sent me a column she had just written and said, "What do you think? Is it publishable? It's funny how you reach a stage where you are just ready and primed for new growth."

Whether we make radical moves or continue along a well-worn trajectory, I have found seven sometimes overlapping paths to career renewal at midlife.

Transforming the Nature of the Work

Everyone knows someone who at midlife made a radical career move into a completely new, previously untested work arena. This is the subject of great (sometimes competitive) dinner-table talk between girlfriends. ("You'll never believe what Anna is doing," one says followed by a story about an incredible change in career direction. "That's nothing, you should hear about Cheryl!" another exclaims.)

Sometimes the moves really are extraordinary. At thirty-nine, modern dancer Joy was tired of poverty and the stresses of constant auditions, cobbling together a living by waitressing, dancing, and writing grant applications. Realistically, she also worried about her age: How much longer could her body sustain the rigors of rehearsals and performances?

With the help of a career counselor she remembered that, as a youngster, she loved to debate anything and everything (her parents called her "little miss lawyer"). She had also dreamed of defending the underdog. As an adult she was deeply committed to women's issues. She decided to go back to school to become a lawyer. Single, with few savings, she got a student loan. She finished her undergraduate degree and ultimately went to law school, supplementing her income by giving dance lessons. Seven years later she has a fledgling practice in family law. She loves her work, and even though she is not making much money and has huge debts, she thinks she is very rich.

Such dramatic career moves, although inspiring and the subject of many features in women's magazines, are actually quite rare.

Indeed, a survey found that only 5 percent of the fourteen thousand people who had received career support from Right Outplacement Consulting Services in 2004 launched completely different careers. Many of the women who participated in my survey had flirted with the idea of doing something completely different, with little relationship to anything they had ever done professionally, but concluded it was too expensive.

As one IT manager said, "I thought of becoming an interior designer, and actually did a fair amount of research. But if I was serious about making a living this way, I would have had to go back to school and then start out all over again since my previous experience wouldn't count for anything. It just wasn't financially feasible." She renewed her work life by creating a portfolio career (see below), which included a small interior design practice. Her comment about the opportunity cost of a major move was echoed by many of the women. They discovered other moves they could make that would have the same satisfying impact on their lives.

But some did try it, like one educational consultant who had always dreamed of being a landscape architect. She went back to school and then gave it a two-year whirl. She said, "It was too hard. I only succeeded in getting three clients. But you know what? If I hadn't tried, I would always have wondered if I could have done it. So do I have any regrets? Absolutely not. I proved something to myself, that I could take risks." She found a job in a different school board where she consults to a client group with more challenging issues and is excited by her work.

But sometimes at midlife there is a spiritual awakening that leads to dramatic transformations. One woman, for example, a hard-nosed investment banker, a Career-builder, had a crisis brought on by job loss. She went on a retreat, and through a series of events that she described as her "destiny" met a spiritual healer who invited her to attend a class she was teaching.

She is now a spiritual healer herself. "I used to live completely above the shoulders, now I live completely below them," she says. A number of women move into body work and the healing arts, such as coaching, at midlife.

The other women who successfully transform their work are artists and slightly older Self-developers in their late forties and fifties who have a financial cushion, albeit modest, such that they are not dependent on their new endeavor to generate retirement savings.

But in my experience, over 90 percent of what looks like a significant career change really falls into one of the categories below.

Shifting or Reconfiguring the Work

"I was miserable, coming home crying every night. I loved the technical part of what I did, I hated the people for whom I did it. I found a similar role working in a completely different kind of culture, with lots of interesting women whom I can learn from or just laugh with."
  —Marketing specialist who moved to an NGO

The great majority of career movers in their late thirties and forties fall into this category, rejuvenating careers either by changing jobs, or reconfiguring their skills in new and interesting ways. Some are deadly bored Self-developers, tired of compromising professional standards; some are burnt-out Lifestylers; and some are Authenticity-seekers, disgusted with organizational life.

Janet, for example, was bored with her work in the public relations department of a bank and questioned the social value of her work. When she first talked to me, she said she wanted to make a career change. What she discovered after she did a rigorous self-assessment is common among bored professionals: she really loved her kind of work in terms of the skills she used. It was just that her feelings about the *purpose* of her work had poisoned her attitude to the *nature* of her work. A year later she shifted to a PR/communications role for a large children's agency. "I wanted my life to have counted for more than giving the bank spin. What I do now is about promoting children's wellness . . . how cool is that?" she said. About 80 percent of midlife men and women who start out thinking they want a career change discover it's not the nature of their work per se that's bothering them, it's where or how they're working.

We saw how many of the women despaired of the lack of values and the compromised professional standards in organizations. Many of these women moved to NGOs, or sought out female-friendly work cultures where they could do their work in a manner consistent with their values and professional standards and where their competence would be respected. Others reconfigured their skills into their occupation's "shadow" or parallel careers. (Shadow careers for teachers, for example, include educational assessment specialist, trainer, or publisher's educational sales rep. Shadow careers for a journalist might include speechwriter, web content producer, or public affairs specialist.)

Take the career moves of three formerly unhappy lawyers who leveraged their skills in the legal profession. (The word *unhappy* commonly appears before "lawyer.") One became a coach to other lawyers, one became a conference producer specializing in employment law, and the third became a writer specializing in legal matters. Many bored professionals who have reached the top of their professional ladder go the reconfiguration route.

Finishing Your Unfinished Business

At midlife, many of us have unfinished business from earlier life stages, ambitions left unexplored. Freema, for example, got pregnant and dropped out of university after her first year. For the next twenty years she worked as an administrative assistant. She had always wanted to be a psychologist: as early as Grade 8 she was the person everyone went to for advice on relationships and other emotional issues. At age forty-one, she decided to make the move.

We have seen that the trigger for a change is often an event in one's personal life. Early in her marriage, Freema discovered that her husband was having an affair. He swore he had ended it, and she believed him. When twenty years later she learned that the affair was still going on, she decided to end the marriage. "Leaving my husband was the beginning of a whole new beginning for me. It opened up the world and possibilities that I had never realized I had. And I didn't want to become one of those bitter old women who spend their lives full of regret," she said.

When her youngest child reached university age, she sold her house, moved to a cheaper city, and, living off the proceeds of her house and part-time clerical work, enrolled in a psychology program. Five years later, with an M.A. in psychology, she is working as a therapist. She is single and loving it. "This is the first time in my life that I feel completely free—free to do work that I love, and free to make my own life decisions. I feel like an adolescent who happens to work and have some money."

At midlife we often come back to the path not taken. Consider, for example, Lynne, a self-described "recovering M.B.A.," who worked her way up the corporate ranks in a pharmaceutical company and then returned to her earlier calling as a humorist.

"I've been a writer/entertainer ever since Grade 3, when I wrote my own commercial and performed it for the class. I used to watch Monty Python and listen to George Carlin when I was far too young to be listening to such foul language. I'm not sure I was preparing to be a writer as much as a humorist, but writing was always my vehicle. For all the reasons everyone does—family pressure, security, etcetera—I ended up going to business school. But it never felt right—the politics, the players, the values."

Lynne went back to school and completed a degree in English. "I never felt so alive as I did in my creative writing class: the language was so articulate, so alive compared to the language I was accustomed to. I was consumed with finding my voice, or shall I say, *rediscovering* it," she says. She quit her middle-management job at thirty-nine to write full-time. But all life experiences count, no matter how awful. Her first novel? *E-Mails from the Edge* (2006), a brilliantly witty book about a woman who works her way up the ranks at a pharmaceutical company only to find such work repulsive.

Often as we mature professionally we drift away from earlier sources of engagement. What were your earliest dreams? Perhaps you saw yourself as someone who was good at helping people, or saw yourself weaving beautiful stories, or standing up for the underdog. These early aspirations provide important clues to underlying career desires and themes. Sometimes, as in Lynne's case, this is the path not taken: sometimes this is going back to the path veered away from.

You may recall the nurse we met earlier who as a child had a Florence Nightingale dream of helping people, and ended up running a hospital at midlife. When she reconnected to her earliest desires, what she realized was that she was a *healer*, not an administrator. She is now a career coach.

Sometimes we are forced into reconnecting to earlier career themes as a result of unexpected life twists. My old friend Candy, for example, started her work life as an artist. As inspiration, she collected antique metal toys that she used in her art. At the age of thirty-one, tired of the waitressing/artist balancing act, she enrolled in a Master of Library Science program and over the following decade focused on developing a career as a librarian. In her early forties, she was diagnosed with multiple sclerosis; looking down the road, she was concerned about her mobility and being able to continue working as a librarian. She now runs a web business that buys and trades old toys, thus combining her skills in cataloguing with her earlier infatuation.

Expanding the Application of Expertise

"Everyone was surprised when I took a job below the level I was at. But I was tired of the management headaches and wanted to get back to the professional side of things. I was sick of the politics and the egos of executives. I wanted to get on with doing a piece of work I knew I was uniquely qualified for and could do elegantly."
—Employee relations consultant

Midlife experts practise their craft with effortless elegance, are poised in the face of problems associated with their profession, are articulate in describing critical issues, and are focused on getting the right results. Some are happy to continue in their craft and look for ways to further refine and develop skills. The very talented, who have devoted their lives to growing and contributing to their professions, may now want to be considered "thought leaders." They enjoy the prestige of being known as a leading expert in their field and look for opportunities to increase their arena of influence, profile, and platform.

I receive about two e-mails a month from professionals asking me for advice on how to get a book published. Sometimes they want to write a book because they think they have something important to say and want to share their expertise with a broader audience. Sometimes the book is a "calling card," a tool to increase their marketability. And sometimes it's because they are bored. I am amazed at the number of frustrated writers there are. In the past couple of years, I have helped five women get started who have gone on to include writing as part of their professional activities. They just needed some advice and help navigating through the system.

But of course not every professional is a high-profile expert. Many women at midlife contribute to their profession or the growth of younger professionals by playing roles in professional associations, presenting at conferences, and mentoring. The satisfaction associated with mentoring runs deep. About 90 percent of the women describe this as a key component of their lives. "I get as much or more from mentoring than do the people I mentor," they say.

We have seen that boredom often afflicts many professionals at midlife, who face the prospect of doing exactly the same thing for the next twenty years. The key element that made these moves rewarding for the women who undertook them was that there was some element of risk involved.

Professionals who reconnect with earlier interests realize they derive deep emotional and intellectual satisfaction from thinking about problems associated with their profession, and don't particularly like dealing with the salad of personalities that is one of the jobs of management. At midlife they eschew the greater status associated with management roles; they choose to abandon the corporate ladder and "reconnect" with their earlier calling, often as self-employed consultants.

The corporate dropouts cite many reasons. One professional captured the issues well: "I'm too old to be dealing with all the ridiculous politics. And I don't really like dealing with all the petty emotional stuff that you have to as a manager. I like expressing my *own* professional voice. When you work in a team, it gets muted." Another, a marketing specialist, said, "I know what I'm doing, not making it up as I go along as most managers do. I'm a pro with a unique skill set that doesn't belong to anyone else. I just want to do my own thing."

Maturing as an Authentic Leader

"I have finally become the kind of manager I always wished
I could have had, or that my kids will have. But I had to get
beaten up a lot along the way before I could get to this great
place in terms of my management style."
  —Director, internal affairs

These leaders—the Seekers we met earlier—no longer have their ego on the line. They will fight as managers to do the right thing, even if at times it's uncomfortable. They express their values in their work. They can make decisions free of concerns about status or competitiveness. They can do the right thing for their staff and enjoy mentoring and coaching them. Typically they are older than the ones still out there proving themselves or else have gone through a serious reevaluation of life priorities.

Authenticity-seeking Self-developer Lauren, for example, loves her role as a vice president of learning and development for a hotel, running a department of eighty professionals. When she was offered a promotion into a line position, she said she "spent exactly a nano-second thinking about it before saying no thank you. I love my work, it continues to fascinate me. I'm doing the best work I've done in my career, except now I'm creating the vision: It would have been a lot more money, but who needs those headaches now?" she says.

She is proud that the work she is stewarding is leading edge and that she has created a culture in which her staff says they can be authentic. She is also proud that she is seen as unconventional in her personality "style" and dress and has not conformed to the behavioral expectations of senior managers.

Leaders like Lauren are taking one more step along a management path embarked on in their thirties. Occasionally, however, leaders emerge from unexpected places. For example, one fifty-three-year-old woman who had been fired from her communications role in a cultural institution went for career counseling. She told her counselor that she would probably pursue a job as a communications consultant. When the counselor looked at the results of the battery of tests she had completed, she said, "You have extraordinary leadership skills."

It took her a while to get her head around this. Although she had always been a leader in her community, it had never occurred to her that those experiences could be transferred to a professional role. With her counselor's coaching and support she decided to pitch herself for a leadership job. She is now running a not-for-profit cultural agency. (This kind of transition, resulting from someone discovering hidden talents at midlife that they didn't already know about, is extremely unusual.)

Some women, such as those who got off the career ramp to attend to family, still dream of playing a role in senior management. They have something to prove to themselves and to the world. They are in a hurry because they know that, due to their age, the window is closing quickly.

Others feel good about what they've achieved as a leader but want to leave their mark. They think this may be their swan song. "I've learnt so much over the past years. I'm a different person. I want to apply all of this and play a leadership role in designing a healthy culture," said one woman. "And I'm not ready to lie down yet."

But there are some women who are still motivated by ambitions to move up. They are unsentimental about their personal lives; their preoccupations are with their work. Forty-one-year-old Alexis, for example, has spent her career moving progressively to more senior management positions, each one in a different city. She says her husband is tired of changing cities every two years and worried about the impact on their kids. When she told me her company was being sold, I asked her about her plans and where she wanted to live. She said, "Who knows what the next step in the adventure will be? I guess I prefer the south, but wherever the best job is, that's where I will be."

Following the Free-Agency Route

"Where can you be most authentic and happy?" In response to my survey question, about 80 percent of the women said "self-employment." One woman who spent twenty years working for an organization before setting out on her own put it this way: "Self-employment is the only place where, as a woman, you can be truly free, where you can be authentic. It's not only about the flexibility, but being able to *design* your own culture that suits your needs and values, who you are. When you work in a collective, which is what an organization is, albeit the wrong kind, the collective 'we' in the team drowns our individual voices: you play a role, like being in a movie. You bring yourself to the role, but there is a frame in which you are expected to express yourself."

We have seen all the reasons why women are attracted to self-employment: to pursue unfulfilled ambitions, to have flexibility, to reap the rewards of their work, to test themselves without the safety net of an organization, or to leave a legacy. As one former manager who left the corporate world to do contract work said, "I was always uncomfortable, the token woman, always feeling like I was living someone else's success story. I just decided 'That's it. I'm gone.'" Today the idea of selling services as a self-employed free agent is alluring, much glorified in the media. But some women, like Dana, who try to move into self-employment, are not suited for this role, or make moves that are far too bold.

It has never been more difficult for midlife people without any prior self-employment experience to make it in this arena, especially if they formerly held roles in senior management. Why? Because the rhythms of self-employment and the behavioral requirements for success are significantly different from those of working for an organization.

As one woman commented, "At forty-nine I left a senior role in academia to set up my own business. I didn't have a clue about what it really meant to run a business, and I was shocked by how competitive it is out there. Quite frankly, the reality has nothing to do with how it's portrayed."

I've watched many women flounder and ultimately return to the corporate world. Sharon, for example, a VP of corporate affairs, is typical. At fifty-one, she engineered a buy-out from her pharmaceutical employer to set up a communications and public relations consulting business. This is what she did in the first six months: spent $3,500 on a Web site; developed a list of fourteen different services; had about three hundred networking lunches with senior managers; furnished a home office to the tune of $6,000. This is what she *didn't* do: research, get feedback, and then develop a list of a few services that she was uniquely qualified to deliver; make tons of calls and then follow up when people didn't return her calls; network with middle managers—the ones who would have bought her services; make *one* sale. Women who have had a long corporate career are unaccustomed to the lack of structure, taking risks, hustling to make a buck, not receiving feedback, designing their own workday, being accountable only to themselves, rejection, and not having their phone calls returned.

So, dear reader, if you are thinking about taking this route, beware. Just as some women have difficulty working in organizations, some have difficulty working outside them. If you have great skills, can describe them eloquently and compellingly, are focused about what you can and can't do, can live in a feedback vacuum, and can obsessively guard the time you planned for your personal life, great. Otherwise, find a better employer.

But if you are genuinely suited to the self-employment route, and you do your homework, the rewards can be enormous. This comment from one woman is typical: "I lost who I am in a corporate environment. Over the years I gained twenty pounds; this was my body armor for dealing with that life. Once I went out on my own I took back my life—physically, professionally, and spiritually."

Creating a Portfolio Career, and Life

The great British management thinker Charles Handy coined the idea of a portfolio career. He wrote that he balanced "core" work, which provided "the essential wherewithal for life," with work "done purely for interest or for a cause, or because it would stretch me personally or simply because it was fascinating or fun."

I have a portfolio career: it consists of writing books and columns, mentoring, tropping (traveling and shopping), running a business, giving speeches, gardening, and volunteer work. Each of these activities meets needs—intellectual, aesthetic, philanthropic, and financial.

Every year I take on one new activity that stretches me, and absorbs me completely, sometimes obsessively. One year it was mounting a landmark conference on work-life balance and promoting children's wellness, another it was refining my garden, the next, writing a book. This is how I deal with boredom at midlife.

I think this is one of the most organic types of career configuration available to midlife women, especially those with multiple interests or the drive to explore new territory. It is based on the assumption that we have many needs and desires and play many roles. As one freelance journalist put it: "I like my work, but it's not enough to satisfy me. I'm a journalist, but I'm also a teacher, a parent, and a volunteer."

Many people already practice this type of career without realizing it. One artist friend, for example, was employed in a graphic design job she hated and on the side did her art. She was always scrambling and feeling that she wasn't doing anything very well. I pointed out that she had an embryonic portfolio career, and she should try to determine how to make a living while meeting her other needs. She identified her income needs, and then the life activities that gave her pleasure; from that she redesigned her ideal "package." She quit her job, started freelancing, got a job teaching art one night a week at a college, and guards jealously the two days she has put aside for her art.

People who effectively work their portfolio are *mindful* of their financial, spiritual, physical, intellectual, or artistic needs, and they design their lives accordingly. The beauty of this kind of career, especially for the restless midlife woman who feels guilty when she is not working or looking after family, is that it liberates them to be in the moment, to feel good about what they are doing, instead of feeling guilty about what they are not doing. I used to resent the amount of time I spent mentoring, even though I loved it, because I would think "I really should be working." Now I think, "I am doing part of my life's work."

What We Wish Someone Had Told Us

"Work has always been a major source of satisfaction in my life, perhaps inordinately so. It provides opportunity for creativity, companionship, and feeling I'm making a difference. I've accomplished much more than I ever imagined, even if sometimes the road was bumpy."

"I wish I could have navigated the politics. Being political gets a bad name. Learn the rules of the game so you can choose to use them if you need them."

"Don't sell your soul in order to make it. The business world needs the compassion, strength, honesty, and leadership of women."

"Refuse to change who you are. Even with the corporate suit I always had the 'F-you' touch, though I'm not sure they got the irony."

"Give serious thought to your priorities and life goals. Life can't be taken for granted. Career choices should be made against the backdrop of your values and what is truly important to you."

"I left a potentially lucrative career in my twenties to make social documentaries with my husband. We never made much money, and now the money has dried up. I'm looking for secretarial work, or anything else I can get. Is it tough at the age of fifty-five to be in this position? Yes. But I look back and think of all the extraordinary people I met, and the important subjects we addressed. So do I have any regrets? None."

"Accept that you may not get the top job, and maybe you don't want it. The higher you get, the more the organization owns your soul. It's part of the deal, whether you are a man or a woman."

"We spend a lot of our lives working, so trying to stick to something that is not personally satisfying is a tough way to live your life. In the early years you need to experiment and not make the major career decision too early. Find the sweet spot which is what you do very well, you love to do, and for which people are prepared to pay what seems to you a reasonable amount of money. Use a combination of your head and your gut when making decisions. Don't get hung up on status and immediate money."

"Be authentic. Present yourself as a multi-dimensional person. On days when I'm frazzled, things forgotten at home by the kids, alarms which didn't go off, I feel comfortable saying to my staff, 'Today I am the poster child for frazzled, discombobulated working mom.'"

"Role model. Mentor younger women, care about the environment, value the whole person, care about relationships."

I asked the women I interviewed, "Looking back over your career, what regrets do you have? What are you most proud of? If you had one piece of advice to a younger woman, what would it be?" Here is their distilled wisdom:

– Know yourself. What are your special talents? What do you care about most? What do you need in your work and your personal life to be engaged and feel good about your life? This is the foundation of making effective career/life decisions. If your work does not require the best of your skills or calls for the expression of characteristics you don't possess, find another role.

– Act on what is most important to you. Satisfying work is a right, not a privilege. Refuse to put on the back burner things that you care deeply about. Make a date with yourself at the end of each week and ask yourself, What did I learn? Which of my values are being met? And looking to the future: What will I learn next week? How can I make my work a better fit with what I need? Don't drift or treat your career or personal life like a force of nature, make *conscious* decisions. Defend your personal time aggressively if your work is not a primary source of satisfaction. Start thinking in your thirties about what kind of legacy you want to leave behind.

– Maintain your integrity. Stay firm on the issues that go to the core of what you believe in. Many of the women lamented that they will always feel they sold a piece of themselves "for the money and opportunities." Maintain your own moral compass and, as one woman said, "stand up to the bullies." A number wished they had had more confidence to do so. Women who did push back cited this as one of their most important accomplishments. As one said, "I have followed my values throughout my career even when that meant making tough and scary decisions. I earned the trust and respect of the people I worked with, and feel that I have truly made a difference in people's lives." "I'm most proud that I maintained my integrity and was able to give back. This often meant fighting to introduce programs that made a difference in people's lives," said another.

– Distinguish between the big issues and those that are a matter of taste. You can't fight all the time. If you go to the wall on every challenge, no one will listen to you. Ask yourself, "Is this really important?" Some women commented that they might have had a deeper impact and been more successful in effecting change if they'd "been willing to sell a little soul now and again." Sometimes you have to compromise. As tempting as it is to let it rip, consider the consequences of doing so, and pick your battles. In a similar vein, *be flexible and open to influence.* As one of the women who had had a rather tortuous career path observed, "If I had been more malleable, not so prickly, I would have had more positive experiences that I could leverage now."

– Find a mentor/Be a mentor. The women who had a "big sister" paid a huge tribute to their mentors, ascribing much of their success to them. Most of the women cited mentoring as one of their chief sources of satisfaction or indicated that they would like to mentor younger women. Avail yourself of the huge pool of savvy women who want to contribute to others' development.

– Don't make work the centerpiece of your identity. Many regret having put their work before their personal life and making too many sacrifices in favor of their work. You can't cuddle or giggle with your job at the end of the day.

– Be able to navigate the political currents. All work environments require skills in negotiating and influencing, knowing who the decision-makers are and courting favor. You can decide when you want to rise above the fray. Let that be due to choice rather than lack of ability. Avoiding politics does not make you a good person, it makes you naive. Treat gossip as simply one source of information. It provides insight into what is going on and what people are thinking and feeling. Don't play when the politics and gossip turn ugly with winners and losers. Better yet, leave.

– Confront the fear reptile and take informed risks. It's not easy, but it's always rewarding. If you don't make a commitment to something, you'll end up with nothing. There is no such thing as complete certainty except when it comes to death and taxes. Virtually everyone said, "Do it earlier rather than later when your age may become an issue." You don't want to wake up one day ten years from now, when it may be too late, thinking, "Where did the time go? What do I have to show for myself? I wish I had pushed myself more." Don't be seduced by money and material comforts. Listen to that niggling voice the first time you hear it saying, "I'm not happy." Pay attention to what you are feeling.

– Invest in yourself. Ensure your future employability. If you lost your job tomorrow, could you find another client or employer? Do you measure the currency of your skills according to industry standards, as opposed to your employer's? When you are in your twenties and early to midthirties, you may need to make compromises in favor of gathering great skills. Women cited their educational achievements and courses taken for personal development among their most important sources of pride. Continuing their education increased employability, but more importantly, self-confidence. This comment was typical: "I put others' needs before my own and didn't take the time to invest in my own personal development. If I had pursued my education at a higher level or a professional designation, I would now have greater career choices and more belief in myself." Don't be a martyr to others' needs. Being self-sacrificing means that you're sacrificing the *self*, not exactly a recipe for mental health.

– Be financially literate. Start saving young. Pay yourself first, as the financial planners say. Put away 10 percent of your income. Your employer's fortunes may crash, you may want to change direction, your personal fortunes may take a down turn. Job loss, death, or divorce should not be the impetus for learning about money. The most common regrets expressed by the women surveyed (almost everyone) is that they were now paying the price for free-spending lifestyles, buying too much crap, not understanding their financial portfolios, and not putting anything away when they were younger. Do you know what your debts and assets are? Can you talk about money, including negotiating your salary and fees, in a matter-of-fact way? Money, quite simply, buys you freedom. Many women find themselves, at an age when they are less employable, scrambling to pay the bills, making decisions driven by a lack of a financial cushion rather than by personal desires. Being concerned about money does not make you avaricious; it makes you intelligent.

– Be yourself. Express who you are in your work. If you can't be authentic where you are, find another employer or work situation. Otherwise you will limit your potential and be miserable. "Don't be a good girl," one woman advised. "It's OK for people (i.e., men people) not to like you. You won't die if you have enemies. In fact if you don't, that's not good." *Define success in your own terms.* Take your own counsel. Don't listen to others, listen to your heart. Eschew career choices based purely on money or status. You need to feed your soul as well as your pocketbook.

– Never be deterred by a lack of confidence. Do you really lack the ability, or is it fear that is holding you back? Give yourself the pats on the back that you should be getting from others. Remind yourself of what you have accomplished and what you are capable of. If you feel anxious, fake it. If you had a lot of confidence, what would you do? Act accordingly.

– Don't worry if you don't know what you want to do "when you grow up." Most of us are capable of getting to that sweet place where our work expresses our talents and needs. It's a question of knowing your interests, skills, and values, as well as trial and error. We learn from failure as much as success. Through successive approximations we get there.

– Think trade-ons, not trade-offs. Forget trying to have it all. Prioritize what is most important at this life stage. Devote each chapter to deeply satisfying one need rather than compromising all your values and living in a gray zone where none of your needs are met. Know what you can and cannot put up with. Take every demand on your time and put it through a sieve. Ask yourself, "How will meeting this satisfy my needs? What will I give up in time and energy to meet this?" Practice strategic laziness and push back against demands that undermine your ability to carry out the roles that are most important to you.

chapter seven

Motherhood:

What We Know and Wish We Had Known

"No one ever told me how hard it is emotionally, physically, and mentally. Sometimes it is so difficult, so painful, I wish I didn't have children. It breaks your heart more than you can imagine watching your child get hurt. But to see your children happy, becoming their own person, navigating the world with confidence and knowledge you never knew they had, there is nothing so precious, so amazing. It was my dream to be a mother."

"Although my career is very important to me, motherhood has an incandescent quality that I don't find anywhere else in my life. It brings me as close to a religious feeling as I've ever had. But I wish I had known how emotionally taxing it is. There is no anxiety like a mother's anxiety."

"I feel like my son is turning into a kind of urban Lord of the Flies lout. He doesn't talk, he grunts. He needs no one *in his life, other than his tribe, especially not his mother. It kills me. I sometimes want to scream when I'm with women whose poised young adult kids adore them."*

"I'm very proud of my daughter. She's made good choices, can look after herself, and has strong values. But my son is a constant source of pain . . . I feel like I've failed."

"No one ever told me just how much of my heart and brain would be consumed by my kids. You think and worry about them every moment."

"No one told me about the constant heartbreak, or the chance for the joyous magic that is motherhood."

"I'm devoted to my child, but I think that life is not only about realizing yourself as a parent. I have friends who say they don't need to love their partners or their work, because they are in love with their kids. That's not enough for me. I love my son, but I'm not in love with him."

"I wish I had had a better understanding of the imprint of my upbringing on my sense of self and what I therefore projected onto my kids. I wish I had a clearer vision of what parenting could be instead of repeating patterns of the past. I wish I had understood what a complex and relentless job mothering is. All that said, my kids, who are now young adults, are the light of my life."
  —Midlife women on motherhood

was with a friend and a group of women we didn't know at a women's cocktail event. The chatter soon turned to the subject of their young adult children. First woman: "My son is about to graduate from Harvard. He's had job offers from think-tanks all over the world. He's really wonderful, a joy to have around." Second woman: "My daughter just won a Commonwealth scholarship to do her PhD at Oxford. Her first novel is being published next year. She wants me to go over and help her settle in." Maybe I exaggerate, but this is how I remember it. One woman turns to my friend and asks, "Do you have children? What are they doing?"

A bit of background: she had been going through a difficult patch with her son, the kind that is common when young men detach themselves from their mothers. It starts in adolescence. The boy needs to separate from Mom, so he becomes hostile. When he's twenty-two, Mummy wants a warm adult relationship with Son, and Son continues with what she experiences as rejection. (Sometimes it's not the son's behavior that's the issue, it's the mother's. He's moved onto his own path, and Mother is mourning her loss—she's the one who can't accept the new adult relationship.)

But I digress—back to the party. Here's what my friend said: "My son? I'm so pissed with him, I could kill him." She didn't intend to say this, she later told me, but "it just slipped out." The women were stunned, as if she had confessed to having robbed a bank. Embarrassed silence followed that felt like the elapsed time of the Boston Marathon but was probably thirty seconds. And then these women started to *compete* about whose kid was more screwed up, difficult to deal with, or a source of pain.

No one has greater capacity to hurt us or engender joy, to affect our emotional equilibrium than our children. Even women who define themselves independently of their children, who do not see their children as an extension of who they are as women, are vulnerable. "How do I feel about my children?" said one mother, who is one of the most together women I know, "it depends on the day." Most of us can relate to this.

Sometimes I lie in bed thinking about my son when he was younger. I look at his pictures, and think how sweet and vulnerable and mischievous he looks. When I received his university graduation pictures, I took one glance at them and then hid them. He looked so, well, hard, stern even. I try to remember if I held him, kissed him. I think I did. In fact I *know* I did, but then how did he grow up so fast?

Other than a bond so powerful we could not have imagined it before becoming mothers, there is no common experience of motherhood except, perhaps, as my father used to say, "When kids get cut, parents bleed."

We have children of varying ages with different personalities growing up in diverse family configurations with mothers who vary widely in their approach to child-rearing. Neurotic mothers. Self-congratulatory mothers. Disappointed mothers. Proud mothers. Mothers who use their kids as an extension of themselves. Mothers with no boundaries. Mothers with a healthy ego and healthy boundaries. Mothers of healthy children. Mothers of children with disabilities. Strict mothers. Liberal mothers. Stepmothers. Mothers such as one woman who said, "I was put on this earth to raise my children." Mothers who said, "I'm not sure I should have become a mother. They are good kids, I think they deserve a better mother. When my children were young, I had a complete loss of identity and was more depressed than in any other period of my life."

What is true of all mothers is that we are held accountable for how our kids turn out. I have never heard anyone say, "Oh those kids are great [or screwed up] because Dad was such a good [or lousy] father," or "those kids lucked out [or lost] in the genetic lottery." If the kids have difficulties, it is the mother we blame. "She's a bitch." "She was too involved in her career." "She's cold and unavailable." "She was a doormat, let her kids walk all over her" are the kind of comments I've heard frequently from women.

Conversely, when kids are well adjusted, we don't praise the mother—she did what she was supposed to, fulfilled her role. Mothers know they are held accountable—it is deeply socialized into their core understanding of what it means to be a mother.

Take this comment, for example: "I struggle with a rather crippling jealousy of my seventeen-year-old stepdaughter who lives with us five days a week. She is a star academically and in the arts. I have an irrational fear that if she surpasses the two kids I have with my husband, he will take greater pride in her than in our kids, and I will be seen as the less competent mother."

The result is that many of us have secrets.

Spinning, Secrets, and Social Comparison

"Mothers see their children as an extension of themselves. Today there is so much pressure for kids to be superstars. When they're not, a mother feels inadequate—not as good as the other mothers. So when mothers talk about their kids and how great they're doing with all that insidious competition, and your kids are just ordinary or having trouble at school or maybe even screwing up, you feel you did something wrong, you failed, and what could be worse than being a bad mother? So you either go into denial or you spin."

"This kid is the product of your DNA and socialization. If he doesn't shine, then you feel you are the failure, because at the heart it's your DNA and parenting choices that have failed him. Even if you know the sperm donor also has a role, it's always the mother who is held responsible."

Leigh, for example, has an eighteen-year-old son and a fourteen-year-old daughter. When I ask her how she is doing, she says she is great. "Oh Dave just won an award for football, and Shaina is doing really well in school." (Note that she describes her well-being in terms of her children's achievements, but that's another story.)

When she opens her purse, I see what looks like a bottle of anti-depressants. Her daughter is a friend of my neighbor, her son a friend of the son of a friend, so I know that he's been caught dealing drugs, while she is having a sexual liaison with a twenty-nine-year-old man, and her marks suck. Why didn't Leigh just tell me the truth? Knowing her, it wasn't an issue of trust; she thinks she has *failed*, that she is a bad mother, that if she had been a better mother, her kids would have turned out differently.

Many of us have secrets and disappointments about our children, especially our young adult children, but we think we will be fired from the motherhood sisterhood if we express them, much less acknowledge them. The idea of "Mother" is so emotionally loaded with its immediate connotation of "good" or "bad": if your children are doing well (translation: achieving), you are a "good" mother; if they are having difficulties, you are a "bad" mother. And nothing in our society is worse than being a bad mother. The result is we would sooner share details of our bank account with strangers than talk about our wounds, anxieties, and disappointments regarding our kids. So we suffer in silence, thinking we are alone. But we aren't. You remember the normal curve I mentioned earlier. Someone out there has to have kids who are having difficulties. In fact lots do. The effect of this dissembling, spinning the truth? Every social comparison–engaging woman who doesn't have the poster-perfect kid feels terrible.

The truth is you can both love your children and acknowledge you are disappointed in them or that they are not perfect. Similarly, you can say "I am or was a decent mother" and "My child is having difficulties." And as we will see later it may be a conceit to take too much responsibility for our children. Your children are not a commodity for you to shape.

In one of my surveys, I asked the questions "If you weren't afraid of being kicked out of the motherhood sisterhood, how would you *really* feel about your kids? What are your disappointments?"

Many women wrote back saying something along the lines of "Wow, these are really bold questions." Interestingly, they didn't think my questions about their sex life were as bold. Some also said, "I can't believe I'm telling you this, I wouldn't tell this to anyone."

Certainly some of us have adolescent and young adult kids who are making sensible life choices, stretching themselves, and doing exciting things with their lives. Many of the women who responded to my questionnaires made comments such as "My kid has great values." "My son is very responsible and appreciative of everything we do for him." "My kids are curious and kind and sensitive to others." At midlife these mothers are deeply proud of their children and enjoy intimate and satisfying relationships with them.

I talk about older kids, because our younger children are more of a work in progress. Our young adult children are by no means fully baked, but the contours are clearer, there is less of a question mark as to who they will become, and the consequences of their challenges are more serious. We worry about our younger children—are they happy? Are they healthy? Are they safe? With our older children we worry if they have the capacity to live independent lives, to contribute to society, to develop intimate relationships.

Many mothers of older kids are in deep pain: their kids are angry and reject them, are having psychological difficulties, or have returned home for the fifth time after the fifth graduate degree, just after their bedroom was converted into a home office.

When I wrote a column about Gen Y, in which I said amongst other things, that they (referring to young corporate types) are very nice, and like and enjoy hanging out with their parents, I received many e-mails from female clients and acquaintances. "Great column, Barbara. By the way, you must be very proud of your son." "I am, but don't worry," I replied, "he wasn't the poster boy." The response could be summarized as "phew" followed by a diatribe about a kid who was, in the mother's estimation at least, if not screwing up, then a disappointment in some way.

How quickly we compare ourselves to others, and then conclude we are inadequate. As one woman said, "I want to scream when I hear women talking about their perfect kids . . . blah, blah is doing this, blah, blah is doing that. Why don't they talk about *who* they are? But at the same time when they radiate that icky mummy superiority about all the crappy parenting books and theories they've followed, I wonder, Would my kids have been different, dare I say it, better, if I hadn't been such an undisciplined, inconsistent slob, just muddling through?"

And sometimes we are not even spinning. The idea that we could have less-than perfect kids is a truth too painful to acknowledge. One woman commented, "I have a friend whose son gives me the willies. Ever since this kid was fourteen he reminded me of the kind of guy you meet at a party who makes you want to go home and take a shower. But his mother always says, 'Isn't David a fine boy?' This kid is obnoxious. I can't figure it out. Is she blind? Is she in denial?"

We also spin about the time we spend with our kids. I've been in countless workshops where a female manager says, "I always put my kids first," and then her staff roll their eyes. One woman confided, "My boss leaves the office at seven-thirty, and routinely calls from her cell on the way to work at seven in the morning. She always brags about how close she is to her kids. Do the time math."

But it's not only about spinning. Sometimes it's about hurts and fears and secrets so deep we feel we can't share them. Almost daily someone will say to me, "You are the only one who knows this," and proceed to tell me about a child's sexual abuse at the hands of a teacher, a son who tried to commit suicide, a daughter who at the age of thirteen is having sex (and Mother doesn't even know if Daughter is using protection). It breaks my heart to hear these secrets, to see these women so alone, to know these hurts run so deep they won't even see a therapist. Because at the core, they blame *themselves*.

Disappointments: The Naked Truth

"I feel I have utterly failed Feminism 101. Try as I might when my son was growing up, I could not get him to take responsibility for helping around the house, or to be sensitive to others' needs. When he had feminist teachers, he would argue and argue about their approach to the world. Maybe this was a reaction to me and my feminism. I'm disappointed that he's so utterly self-centered. The one big thing about me is caring for others, being thoughtful, doing for others. Not my son! Nope. Uh-uh."

"I'm proud of my son, but I wanted him to do something singular. He's not going to be a Mozart, just a regular person. And so are my daughters. I thought they would be tough, adventuresome, but maybe I failed to teach them to be proud and strong."

"My son doesn't want to go to university. So the gut part of me says he'll be blue-collar, barely literate, semiskilled. He'll have bad teeth and not give a rat's ass about Tolstoy, Shakespeare, and Dickens. He won't understand the pleasures of the mind."

Not all women spin. Carrie, one of the Seeker types we met earlier, says this about her daughter: "I'm an adult looking at another human being and can see her for who she is, just like appraising anyone else. I think my daughter is judgmental and intolerant. Sometimes, and I can't believe I'm saying this, but sometimes I find her obnoxious."

And then, predictably, lest the motherhood gods banish her and put a hex on her kid, she added, "But of course I love her." Of course she does, and she doesn't need to tell me that.

Others see characteristics of their partners in their offspring. A recently divorced woman commented, "I see in my daughter all my ex's worst traits. Actually that doesn't leave much, because all of his traits were bad." She says, "I love my son but sometimes, when he's angry or upset, I have to take a deep breath and realize it's my six-year-old I'm talking to, not my husband."

And then, of course, there is just getting through the whole teenager thing. I have a friend who is having a particularly difficult time with her daughter, who is showing anorexic tendencies, and her son, who has been diagnosed with ADD. She often asks her husband, "Whose stupid idea was it to procreate anyway?"

What are we disappointed about and why? Often we are disappointed in those characteristics our children display that we do not like in ourselves. Ellen, for example, was so upset about what she saw as her daughter's inadequacies that she sent her for psychotherapy. The therapist said, "I'll work with your daughter, but only if you see a therapist as well." What she learned in psychotherapy was that everything she was complaining about regarding her daughter—her aloofness, her inability to get excited about anything—were exactly what she didn't like about herself.

Some mothers, especially the authenticity-seeking moms, have expectations that their children will be "special" (usually projecting their own desires to be special) and are disappointed if they are not.

One woman captured the dynamic well: "I am disappointed that my daughter isn't more ambitious, more academic, more accomplished. As a young mother I felt my daughter was brilliant, gifted, and exceptional, and I expected so much, too much, of her. Indeed, I thought she would change the world. That put tremendous pressure on her. I didn't want her to be ordinary or, worse still, a failure. Maybe it was because I was a single mother, I didn't want her to become a statistic, someone less likely to finish school, someone who would do drugs, all that mixture of myth and fact."

And perhaps the most painful disappointment is when we think our kids reject everything we stand for. We want to be role models for our children and then when they make the same mistakes we did or reject what we have tried to instill, we experience it as the deepest form of rejection, a repudiation of who we are. As one mother said of her twentysomething kids, "I worked so hard to accumulate wisdom and to share it. How dare they start out all over again making the same stupid mistakes in relationships, financial matters, work choices. I guess mother as role model is not as important as individuation or else it's 'let's not be like *her*.'"

Stepmothers express the greatest disappointment, to the extent that many say if they had to do it all over again, they would wait until the stepchildren were grown up before entering a committed relationship. This stepmother's comment was typical: "I read all the books that said how difficult it is to raise someone else's children. But I thought I would be different. I did all the 'right' things—I didn't try to replace their mother, or to force the relationship; they knew I cared about them and was available for them. But no matter what I did or didn't do, they always resented me, treated me like I had no right to be there. This is one of my great disappointments."

But it's not as if every mother or stepmother is profoundly disappointed with her children. In fact every mother I interviewed felt proud of their kids in some way, often referring to aspects of their personality—such as being brave enough to take the road less traveled, their creativity, or their sensitivity and caring. Indeed, a few women made comments such as "Disappointments? . . . I can't think of any. I am disgustingly proud of my kids." (In fairness to those social-comparison-engaging moms of adolescents who are reading this, I should tell you that her children are under ten years of age.) Or, as this stepmother, who at forty-one married a divorced man with three young children for the sole reason that she wanted to raise his kids, said, "Parenting these kids who have turned into wonderful people is my peak life achievement."

What we are proud and not so proud of in many ways reflects our own personalities and insecurities—they shape who we are as mothers and our parenting styles.

Contemporary Mother Archetypes

What are the dominant types of mothers? What are you like as a mother? You will likely find yourself and your mothering style, not to mention those of your friends, in a couple of the following types. (Of course, we are complex beings, none of us is exclusively one type or another.) Be honest with yourself. The good news is that just as we mature in our desires and behaviors regarding work from the first half of life to the second half, you may find yourself now moving from one type to another.

Good Girl Supermom

You already met her. She lives in the same upper-middle-class neighborhood that she grew up in and wants her kids to have the same domestic childhood experiences she did. She usually chooses a traditional female occupation such as teaching, nursing, or part-time admin that allows her to spend as much time with her family as possible. Or she may take a career break from her demanding job. (About one in four high-achieving women leave the workforce at some point, almost half for reasons of family.) She frequently comments, "When there are kids in the picture, you are always torn. You need to make a living, but you need to be there for your kids." She always knew she would be a mom.

She bakes cookies, is active in the parent-teacher association, starts planning her kids' birthday parties four months in advance, is "available" to her kids whenever they want to talk to her, and is warm and nurturing. Her kids' friends love hanging out in her house—it has a great rec room with every electronic kid-pleasing toy imaginable, and the larder is always full. Although she encourages her kids to be accepting of others, she gossips about mothers who work long hours, making nasty comments about their fitness as mothers. She's read three hundred parenting books and loves to quote from them. When she asks you how you feel about returning to work after your maternity leave, and you say, "I'm glad to be back," she looks at you as if you were a felon.

She loves doing "fun" things for and with her kids. When her daughter had her prom, she and the other moms in the neighborhood regularly consulted each other about who was wearing what and who their children were "going" with. She was so enthused on prom day, she said, "I'm so excited, I think I'm going to pee." When her kids go away to university, she suffers terribly—so much of her identity is tied up with her children. She e-mails them every day, and sees them regularly on weekends. Her deepest fear is that her children may move to another city.

Although she would describe herself as close to her kids, she has never really had a truly intimate or provocative conversation with them. She knows a lot about what they do, not *who* they are or what they think. Her kids describe her as "nice," as do her kids' friends. She is very proud of her kids. She would not entertain the possibility that they are less than perfect.

But some women who took the supermom route were not natural supermoms. They gave up satisfying and demanding careers, at least for their children's early years, as a result of pressure from partners or other good-girl desires to conform to expectations of moms. Or else they felt they could not fulfill their mothering role in the manner they wanted to when they were working.

It was a tough decision to leave her job. At first she stayed in touch with her former colleagues, but it was too sad for her; after every get-together, she would come home and bawl her eyes out.

She pursues motherhood with the same Type-A competitive achievement striving as she would have closed deals on Wall Street. Her kids' never-ending round of extracurricular activities are testament to how well she engages in the ongoing Mummy Wars in her neighborhood. She describes it as "giving her kids a leg up." Privately she feels her investment banker husband doesn't appreciate how she sacrificed her great career for the kids, but she tells her friends how "helpful" he is on the weekends. This also wins her credits in the Mummy Wars—she has trained her husband well. She's not a pushover, this one.

At midlife, if she has a good relationship with her kids, she is satisfied. She looks forward to or is enjoying being a grandmother. But if she does not enjoy a warm relationship with her kids, she is bitter and resentful about what she has given up. She is angry at her husband (or ex-husband) who turned all the parenting over to her, and she thinks her children, too, are unappreciative of her career sacrifices. If she is divorced and has spent every penny of the value of the house on lawyers trying to get proper child support, she feels angry and betrayed. Simply put, she did not get the return on her investment she feels entitled to.

Supermoms, the ones who are by inclination real supermoms, describe their parenting style as "lots of hugs and kisses, with clear guidelines for what is acceptable behavior."

Yummy Buddy Mom

When her kids were young, she dressed them in European clothes. When her daughter turned twelve, she got a Fendi bag for her birthday. To the extent her kids looked good, she felt good. She describes her daughter as her best friend. She takes her to the spa and on shopping trips (even though Daughter complains about this to her friends, she goes along with it, knowing she can get Mom to cough up the money for some new designer clothes). She has few boundaries: she talks to her kids about her sex life and asks them intrusive questions about theirs.

If her husband left her for another woman, she told her son he was now the man of the house. He accompanied her on social occasions, and she introduced him as "her date"—with an almost flirtatious smile.

Her parenting style is inconsistent. For the most part she indulged her kids, ignoring bad behavior, but when that bad behavior would inconvenience or embarrass her (for example, when her son was found cheating at school and her friends knew about it), she would have what her kids would describe as "a major freak out."

She desperately wants her kids to like her. The biggest compliment she can get is her kids' friends saying to them, "You have the *coolest* mom."

If her adolescent children rejected her, she became even more prone to alternating between sucking up to them by buying them expensive toys and clothes and taking them on fancy vacations, and "freak outs." She bribed them to see a shrink, saying, "You have issues, honey," and then told them about her own "issues."

She often asks her kids if they think she still looks hot. She is secretly disappointed with her children, but she wouldn't tell you. If you ask her how her kids are, she will talk about their *accomplishments*. It wouldn't occur to her to consider their emotional well-being as something of interest. She has little insight into her parenting style. No matter how her kids might have turned out, she doesn't lie in bed at night wondering what she could have done differently. There are no self-doubts for this mother. She is self-centered and obsessed with outward appearances. If you had to describe her parenting style in two words, it would be "sucking up."

If she does not have a good relationship with her children when they are adults, she is deeply hurt and therefore mean to them. She is constantly critical and says hateful things. She controls them by money. If she does have a good relationship with them at midlife, she and her children describe each other as "best friends."

Overly Identified Mom

She shares many of the characteristics of the Yummy Buddy Mom, using her children to fill an emotional vacuum. But whereas for the Yummy Buddy Mom it's all about sublimating needs for status onto children, for this mom it's more about feelings of adequacy as a woman and a mother. She projects onto her children her own needs and treats her kids as a project. She is intensely involved in her children's life, so intensely, she *smothers* them. Her sense of well-being is intimately tied to how her children act with her— loving or rejecting.

She loves her children, obsessively and to a fault. She will explain away all kinds of intrusiveness on her part as love. She has been reading her daughter's diary since she was eleven. (Her daughter found out about it, and now has a "Mummy can read" diary, and a personal one.) She started checking her son's pockets for condoms when he was thirteen to see if he was having sex yet. When her daughter didn't get into private school because of her marks, she was so ashamed that she told no one. It was as if *she* didn't get into private school.

Her sense of self is so closely tied to her children's success that she has been known to go into a rage with her kids and their teacher if there is a less than stellar report card. When her children achieve, she feels good about herself; when they fail, she feels personally inadequate. She works very hard to solicit her children's love: like the Yummy Buddy Mom she uses money and gifts as a major form of control.

She peppered her kids with questions about what they did in school, who they talked to, what they did after school. When her kids went through adolescence, she became depressed—she couldn't stand not being in the know about her kids' lives. And she couldn't stand their rejection. She worries obsessively about her kids. Will they get into university? Will they get a good job? Will they date the right (read: successful) kind of people?

As her children enter adulthood she usually relates to them in the way she did when they were younger, trying to recapture childhood closeness. For example, when her son says he doesn't care for sports, she says, "But you used to love playing T-ball." She cannot see and accept her adult children for who they are. It is too painful for her to think about how she might have behaved differently. No one knows how she really feels about her kids. No matter what their situation, she will always answer the question "how are your kids doing?" with a bright "great!"

If she grows as a mother (this happens occasionally), and her children have either flown the coop or rejected her, she may now be in psychotherapy, learning to accept that her children are not an extension of herself while developing an identity independent of her children's success and approbation.

Executive Mom

She runs her house and her kids the same way she runs her work—with about as much joy and spontaneity as a military operation. In fact she often likens her approach to motherhood to a well-oiled machine. She is poised, demanding, and emotionally detached. How does she do it all? Well, for one thing, as she always lets you know, she never sleeps more than five hours. For another, and this she probably does not let you know, she has a double nanny shift.

If she works outside the home, she says she really yearns to spend time with her children, to have work-life balance. But she has no choice: she *has* to go on extended business trips, go to work at 6 a.m., return at 7 p.m. After all she has an important, demanding job. (Not all Executive Moms work: think Bree on *Desperate Housewives*.)

She is intimately aware of her kids' activities and marks. She has an Excel spreadsheet of their activities, updated every Sunday evening, but she doesn't know the names of their teachers or who their friends are. When she does spend time with her kids, she is distracted, thinking about work problems or problems with the nanny. "What did you just say, honey?" she often says.

When a teacher called to ask her to a meeting to discuss her son's difficulties at school, she got annoyed that the teacher wouldn't come to discuss the problem at her office.

She uses conditional love as her parenting style. Great marks and great extracurricular activities win lots of approval (usually in the form of money—if she works, she's too busy to buy gifts, and in any case doesn't know her kids well enough to know what they would really want); anything less is met with rejection.

In her mind, she is a great mother, putting her kids' needs before her own. As a general rule, she is not terribly reflective. She needs to see herself, and her kids, as perfect. But sometimes at midlife, a reversal in work fortunes or in her personal life make her look back and wish she could do it over again. As one woman said, "I think about their childhood and realize I missed all the moments. What do I remember? Not much, just all the rushing, scrambling, and being chronically tired."

If her husband has left her for a younger model, or she doesn't have a close relationship with her kids, she is resentful. She may have put her career on hold to raise a family and is anxious to make up for lost time. Unfortunately, it may be too late to get back on the career track at this life stage.

Helicopter Mom

Her hovering and micromanaging can be the result of the insecurities associated with the other types of moms, and in some ways she is a composite of a number of them, but not all of these other moms manage their kids' agendas so obsessively. Helicopter Mom wants her kids to get into the right preschool, which will get them into the right school, which will get them into the right university, which will get them into the right job. Her behavior is similar to that which the other moms may engage in, but the *motivation* is different; she is driven by anxiety and fear. (When Supermoms who got off the career fast track or Executive Moms engage in this behavior, they are driven by an innate competitiveness.) Every step her child takes is evaluated in terms of whether she's on the road to ultimately becoming a successful professional. And every misstep is a harbinger of future failure.

Daughter doesn't want to go to soccer? Disaster! Think about all the friendships she'll miss out on, not to mention the team-building skills. Son comes home from camp proudly displaying a chair he made? Ohmygawd! He's going to become a carpenter. She bought her infant an iPod so she could play Mozart to him—it lays down neural pathways ya know.

She's done icky and questionable things to ensure her kids prosper. She wrote a poem for her son's portfolio when his name was put forward for the gifted program. When he wasn't accepted, she called the head of the committee several times, saying, "You let Peter in. I know for a fact his IQ is far lower than my son's." (It didn't work; when she learned her son was not going to be accepted, she cried herself to sleep that night.)

She called the summer camp so often to find out how her daughter was doing, they made a camp rule: no calls from parents, no exceptions. On visiting day she gave the counselor a "performance appraisal" form she had written to get feedback on her daughter's initiative and social and leadership skills. When her daughter went to university, she checked the cafeteria food to ensure it was nutritious, e-mailed professors to find out how her work was going, and got angry when told she couldn't take notes for her daughter when she had the flu.

Of course, most helicopter mothers aren't this extreme. Whether it's slavishly following parenting books on how to promote cognitive development, involving kids in a never-ending round of extracurricular activities, or ensuring their children are involved in resume-enhancing volunteer work, nothing is done for sheer pleasure. Everything is purposeful and instrumental and focused on the long-term.

So when she says, "All I care about is that Jonny grows up to be a happy, independent person," you think, yeah right! And of course, nothing would be worse for little Jonny than for him to suffer from low self-esteem.

At midlife, she may be questioning the utility, not to mention desirability, of her tactics. If she has developed as a person, she understands her child is not clay to be molded as a future economic unit, and that her child will be okay without her interventions. And maybe, just maybe, she realizes there is more to life than getting a great job.

Emotionally Intelligent Mom

She read the books on breast-feeding and when the suggested positions didn't work, she took her own counsel about what to do. "Screw this. My son doesn't come with an operator's manual," she said. When her unathletic son didn't want to play baseball, she accepted it. When her introverted daughter didn't want to join after-school clubs, she encouraged her, but she didn't *make* her. She adjusts her parenting style according to her child's personality. She makes comments such as "All three of my kids are different with different abilities. What is amazing for one is mediocre for the other, but it doesn't matter; they are each special as individuals."

She is there for her kids, if not as much as she would like. She doesn't confuse quality time with quantity time because she knows that her kid isn't programmed to open up and share whatever issues concern him when it's convenient for Mom. She agonizes frequently while her kid is growing up. Her parenting style ranges from "benign neglect" to "sensitive interventionist." She may even have done a couple of neurotic things. In fact I'm pretty sure she did. I've never met a mother who has not had a neurotic moment at some point about her kid.

What makes this mom different is she has *boundaries*. When she has a conflict with her kid, she can say to herself, "I'm the adult in this situation." She can distinguish between her needs and issues and those of her children. Her identity is not tied to her kids' accomplishments, and she is not using her kids to fulfill repressed ambitions. When she has done something wrong, she can say "I'm sorry." She is very much like the Seeker you met earlier. "Trust" and "appropriate support" are her guiding principles.

These moms have taken the full range of work routes from career at full throttle to part-time work to unpaid work. Most feel good about work decisions vis-à-vis the impact on their kids. They can distinguish between guilt (the failure of moral standards) and shame (concerns that other people won't approve of you). Whatever their decisions, they don't feel a need to dissemble. Amongst those who work throughout their children's lives, most say they work for fulfillment as well as income. But a few, like this forty-eight-year-old scientist, commented, "If I could do it over again, I wouldn't have chosen such a demanding profession, I would have taught science instead, so I could have been there emotionally and physically for my kids."

She may not always have been this kind of mom. At midlife she may have become so—she can reflect on what she did, wise and unwise, can take responsibility for her actions, and will try to recalibrate her parenting style.

Taking Too Much Responsibility for How the Kids Are

*"We never fully comprehend what we are in for because
we cannot even begin to imagine who our children will be.
We do not own our children and our children do not own us.
We are not responsible for who and what they become and
try as we might, we can't change them or protect them."*

"I carry luggage from my own childhood." (A Holocaust survivor
mother who invested all her energy into her kids and had fierce
ambitions for their success.) *"This leaks into my interactions with
my kids. I place excessive emphasis on their success, especially
in academics and the arts. I try to be aware of and temper this
attitude. I wish I were calmer and less 'identified' with my kids.
I think I take too much pride in their successes, which even
though intellectually I know they are separate people,
I experience as MY success."*

I asked a fifty-five-year-old social worker friend, a woman I admire
who has three grown-up kids, "Do you ever lie awake, wondering
whether you could have done or do things differently?" She said, "Of
course. Sometimes doubts, and sometimes verging on panic attacks.
Doesn't every mother?"

There are some self-satisfied mothers, and some of us are less
prone to introspection, but most women do second-guess some of
their decisions and parenting style. "I shouldn't have been such a
control freak; I should have been more trusting." "I shouldn't have
insisted we live in a fancy neighborhood so my kids could go to a
fancy school. I was always tense and worried about money so I
couldn't just relax and be with them."

And of course there is the whole divorce issue. Almost every
divorced mother wonders if she should have hung in longer for
the sake of her kids, or if she hung in *too* long. Did her depression

and anger have a significant emotional impact on her kids' well-being? Would it affect her kids' capacities to develop healthy adult relationships?

Siobhan expressed the familiar dilemma divorced women grapple with: "If you are unhappy, or depressed, what impact do you have on your kids' emotional well-being? Ditto, if you are screaming all the time? But if you don't have an amicable separation, what is the impact on the kids? Mommy is angry at Daddy, and Daddy is angry at Mommy; they're always fighting about money, and Daddy takes out his anger on the kids."

But as one woman said, "I beat myself up for all kinds of things. And then I tell myself, how do I know if I had behaved differently, my kids would be different?" There is only so much we can do to contribute to who our kids become.

I think there is a misconception that many women suffer from—that they are 100 percent responsible for how their kids turn out, whether they are happy or sad, engaged or not, independent or living off their parents.

The nature/nurture subject is much too big to address here. Of course you influence your child. Yet as social biologists are discovering, nurture may have been significantly overrated in its contribution to who our kids become. One mother said, "As women, most of us try too much to control the outcomes, intervening all the time. I used to think it was 50/50 nature/nurture. With three kids with widely different personalities, I now think its 90/10, and I appreciate the randomness of genetics."

In my workshops with women, as with the women I interviewed, many say "my children are my greatest accomplishment." I have always had trouble with this concept. I am deeply proud of my son, in much the same way I am proud of my close friends when they do tough or interesting things, or of my husband when he writes a book—well, perhaps it's not quite the same. It is a *visceral* swelling of happiness, a pride which has a special character, but I don't think I *made* my son or can take particular credit for who he has become; some perhaps in influencing him, but not much. That takes away from his personal responsibility for having become such an interesting, bold, and independent-minded person. He's not my accomplishment, or my husband's, or our collective accomplishment. And in any case, why should you be proud of your genes?

This is not to say we shouldn't be good parents, but we shouldn't pat ourselves on the back so much. To be mean or self-absorbed or neglectful is simply wrong. Similarly, parenting should not be carried out with an eye to our eventual accomplishment. We should be good parents because that is the *right* thing to do, not because our children are commodities whom we need to shape. We should read to them, not because we want them to get into MIT, but because this is joyful. We should show kindness and tolerance, not because we are role models, but because these are our values. We should expose them to rich experiences, not so they can improve their cognitive and social skills, but so they can have a full childhood.

My friend and I had an interesting discussion one day about the idea of being proud of our kids. "There is a right and a wrong way to be proud of and disappointed in your kids," she said. "The right way is you feel happy for them when they are happy. You feel happy for yourself that they are good human beings. When things don't work out, you feel sad. But your kids' accomplishments and disappointments belong to them, not you. And what you may find disappointing may say more about who you are than what your kid has done."

And who our children become as adults is not an extension of who we are. One mother of three young adults, for example, says she loves her children but doesn't like them. "I am disappointed in how liberal-minded they are, how they have to challenge the thinking of everyone older and wiser than them." I think her kids have performed the task of adolescence and young adulthood admirably—which is to *individuate*, to separate from one's parents, carve one's own path, and develop one's own values.

Independence vs. Dependence: The Most Significant Struggle

"Letting go and stepping back from her life as she became a young adult was very difficult for me. I felt I had all the right advice about what she should do, and of course she didn't want to follow my advice. But then again I raised her to be independent and think for herself, so no wonder she wasn't going to fall for my agenda!"

"The world is a very scary place. How do you balance their needs for independence and your concerns about where they are, who they're with? Are they safe, are they making good choices?"

"As my children get older, they are less dependent on me. I view this with a mixture of wistfulness and pride."

"It's their (the kids') job to break away and make mistakes."

Like all mothers, when my son was born, I was tantalized, seduced, madly, passionately in love; he was the center of my universe. And I remember thinking how difficult it would be to do what I should do—promote independence—knowing that one day I would be fired from the role of "needed mother." (Fortunately along came adolescence about which I have a theory: its purpose is not only to help kids individuate and become their own person. It is to help parents let go, because by the time it is over you can imagine them leaving the nest—a reality you couldn't possibly have entertained when they were younger.)

As Marni Jackson said in her wonderful book *The Mother Zone* (2002), "Motherhood is like Albania—you can't trust the brochures, you have to go there." There are no easy answers.

The thorniest questions we deal with are when to intervene and when to allow our children to make their own mistakes. This is what goes through my mind when I want to offer my two cents to my son: If I offer advice, will it just piss him off and make him more resolved to continue on his chosen path? Am I becoming my overbearing mother whose advice I did my best job to aggressively ignore? If he follows my advice, am I robbing him of the opportunity to feel good about his choices, or at least to know it was *his* choice? If I don't offer advice, am I abdicating my responsibility, am I sucking up so as not to alienate or annoy him?

A social worker says, "When they were little, you could just wipe their tears—what to do was so straightforward. Now they are big, it's so much more complicated. The biggest dilemma is between helping them or not. And if you help, how much? When is money a spoiler, and when is it a hand up? And with advice, do you like the boyfriend/girlfriend? How do you raise concerns about their choices, whether with relationships, work, or whatever without being judgmental or driving them away?"

I have watched many friends and clients have their hearts broken as their children go along a road that they think leads nowhere, or worse, to disaster, knowing they are powerless to change their course. It could be a daughter suffering from depression who refuses to get help, a bright son who insists he doesn't want to go to university and ten years later has three kids, no skills, and is living on welfare, or a daughter falling in love with a very dangerous man.

Partners, if they are in the picture, divorced or not, seldom agree on ground rules. If there is one boiling cauldron in relationships, it is that most parents do not agree on what is an appropriate level of intervention. About 75 percent of the respondents to my survey said they and their partners have different views on when and how much to intervene. "He's too passive," said some. "He's too strict and controlling," said others.

And nowhere are these conflicts felt more sharply than in blended families. As one woman with two grown-up stepchildren commented: "Not only do you have your different parenting styles, but you are inheriting the product of that style. And I hate to say this, but all of my friends in blended families agree—they're not your kids, you don't feel the same way about them. So if you are mature, you have to ask yourself, what am I really responding to here? Am I projecting that I don't love the kid in the same way as he does, or how I feel about my own kids? Am I feeling guilty about those feelings?

"My husband continues to support his twenty-seven-year-old daughter, which really pisses me off. When she moved back home, I said: 'You have to hold her accountable, you can't just keep bailing her out.' He said: 'She's not your daughter.' So maybe I would behave differently if she were mine. Or maybe I just resent her intrusion into our relationship. It wasn't what I signed up for."

Disagreements aside, most of us boomer parents are guilty of some measure of overprotection, with consequences for us and our Gen-Y children.

Relax, Your Kids Are Doing Fine but if You Want to Blame Someone, Blame Boomer Parents

"I was always in a rush, always worried about what activities and experiences my kids were being denied compared to the other kids. And then feeling my kid would end up screwed up because I didn't do enough, didn't follow the books enough. What if dance lessons, skating lessons, piano lessons, religious

*studies, skiing lessons, art classes—you get the point, my kid did
everything possible—what if it wasn't enough?"*

A friend's twenty-one-year-old daughter accepted a part-time job on
the understanding that she would work only on weekends. When
she arrived for her first day on the job, her boss said, "You have to
work on Thursday and Friday nights." When the young woman
protested, referring to the agreement, her boss said, "We never
talked about anything like that." My friend's daughter quit, saying,
"I really don't appreciate you talking to me that way and questioning my honesty."

If you are a boomer mother with a child of a certain age, you
probably recognize the syndrome even if you are perplexed by it—
the sense of entitlement, the concern with personal feelings. Your
thirty-year-old son, with four degrees, can't commit to a career
because none of them "feel" right; your twenty-two-year-old fashion-
obsessed student daughter continues to expect an allowance so she
can buy designer clothes.

They may be driving you nuts. Blame it on yourself. I know I
said earlier you can't take too much responsibility for who your kids
become, but this is one arena in which all of us need to fess up.
Namely, that as a generation, we made our kids' feelings and success
our hobby, scrutinized all their experiences, and constantly took
their emotional temperature. We worshipped at the altar of "promoting self-esteem" (God forbid they should ever feel they'd failed),
and because we felt guilty or uncomfortable about our long work
hours, tried to compensate with expensive vacations, clothes, and
electronic toys.

We told our kids they were brilliant because they could
program the VCR. We gave them the vote on everything from choice
of family vacation to the color of the new car. So here's what our
kids learned: their feelings matter, they should feel good about what
work they do, unrequited desire is bad. They also learned that work

sucks. They witnessed parents who were overworked, who complained about jerk bosses, and often saw them terminated by thankless employers at an age when finding new work was difficult.

And since most of us are in part helicopter mothers, when grappling with the question of promoting independence, most of us give into ensuring our kids don't suffer or need to fend for themselves.

So it's not surprising if, as they say, fifty is the new forty, and thirty has become the new twenty. When one mother of a twenty-nine-year-old told her daughter enough was enough—she had to grow up, get a job, and she didn't have to love every minute of the workday, the daughter responded, "I wish you hadn't taken care of everything, solved all my problems. Now you expect me to look after myself, but you never really taught me how."

The effect of our micromanaging is that many of our kids never really individuated. When I do workshops with twentysomethings, I am struck by the fact that this is the first postwar generation that, as a whole, has not rebelled against its parents' values. These young adults have less edge than we did at their age, and express lifestyle desires very similar to those of their parents. What they want is to be *comfortable*, as they are accustomed to being. I sometimes wonder if these kids will have a serious crisis later on to compensate for the fact that most of them never fully rebelled?

They are adult in their poise, but childlike in their continued dependence on their parents for money and lodging while they do the endless round of graduate school, job hunting, and figuring out what they want to do with their lives. Indeed, in 2004, the editors of Webster's *New World College Dictionary* chose *adultescent* as its word of the year in response to what they described as the "Peter Pandemic." If you google Gen Y, you will find many not necessarily complimentary monikers that reveal how this generation is perceived by older people: "the twixter generation" (*Time* magazine, seeing them as betwixt and between childhood and adulthood); the "the what's in it for me generation?"; "the generation that won't grow up."

But it's not all bad. As I mentioned in Chapter 1, I worry more about kids who know what they want to do than those who don't. The point of your twenties, at least today, is to try on different roles, test oneself, and, from the kids' point of view, to do it as much as possible on your parents' dime. (Although more twentysomethings today are uncertain about their careers, remember that many of us stumbled. The major difference is that we didn't look to our parents to support us.) Kids will get there, but we must stop taking their temperature to see how far they've come, or how far they still have to go. Stop focusing on what to you seems like a misstep, a potential harbinger of long-term career disaster.

And never, and I mean never, start a sentence with "When I was your age." The world was different, there were far fewer work choices, the perceived career stakes were not as high, and the work world was more civilized.

Oh, and for once, your kids were listening. You remember how much you complained about the idiots you work with? They heard you. When my son was in Grade 6, I talked to his class about work. I asked the kids, "How do you think your parents feel about work?" They almost started to compete about whose parents were more miserable. "My mom hates her job." "Oh yeah? Both my parents hate their jobs." "Oh yeah, my mom was fired, and it was really mean, and now she can't find another job."

Sometimes we complained about how awful our jobs were because they were truly awful. But sometimes we told our kids how demanding our jobs were because we felt guilty about not being there for them.

Is it Really Guilt?

"When I went on business trips, people would say, 'You must feel really bad being away.' And I would say, 'Oh horrible,

I really feel guilty.' But I knew my kids were well-cared for,
so actually I loved it. This was my retreat, my respite, no fighting
kids, no one making demands on me. And room service beats
cooking any day."

"Sometimes the pain of being away from my kids was so
powerful, it was almost paralyzing. I was colonized by guilt,
consumed by guilt. My body was in the office, some of my
brain was as well, but my heart, my soul . . . never."

It is fashionable today, and has been for some time, for working mothers to talk about their guilt. Certainly many do feel guilty. But sometimes I wonder if it's just a kind of verbal hiccup to qualify them for the working-mother sisterhood, bragging rights if you will. Certainly some of the women said they always felt torn, inadequate, and sad, always felt they were doing something wrong, their mind drifting throughout the day while they worried about their kids.

But several commented, "I know I'm supposed to tell you that I felt guilty about my long work hours, not being there for my kids. Sure I would have liked to have spent more time with them, but they're great kids and turned out fine, despite the long work hours. Work is important to me in terms of how I feel about myself. Would I have been a good mother if I made significant sacrifices in terms of my well-being for them? A resentful, bored mother does not constitute a good mother."

Is it really guilt? When my son was young, I would bring cookies to class in their grocery packaging. I remember someone asking me, with some wonder, "Don't you feel guilty not baking cookies, not having the time to do this?" I would think, are you a complete idiot or is there something that I'm missing because I feel NO discomfort. I concluded she had a different concept of what is important. For me, my "mothering quotient" was not measured by my ability to bake cookies!

Often when we talk about guilt, we really mean "shame." We haven't failed in our values, but we just feel social pressure to behave a certain way. As one woman said when she returned from mat leave, and people asked her how she felt, "I told them how guilty I was. I didn't want them to think I was a cold, uncaring mother!"

If it's guilt, act on it. If it's shame, consider the energy you are misspending.

What We Know about Being a Working Mother

Motherhood is different for all of us. Some of us have experienced an easier path, while for others it has been fraught with heartbreak and difficulties. Some of us feel good about decisions we made regarding work, while others have gut-wrenching regrets. We were neurotically anxious about our kids (and now regret that), or relaxed enough to enjoy the magic of watching our children grow up. Some of us cite children as our greatest life achievement, while others, like me, are queasy at this idea.

What is clear is that most of us, myself included, feel that motherhood was and is one of our greatest and most important sources of life satisfaction.

In *Perfect Madness: Motherhood in an Age of Anxiety* (2005), author Judith Warner paints a picture of motherhood that makes it about as appealing as a vacation in a war zone. She interviewed 150 upper-middle-class women in the American East corridor. She concludes that they are "living on a choking cocktail of guilt and anxiety and resentment and regret" that is destroying motherhood for women today. One friend said, "the book was so depressing, it could be the best contraceptive in the world."

My surveys were not scientific (neither were Warner's); I did not find, however, the same deep sea of misery amongst the midlife working mothers. Indeed, most described mothering, as one put it, as having an incandescent quality that she doesn't find anywhere else in her life, even if at times it can be a scary, emotionally demanding, and guilt-inducing role. (There is research that indicates that people with children are happier than those without. In comparing identical twins, sociologist Hans-Peter Kohler found that mothers with one child are about 20 percent happier than their childless counterparts. Second and third children don't add to mothers' happiness. These additional children seem to make mothers less happy, although still happier than women with no children.)

The kind of alpha helicopter mothering that Warner describes has been part of the mothering landscape for a number of decades. But there is a difference between "then" and "now." The messages that you will be kicked out of the motherhood sisterhood if you don't play the game have grown steadily stronger and more insidious. Expectations of what mothers need to do to ensure that their kids are well brought up and will have long-term educational and economic advantages have turned motherhood into an extreme sport.

We also now have work as extreme sport, as we have seen. Put this together and you do indeed have a toxic cocktail. But there are *choices* to be made. I look at mothers who are run ragged, who complain about how tired and busy they are almost as if it is a badge of honor. And I want to ask them "Why are you playing this game? Is this really for your child's benefit or for how it looks to others or what you think you are supposed to do? Will your child be disadvantaged because your house is not worthy of a photoshoot, or the kid does not play soccer?"

So in answer to the many thirtysomething working women who ask me today, "Is it possible to be a mother, work, and *not* have a nervous breakdown?" I answer with a resounding yes. But it is tougher than before. As we have already seen in Chapter 5, you may need to revisit your concept about what a good life looks like, and know what is really important to you.

You also need to be able to push back against work demands. I call this practicing *strategic laziness*. Before you agree to any work demand, ask yourself: How important is this? If I do this, what will be the impact on my other work commitments? How will this affect my time and emotional availability for my kids?

As one woman commented, "At the end of the day, your career is only for a period in your life, but your kids are forever. It's important that you don't sacrifice your children for your career, and you don't sacrifice your career for your children. If you can't have both and want both, then get another work situation."

This thought was echoed by many, including Elisa, a stay-at-home mother who had her children in her twenties and early thirties. With two master's degrees she now finds herself trying to kickstart her career. It's very difficult, but she has no regrets. "At thirty-three I was diagnosed with ovarian cancer and had a hysterectomy. Every time I resent my friends who started their careers before they had kids and kept on working I think, I would never have had these three gifts . . ."

But it's not only about your career. If you are living with your partner, it also means there is shared responsibility for housework. Researchers in Australia found that even when so-called traditional roles are swapped—fathers stay at home, mothers work—women still did the lion's share of the housework.

I hear many women make comments such as "My husband is really good about helping me around the house" or "I wish he would help more," and I shudder. He's not supposed to be *helping*. He should have as much ownership of household tasks as she does. And they are his kids, too.

Women on Their Work/Life Choices

Work at full-throttle, at a demanding but manageable clip, part-time, or stay at home. We all made different decisions about the importance of our careers. Some of us are happier with these choices than others.

"I sacrificed too much of myself for my work. My children suffered. I lost my marriage. And in the end, it was just work, and who cares? I haven't enjoyed my life as much as I had expected."

"I know it's unfashionable to say this, but I would have been a horrible mother if I had designed my work life around my children. I needed the intellectual stimulation and to be 'out there.' I haven't neglected my kids, but they weren't the center of my life. That said, they've turned out great, so they haven't suffered."

"I'm proud of what I accomplished in my own business, working on my own terms to my family's benefit, so that if a child was sick I could be there for her."

"I chose the tough route, designing my work life around my children, first when I was working for someone, and then in my own business. If this meant taking a pay reduction . . . fine."

"I insisted on working part-time, even though there was a lot of pressure—from the company, not to mention my pocketbook."

"You can have it all, but we have to throw out the image of Mommy in power suit making $xx amount a year and carrying a briefcase and diaper bag and doing it all. So an admin

assistant or whomever who works part-time and has kids can 'have it all' as long as she is happy that her decisions and the way she is living honors her values."

"Treat your caregivers like gold. Get over being jealous and petty with them."

"Get a nanny. I needed to work for the intellectual and social stimulation. With a demanding career, I still did it all myself. A nanny would have given me more time and energy to be in the moment with my kids and husband, and less time with a short temper—even if every penny went to the nanny, it would have been worth it."

"If you have kids—put them first. That doesn't mean you can't have a deeply satisfying work life. But if there is a conflict . . . what is most important?"

"You can't do all jobs equally well—your work, kids, friends. Decide which job is your number-one priority and accept that responsibility. So many have a desire to have it all. You can't really. Figure out what's most important, focus on that, and then you can be satisfied you've done a great job there."

"If you are a mother and your work is killing you and you come home tired and grumpy, you are neither fulfilling your professional role nor that of being a mother. Find another job or work part-time—you are no good to anyone including yourself in this state (except perhaps to pharmaceutical companies who sell antidepressants)."

"The media image of modern motherhood today—that we are overtired, obsessed with our kids' needs, have no time

*for our partners, and have to forget about having a good
career, is dated and doesn't resonate with my life or that
of many of my friends."*

*"My friends say you cannot provide your children with a
decent lifestyle without a double income. I chose to stay at
home. We struggle to get by sometimes, and don't live in
the fancy neighborhood or have the fancy vacation,
but my kids get what's important—love and attention."*

What We Wish Someone Had Told Us

I asked the mothers: "What regrets do you have? What advice would
you give to a mother with a younger child? What would you do differently if you could do it over again?" Our collective wisdom can
be summarized as follows.

– Don't be overprotective. Allow your kids to experience
difficulties. We were so concerned about our kids developing self-
esteem, we may have undermined their ability to participate in
the world as adults. Failure is a part of life. As one mother said,
"Of course they have a sense of entitlement. We gave it to
them." Helicopter mothering also robs children of a feeling of
accomplishment and belief in themselves. The foundation of self-
confidence is the ability to say, "I was successful because I tried
hard, weathered adversity, and used my skills," not, "My parents
helped me."

– Don't overprogram your kids. They need the freedom to play,
explore, and discover who they are. They also need to learn how to
organize themselves and create structure out of a blank canvas of
time. How will they cope as adults in a world that places a premium
on creativity, self-management, and problem-solving skills if they
have had everything organized for them?

– Don't treat your kids as your best friend. Forget the popularity contest of being the coolest mom on the block. You will end up an embarrassment to your kids and their friends who laugh at parents who dress, talk, and listen to the same music they do. Maintain appropriate boundaries, and be respectful of theirs. Don't make your kids your confidants. They should not know about marital or other difficulties until they are old enough to understand what they mean.

– Don't overestimate your own importance. What you do is important, but parents attribute too much of their children's outcomes to themselves. Parents play a role, but so do peers and genes. (And regardless of what you do, they may still blame you if they have problems later in life.)

– Don't project your own needs onto your kids or define yourself through them. You cannot live your kids' lives, and nor should you live through theirs. Your kid's success or failure is independent of who you are. You are not a failure if your child doesn't get into Harvard. Nor are you a better person if she does.

– See your kids in terms of their own needs, attributes, and personality characteristics. Cherish them for who they are, rather than bemoaning who they are not.

– If you really feel guilty, do something about it and change your behavior. But if you do not feel you are doing something wrong, then all this "I feel so guilty" chatter is just a meaningless way of making you feel better about yourself and trying to look better to others.

– Lighten up. Don't evaluate every step your kid does or does not take in terms of their future capacity to make a living. Whether or not they get into the gifted program, the elite private school, or the school play will probably have little impact on who they become. Your disappointment and distress, on the other hand, will send a strong message about what you value in them—they are lovable only to the extent they are achieving or pleasing Mother, not lovable when they are not.

– Take your own counsel. Be appreciative of others' advice, but recognize that their parenting style and child's personality will be different from yours. There are no universal truths when it comes to parenting.

– Refuse to play in the "Mummy Wars." Don't evaluate your child or your parenting by other kids' achievements or activities, or what other mothers are doing to give their kids a "leg up." Don't engage in social comparison—feeling better about yourself to the extent your kids are achieving more than others, worse about yourself if they are not. I know many mothers who are depressed because their kids are not academic superstars. Remember the normal curve. Maintain a sense of self independent of your kids.

– Be "in the moment." Almost every working mother wishes that she had been able to enjoy her kids more. These comments were typical: "I was always distracted, thinking about my work or what else I still had to do." "My body would be there, my mind somewhere else." "I was always worrying about what they *weren't* doing, what extracurricular classes they were not taking, or what marks they were not getting, rather than the good things they were doing." For children there is no difference between quality time and quantity time.

– Don't make financial or other sacrifices that impact your emotional well-being. Your children need you to nurture as well as to provide. Forget a fancy neighborhood, expensive vacations, or private school if the only way you can provide them is by being constantly stressed. If you come home grumpy or are resentful of your life, your children will suffer much more than if you are making work/life choices you feel good about. Be honest with yourself about whose needs you are meeting—theirs or your desire to "look good." Many mothers are in essence sending themselves to private school. The kids ultimately pay the price. A comment I have heard from many young adults whose parents made significant financial sacrifices is "It puts so much pressure on you to pay them back for what they gave up. I don't know if I'm pursuing this career because I want to, or because of that parental voice in my head that says, 'You must achieve. You must be successful because of what I've done for you.'"

– Don't allow yourself to be swallowed by your kids. Define yourself broadly. Nurture your romantic and other relationships. Some women made sad comments such as "I always put my kids' needs before my own. I lost my sense of who I am somewhere between the dance class and soccer practice. And one day they are grown up and you find yourself very lonely, in a shell relationship with your husband, and without any sense of purpose."

– Remember that they are *his* kids as well. Imagine a man saying about his wife, "She's really good with the kids and helps me a lot around the house." If you ever find yourself making a statement about your partner, which when flipped around would sound odd, stop for a moment and ask yourself important questions about the division of labor in your home. Whose expectations are being filled? What is your role and your husband's role in maintaining this state of affairs? (Sometimes it is the women who are guilty—they guard jealously their position as chief parent and household manager even if they bitch about their husbands doing nothing.) Are you comfortable with the arrangements? If not, how can you renegotiate these expectations?

What We Would Have Done Differently

"I wish I could have lightened up a bit with my kids. As a single parent from a poor family I was always driven, expecting the same standards from my kids, tough to the point of overkill.

I wish that I could accept they did the best they could, accept their views, and be more open-minded. I realized recently that I am more accepting of individual differences and flaws in my staff and the people I work with, than my kids."

"I shouldn't have been so concerned about living in a fancy neighborhood—I was always worried about money. So I stuck to a job I didn't like, was always stressed out and grumpy, and you can never have those years again."

"I see my 'always in a rush, always needing to achieve personality' and feel awful. When my daughter says, 'Mummy, it's no big deal if I don't do this,' I am worried that she thinks my expectations are too high."

"I have never verbally or physically abused my kids, but I understand how people get there. Sometimes I think I would have been, or would be, a better mother if I worked."

"It really does take a village. I used to think my spouse and I were the best caregivers, but now I'm not so sure, maybe they would be better with a nanny."

"I spent several years second-guessing whether I should work or not. I still second-guess my decisions. My kids picked up my ambivalence and resentments. I wish I could have just accepted and felt good about my decisions."

"I wish I had known how emotionally draining and daunting motherhood is."

"See your children. Get to know them and acknowledge them as individuals with their likes and dislikes, skills and setbacks.

Loving your children is not about buying them things or enrolling them in the right schools."

"I stayed much longer in an unhappy marriage than I should have because I didn't want to hurt the children the way I was hurt when at thirteen my parents split up. But I learned that the unhappiness we were all living in was far more destructive than two happy parents living in separate houses."

chapter eight

Childlessness:

It's a Complicated Story

"People think that because I don't have children I must somehow be unfulfilled, selfish or an angry and narcissistic bitch."

"I never felt any pressure to reproduce. When I was younger, I used to worry about whether I'd be treated differently. But it's never been an issue. The stereotypes of being selfish or lonely that existed in my mother's generation don't exist anymore."

"When I was married, my husband and I never got the baby urge. I perceived motherhood as a complete loss of self. People told me I would change my mind. I didn't. Now that I'm divorced, people assume I'm racing against time to find someone to have a baby with, that I'm missing the best life has to offer me. But others understand not everyone is meant to be a mother."

"I can't say my life is less fulfilling. It seems very rich and complete to me."

"I never felt maternal, never wanted to babysit when I was younger. I took more satisfaction from work than I did children."

"My partner had kids. That met my needs and was enough for me."

"I never had any desire to reproduce. But I'm very close to my nieces and nephews."
      —Women on their decision not to have children

I was surprised to discover some years ago when I conducted a workshop for senior women in the educational sector that more than half of these department heads, vice principals, and principals did not have children. I knew some women chose not to go the mother route, but I had never really thought about or realized just how many women made this choice. As it turns out, about one-third of professional women over forty-five years old living in urban environments do not have children, about the same percentage as the women who answered my survey questions. Their reasons are varied.

For some, it was a question of happenstance. They were not in relationships, or the relationships were not appropriate, or when they entered relationships, it was too late to try to conceive; they also did not experience a burning desire to have kids. Lu-an, for example, is a writer who spent her twenties and thirties working, studying, and traveling in Europe and the Far East. She loved her life and never felt the nesting or baby call. She returned to North America at the age of forty-one, and shortly after that met her husband-to-be. By the time they moved in together, having a baby "wasn't an option." "But it wasn't really about my age or not being in a suitable relationship. I have single friends who adopted and friends who found a sperm donor. Basically my life felt good the way it was," she says.

Similarly Wendy says, "I was never really interested in children. When I visited friends with babies, I was happy for them but relieved for me; I also noticed that other childless women were googoo-gaga and was mildly perplexed at my lack of connection." She was in two serious relationships and each time asked, "Would I want this person to be my child's father?" The answer was "no" until she saw the Big Chill. She decided to see if she could have a child "by proxy." She lent out her partner to a friend who wanted children. "She didn't conceive. I was disappointed, but only slightly. I'm fine with how my life turned out."

Regret or Choice

According to Sylvia Hewlitt, author of *Creating a Life: What Every Woman Needs to Know about Having a Baby and a Career* (2004), the vast majority of childless women suffer from *baby lust*. When the book was released, it created a huge media buzz. Hewlitt argued that fertility rates drop dramatically after the age of twenty-seven; childless women devote themselves to their careers in their twenties and thirties, only to discover the heart-wrenching truth in their forties that their biological clocks are ticked out. (One childless thirty-four-year-old who wanted children said, "It was so depressing it made my ovaries curl.") I have not found these tidal waves of pent-up baby lust or baby regret in my research.

As with the senior educators at the workshop I gave, for many childless women it was a matter of choice. They never saw themselves as mothers or else looked to their relationships, careers, and personal interests for fulfillment. Darlene is typical of the women who married. When she met her husband at the age of twenty-five, they discussed the baby question and agreed neither were interested for lifestyle reasons. She and her partner have a wide circle of friends. They built a cottage together. She sings in a choir, and he moonlights in a band. "We knew we would have a rich life—and we did and do. We always have a project on the go and travel frequently—we could not have done this with kids," she says.

When Sarah got married at twenty-eight, neither she nor her husband felt any great "call to be parents," but everyone told them they would change their minds, and they accepted this as a possibility. They decided that if either of them felt the urge, they would wait three months to see if the other person felt similarly compelled. It never happened.

"Some people said we were selfish, that we were too devoted to each other. But it's not a question of being selfish. It's selfish to reproduce yourself for the sake of passing on your genes. If neither of us felt we wanted to be parents, would we have been good parents? That's selfish—having children when you are not fit to be parents."

Larissa, in contrast, never had a long-term committed relationship, and she always knew she would never want children. She values her time, freedom, and most of all, solitude. She's extremely introverted and describes herself as her own best friend. "I didn't want to be at someone's beck and call. I live an interior life, and enjoy the hours I spend in solitude," she said.

These women simply did not feel an urge to be a mother. A typical comment was "I never went gaga over kids the way some of my friends did, never felt maternal, so I never had a compelling reason to try to have a baby. I don't think I was put on this earth solely to reproduce."

Nor do they accept the stereotype that they will grow old and be lonely. As a friend commented, "Whenever some idiot asks me 'Who will look after you in your old age?' I think, what a stupid reason to have children. Children aren't tools to look after aging or lonely parents." And in any case, as many said, the chances that they would be living in the same city as their kids were low, or their kids would see them as a nuisance and would not be around to look after them any way. Perhaps it would be even worse. As one woman said, "My mother lives in a retirement home. She said, 'We (the mothers) are the loneliest. We expect our kids to visit and when they don't, we feel alone. The women without kids seem the happiest. They're not sitting there waiting for their kids to show up.'"

As a psychotherapist who specializes in midlife women observed, "I see as many lonely mothers in my practice as childless women. 'Alone' does not equal loneliness. Friends, relationships, passions, family, all contribute to having a rich life."

But a minority worries deeply about being lonely. "I know children aren't there for you when you are old, that's not why you have children. But I'm single, and childless. I don't want to spend the next three decades without anyone to love or care for me. I know I could have adopted a child from China or somewhere else, but I didn't feel I was strong enough to do this."

Worries about loneliness aside, many childless women enjoy close relationships with nephews and nieces, or stepchildren. They like kids, but they just didn't feel a call to motherhood. Their relationships with others' children are an important source of satisfaction, but it is not compensation for never having had children of their own.

I confess I expected more of the childless women to cite some kind of trauma or to refer to a painful relationship with their mothers. While a few women did describe their mothers as cold and detached, and therefore felt they lacked nurturing role models, many said they enjoyed a very close relationship with their mothers. As one commented, "My mother was the most powerful person in my life . . . the ultimate role model in shaping who I am."

Obviously there *are* women who chose not to have children because of emotional trauma, but they are in the minority. One woman, for example, who grew up in an abusive household said she did not feel "whole enough to mother someone else." Another said, "My mother never taught me to value myself, that I was important or special. I am just coming into my own now after more than two decades of spending time with the wrong men. I'm starting my happy childhood, this is my life, and I want to live it for me."

For a few women the reason for their choice is complex. For example, Katherine's brother died when she was fifteen. "Our household changed. I saw the agony. Did this influence my decision not to have kids, witnessing the impossible heartbreak of losing a child? I don't know. I just know I never wanted kids, and my partner felt the same way."

Some childless women who developed relationships with men at midlife tried to conceive, but never felt such a strong desire to have children that they went the fertility route. Hannah, for example, had been in a number of relationships in her twenties and thirties. When the last one broke up when she was thirty-seven, she says, "I thought, given my age and the number of emotionally competent available men out there, I'm probably more likely to be hit by lightning than to enter a stable relationship. I was comfortable with this. I never had had this burning desire to be a mother. I had always thought, if it happens, great, if not, that would be OK too." At thirty-nine, she met a man who ultimately became her husband. They tried to conceive for a few years and then gave up. "I was disappointed, but not devastated. I guess because I had never expected to be a mother, it wasn't a huge trauma."

Many who were ambivalent about having kids, or decided to try later on in life were, like Hannah, disappointed for several months and then bounced back. As one forty-nine-year-old woman who tried unsuccessfully to conceive said, "Maybe I missed out on something; when my husband and I got together, this wasn't the life we planned. But it was a different and equally satisfying life. I think about it from time to time, wondering what it would have been like, but it's not a major issue for me, or source of significant regret."

There are many reasons for this ambivalence. Some women questioned whether they would be good mothers, or were prepared to sacrifice their lifestyle. Others, like one acquaintance, hooked up with egotistical men who wanted the undiluted focus of their partner's attention. They wanted their wives to look after them as if they were the child.

One friend explained her ambivalence in terms of being a "genetic dot." She and her sister were both adopted and, as she said, had no genetic connection forward, backward, or sideways. Pregnancy offered the possibility of a connection forward, but being adopted gave her an almost pathological fear of pregnancy for reasons she herself doesn't quite understand. She did eventually get pregnant late in her productive life. She miscarried, which she says she had half expected.

"I'm an accident. I was fatalistic about motherhood. I was heartbroken, but it meant something different to my husband. It was easier for me to deal with it because motherhood is such a complex issue for me."

The Heartbreak for Some

"Not being able to have children was my great tragedy. But you learn to live with it."

"We all have to live with some tragedy in our lives whether it be the premature death of parents or your failure to conceive."

"My husband died very young. I wish he had left me some part of himself. As I move into my fifties, I feel very lonely."
   —Midlife women discussing childlessness

When a friend was told she would not be able to have children, she quit her job and spent the next three years crisscrossing North America in search of treatments. She was fortunate. Because her family was affluent, she was able to undergo repeated and very expensive fertility enhancement treatments; she gave birth to twins. Many friends and acquaintances have told me that it is impossible to understand fully the anguish of not being able to have a child when you want one, unless you have "been there." But I certainly witnessed her heartbreak and desperation.

For some there are extraordinarily tough decisions to be made. Some women, for example, marry men who have already done the "father" thing. The deal is "no children," a heart-wrenching choice for women who want to be mothers.

Consider Katrina, a woman who married a man fifteen years her senior when she was thirty-three years old. He had two young adult sons and was so adamant about not becoming a father again, he wanted her to sign a contract agreeing that they would not have children if they got married. She agonized for a year over whether to marry him. Her parents were so upset by the match they didn't speak to her for several years. Now, at forty-five, she is still torn apart that she has no children, especially when she is around her nieces and nephews and thinks, "They could be playing with my kids." She lies in bed wondering if she did the right thing, knowing at her age it's too late to make different choices.

For some women it's not about choices: they blame their childlessness on personal inadequacies. Take this sad comment from a forty-two-year-old: "I have major grief about not having children. It wasn't because of my career or that I was ambitious but because of my inability to be intimate. I came to understand the effects of that too late. To me this is my most significant failure, more so than anything in my career. But I have faith that I will find graceful acceptance with help from my friends, family, and God. Everyone has their cross to bear."

Infertility represents the greatest emotional trauma in the lives of some women. Cerise, for example, kept hearing in her twenties and thirties that women could get pregnant even into their forties, so she didn't feel rushed. At thirty-eight, she started trying and subsequently went through years of fertility treatments that she thinks might have worked but "there were so many months between the appointments; the years ticked away until it was too late."

At forty-seven she says, "I have a stepson, but not having children of my own leaves me feeling empty inside. My husband has been supportive throughout this, but I don't think he understands the depth of my emotions. No one can give me those years back. I always ask, Who is going to visit me in the old folks home?" She threw away her camera when she had to have a hysterectomy. She knew it wasn't rational, but she thought, "Who would want to have the memory of me captured in pictures?"

She is angry and thinks a whole generation of women was fed misinformation about the success of pregnancy at an older age; she cautions women who want children to start young. (Her story is tragic, but to put it in perspective, several women who underwent successful fertility-enhancement treatments in their late thirties and early forties said, "Keep on trying. It's worth it if this is the one thing in life you want.")

The pain is palpable. As one woman said, "No one understands the pain of failing to conceive: it raises very emotionally loaded issues that go to the heart of what it means to be a woman, your womanhood, who you are. You feel like a failure in the most visceral way."

One forty-three-year-old tried the fertility-enhancement route, but after what she describes as "several horrendous months of being poked and prodded and topped up with hormones that at times made me feel like chewing off my arm and at other times f...ing the guy at Wal-Mart who wheels the empty carts," she decided it was too painful. Because of her age, they had started her off on the maximum dose of follicle-stimulating hormone that made her "produce over two baseball teams of potential eggs. Nineteen to be exact." She freaked out. "I insisted they induce ovulation to reduce the risk of becoming Madame Ovary, the freak of fertility. A day later I had an insemination procedure that they said would feel like a pap test but was more like being f...ed by the Terminator. And after all that? No pregnancy."

But just as mothers have secrets and pains too difficult to share, so do those who want children. She didn't tell a soul. "Who wants to listen to my travails at the assembly line 'F...-thru' fertility clinic. Not even the people at the fertility clinic want to know what I went through," she says.

Several women who said they had desperately wanted to have children have come to terms with their inability to do so, most with the help of therapy and support groups for women who can't conceive. However, for some it still represents a gnawing ache. It's a different life from the one they had envisaged.

A Clash of Womanly Values

"When I was younger and my friends were having children, they would ask me why I wasn't. But with the changing role of women, no one seems to ask that anymore."

"I get it all the time—nosy, obnoxious questions, and passive-aggressive comments, especially from women who have kids. 'Gee, I wonder what it would be like to sleep in till noon on weekends.' I think they're actually jealous of me and the freedom I have."

"The major times I feel uncomfortable are when my friends' kids ask: 'How come you don't have kids?' What am I supposed to say? 'Sorry, kid. I don't like kids.'"

*"Because single women can opt to have children through adop-
tion or sperm donors, some women wonder why I haven't taken
that route so that I could become a complete woman. I think
they disapprove of and pity me."*
  —Women discussing how others react to their childlessness

Although virtually all the childless women I spoke to had been the
recipient at some point of snide comments or rude and prying questions about why they didn't have kids, their experiences can be
divided into two camps.

Many were like one forty-eight-year-old woman who said that
when she was younger, a few people asked her prying questions, but
now people accept that women choose to have a child or not in
much the same way they choose to have a career or not. Like the
majority of other childless women, most of her friends also don't
have children. She comments, "Birds of a feather flock together? My
friends have a similar lifestyle. Because you are freer and have more
money than people with kids, and you're not worried about the
kind of stuff mummies talk about, you tend to hang out with people
with similar interests."

The second camp does feel the strains. A number of women
made sad comments like this one: "Some people think there must
be something wrong with me, unnatural as a woman, given that my
partner and I have been together for twenty years. There is still a
taboo—you can't really be fulfilled as a woman [unless you have
children]. So I imply that we had medical issues. I find it easier and
people seem to be more accepting of this, than the idea I would
choose to not have kids."

Some women felt that it is the mothers who are "suspicious"
of them, who wonder if they are "whole." Maybe these mothers
are insecure, unhappy Supermoms or Overly Identified Moms,
who feel others' choices *not* to have kids are a repudiation of their
own choices.

A friend says she often feels pity from mothers, like she has missed out on the most important thing in life. And paradoxically, when someone pities her because she doesn't have children, she feels hostile. She calls it the "tensions between the barren and the breeders."

Do some mothers "pity" the childless? I was surprised by this comment. Personally, I don't. I think people create the life that is best for them given who they are and happenstance. I asked a number of mothers about this. One replied, "They're ignorant of a whole dimension of life, because you have to give more. But you get more, something you can't even define because it is so big. So I think, 'if you knew what we knew, you'd choose to have kids.'

"And there is also some contempt. I think they are selfish, not in the sense that they selfishly deprived the world of their genes, but in the sense of being self-absorbed. My attention is divided between three million things, while all they have going on in their head is 'I wonder about that cute trainer or if I should buy those stilettos or if everyone liked my presentation.'"

But others said that they have received more comments from men than women: "Men say things like 'You would have been a great mother.' 'How can you be so sure you don't want kids?' 'How unusual to not want children, why get married then?' 'You chose not to have children, huh?'"

One manager made an interesting observation about these men's female role models—their mothers and wives. "Their mothers stayed at home, and they have stay-at-home wives or wives who moved off the career fast track to accommodate family responsibilities. They're resentful since they're financially strapped with children and non-working spouses, with the additional strain on their leisure and work activities. So it's probably a combination of envy and lack of under-standing because this is foreign territory.

"But I also think it's partially sexual. Mothers are not deemed as sexy or desirable as women without kids. So the men think, 'I bet she's not saying, Sorry honey, I'm bushed tonight.'"

Given that there are such deep-seated socialized beliefs and prejudices about women who don't have children, is it odd to choose not to? As I conclude this chapter, something occurs to me: in my survey questionnaire I asked childless women why they *didn't* have children, but I didn't ask mothers why they *did* have them. One of my best friends does not have children. Why, until I wrote this book, did we never have a conversation about this? I think it is because, subconsciously perhaps, I assumed that this was a sad issue for her, something had gone wrong, and that it would be in bad taste to probe. In fact, she, like many women, chose not to have children.

Perhaps, as in organizations where the gold standard is male behavior and anything else is deviant, in womanhood, the gold standard is motherhood. How sad. I guess we haven't moved as far as we think.

chapter nine

Relationships:

What We Want, Know,
or Should Know by Now

- *"My partner is my second skin."*

- *"My husband bores me but it's convenient. I have a rich life—the marriage is irrelevant."*

- *"We are passionately in love in all ways—intellectually, emotionally, and physically."*

- *"My husband thinks my aspirations are less important because I make less money than he does."*

"I think my husband is threatened by my success and the fact that I challenge him and don't take his B.S."

"My relationship? Although we are married, we have no emotional connection, just through the kids. We need to do something about that but quite frankly I don't have the

energy, or maybe not the interest. I'm terrified one day when the kids are grown, I'll look at him and think, 'I don't like you anymore.'"

"Twenty-nine years later, we still delight in each other."

"I'm so lonely. I think I'm going to die alone. I'm still looking, but I don't think I'll find anyone. This is my tragedy. I wish I could be one of those sparkly Sex and the City girls who obsess over guys but don't really need them."

"At this age, it's unlikely I'll meet someone. I'm a heavy-set woman and don't have the kind of perky boobs guys are attracted to. I would like a partner, but I don't need a partner."

"I loved my husband fiercely. When he died, a part of me died as well. It's three years later, and I have made a life for myself. But I will always feel this profound ache."
　　—Women discussing their relationships with their partners

When I was thirteen years old, my parents sent me to an artsy summer camp in Vermont. The other kids all came from affluent New York City families, their left-leaning, intellectual parents working in media, academia, or entertainment. At night my bunkmates would swap stories about their shrinks. When my parents came to visit, I reproached them, "How come I don't have a shrink?" When I was in my thirties, I sometimes used to wonder, in much the same way, given the statistics and that almost everyone I knew was divorced and working on their second or third committed relationship, "How come I'm not divorced?"

From every demographic and statistical point of view—education level, social class, liberal nonreligious background—not to mention (in case you have not figured this out yet) I'm a tad neurotic (although charmingly so I like to believe), I clearly should have had a marital breakup. As well, at thirty-one I experienced every stress event on the Holmes Rahe Social Readjustment Rating Scale, which predicts, among other things, marriage dissolution, financial difficulties, completing a thesis, renovating a home, and the death of a father-in-law. So I worried. "Was I *settling*? Was everyone else bolder than me? Did I have lower expectations?"

The truth is that my husband and I had and have the kind of relationship in which one feels centered and calm. Of course we have "issues," but there are "issues" in every relationship. So my questions had less to do with the nature of our relationship than the social comparison one engages in at that life stage, and being a statistical anomaly.

A friend, who is also long married and is in a similar type of marriage, introduces her husband as "this is still my first husband." In her circle of professionals, she says, "I am the only person I know who is still on their starter marriage. Sometimes it's almost embarrassing."

I think of relationships like a fragrance, which has upper tones, midtones, and undertones. My husband and I have primarily what I call a companionable relationship, one of nine types I describe below. But relationships, as every woman knows and loves to dish about, are complex: changing or not, meeting our needs or not, important to our well-being or not. They are rarely one pure thing or another. Most of us have undertones and midtones of other types of relationships. As with career satisfaction, our happiness depends on the balance between the various aspects—great, good, not so good, irritating, and just plain awful—and what's important to us at this life stage.

The nature of our relationships with our partners is shaped by who we are, what we want from our lives, as well as our partners' personalities, what we project onto our partners, and what we accept in our partners.

Archetypes of Midlife Relationships

One of my hobbies is playing "relationship yenta." Throughout my life people have come to me for advice about their relationships. I love to observe, think about, and discuss (withholding names, of course) people's relationships. What holds them together, what makes them dissolve, why do some women hang in while others walk away?

As always, patterns emerge. I found the responses I received from women about their relationships could be classified into "types" consistent with my observations about people's relationships. These composite sketches are based on what the women said about their partners and what women have said to me when they have sought my counsel.

Identify the kind of relationship you are in. If you have been in several, are there any recurring themes? Look at the upper tones—the main event if you will, then at some of the subtler mid- and undertones. Lesbian relationships follow most of the same archetypes. For simple readability I have used "he" and "she" here and throughout this chapter to signify the other partner.

The Deal

Most of the women who have "the Deal" are the Supermoms, who downsized their ambitions and left high-octane careers to look after children, the Yummy Buddy Moms, or the stay-at-home Executive Moms we met in Chapter 7. A few are childless. Occasionally women enter Deal relationships at midlife, hooking up with an older, more affluent partner. He's a divorcee or widower who wants companionship, someone to accompany him on trips and to business functions and look after the home; she wants financial security.

Most of us are familiar with this one. We have friends, or friends of friends, or have watched with amused interest the mothers at school who volunteered for everything and were constantly on the go with their kids' overscheduled lives who live the Deal.

The Deal usually works as follows: he makes serious money in his "player" job as a lawyer, investment banker, CEO, or doctor. They are both competitive and value status, but because they value money, and he makes LOTS of it, she is the second-class citizen, and he is the important person in the relationship. Making money, after all, trumps mothering.

She sacrifices her desires in favor of his choice of vacation, club membership, or whom to entertain. In return she gets a beautiful home, an opportunity to enhance her status by volunteering for "name" charities, and the clothing and jewelry necessary to frame his ego and her status with their friends.

Ever wonder about all those brand-new Prada and Chanel bags at designer resale shops? She bought them and then immediately sold them for cash (he controls her by not giving her access to cash, but she does have plastic—at least until he wises up to it and reduces the credit limit). This is how she finances purchases she doesn't want him to know about (a cosmetic procedure, a fancy lunch with friends, a hotel room because she is having an affair with a neighbor).

He often treats her like garbage—not showing up for dinner, changing mutually agreed upon plans, having affairs. Her job, if she wants to keep it, is to overlook his peccadilloes or use them as a bargaining chip for another diamond trinket or plastic surgery.

The problem is she has her own fairly hefty ego needs—she is not the agreeable good-girl Supermom who happily subordinates her needs to those of others. They have many knockdown fights in which they don't hear each other, so loud is the clash of their egos. She says, "You're never around. You're oblivious to the kids, you don't understand how hard I work. You treat me like shit." He says, "You're hysterical. What are you complaining about? . . . All you do is play tennis and go to the spa. Calm down," which does in fact make her hysterical.

For many years she and a group of friends, also in Deal relationships, have been going to Paris for a long shopping weekend. They love to bitch about their husbands; in fact, they compete—whose husband is the bigger prick. When she was younger, she said, "What an asshole. When I leave him with the kids, he says he's babysitting." Now she talks about his apparatus. They howl with laughter.

At midlife, if they are still together and he has not left her for a younger model, the effect of the continued subordination of needs throughout the marriage has been either to gradually erode her self-esteem, make her bitter, or both.

She may have an affair to make herself feel better, desirable. Her husband, who used to tell her how sexy she is and buy her lingerie, now uses her only as a sperm receptacle, that is, *if* they are still having sex.

But sometimes this competitiveness and rage galvanize her at midlife. We have met these women earlier who say, "It's my time now." They start businesses in what is often a competitive bid to prove themselves to their partners or to keep up with their friends who are now also starting clever fashion and décor enterprises. Or they chair a high-profile volunteer board.

He's not happy about this turn of events, which has changed the dynamics of the relationship now that she is "coming into her own." In fact, he is seething with anger. She wants to be treated as an equal, to have her time commitments and accomplishments respected. He belittles what she does and refers to it as her hobby. "If you didn't have access to my pockets, you couldn't have done this. You don't have a clue about what it really means to put yourself on the line," he says. He needs to restore his power.

Will the marriage last? Probably not, unless it turns into a Shell or a Toxic relationship. If she is doing something interesting, her self-confidence often returns. She doesn't need him. The price, her self-worth, is too high. The divorce is bitter and *very* expensive. The kids are drawn into the nasty power struggle and are forced to take sides.

The New Deal

These relationships grew out of the restructuring of the workplace throughout the nineties that disadvantaged men of a certain age. He was terminated from his executive job and couldn't find another job, and/or he has set up a home-based business, Joe Blow and Associates, that produces a meager and unpredictable income flow. Or he just gave up the job search after a year of rejections, and has turned his attention to hobbies and volunteer engagements.

She, on the other hand, has never felt better about herself and the work she is doing. The new deal? She provides the lion's share of the household income, he plays Mr. Wife—he cooks, cleans, and does everything he can to make her life easier.

She and a group of friends in their late forties and early fifties were talking once and they realized that all of them were in great jobs, while their partners were not making a living. "Who would have thought this would have happened ten years ago," they marveled. And then they laughed, with some embarrassment, about how at least they no longer had to cook.

There is always a challenging transition to the New Deal—sometimes it is successful, sometimes it isn't. These relationships are different from those equitable relationships in which partners decide to switch so-called traditional gender roles in order to fulfill family responsibilities. This decision was made *for* them.

He was previously a powerhouse and work was the centerpiece of his identity. She enjoyed the status of him having a BIG job. Both of them may have trouble dealing with his loss of status and miss the powerhouse personality. She may see him as emasculated and no longer wants to have sex with him. She may nag him about his job search every day, and even set up an appointment with a career counselor for him, telling the counselor, "He says he doesn't want to work. But I know he does. Talk to him. Make him find another job."

He has suffered a huge blow to his ego. He is a traditional guy who believes in the importance of being the breadwinner, and whose sense of self is tied to the status of his work.

Sometimes he becomes depressed, mopes around the house, and watches daytime TV. Friends comment that he has become a shell of his former self. He and his wife have nothing to talk about. He's not interested in her coups at work; hearing about her successes makes him angry, resentful, and jealous. When they go for marital counseling, the therapist says, "He's packed his bags; he's emotionally left this relationship."

But many men after a period have adjusted to, accepted, and even welcomed this role reversal. They develop new hobbies and flower in the way midlife women do. They cook gourmet meals, volunteer, explore new business ideas, and deepen their relationships with their family. After a life spent playing a role at work, they discover the pleasures of an unstructured day.

Because she is traditional in terms of her gender expectations of what men and women do, if she accepts this turn of events, a woman in a New Deal relationship may be sensitive to how her partner might feel to be put into this new role. If he is in pain, she feels it and shows empathy, behaving in traditionally female ways. She defers to him, she allows him to buy things that she thinks are hideous, she turns all financial matters over to him, she flirts with him.

If they both welcome this new arrangement, they experience their relationship as satisfying, sometimes even as renewed, and meeting mutual needs. If they do not, because one or both of them cannot accept his new role, the relationship becomes toxic with her nagging him, or feeling like he is now her child and consequently resenting him.

The Toxic

Every woman has witnessed a Toxic relationship, of a family member or friend, or has been in one herself. So we are familiar with the dynamics.

How did it get that way? There are many paths to Toxic relationships. Sometimes it starts with an affair that leads the hurt party to lose trust in their partner or engage in a tit-for-tat relationship. Sometimes she connected with her partner for all the wrong reasons. She saw him as needy and wanted to mother him, to make up for the fact that he'd been brought up by a "den of wolves" as she puts it. He's her project—she will fix his low self-esteem. It starts well enough, but over time he starts to resent this Pygmalion in his life. "I'm not your puppet," he says. She wanted to "save" him. He didn't want to be saved. It became a power struggle. Or, she was by nature bossy so she chose someone who was naturally submissive. But eventually she came to hate that about him.

Sometimes he changed—he is no longer the great guy she met. It started as an affair. He was still with his wife, who got the brunt of his controlling nature. With his new partner, he was conscious of trying to woo her. When they started to live together, all of the hostility that his former wife had experienced was now targeted at his new partner.

Or when both partners have changed—as in Deal or New Deal relationships—there is a failure to renegotiate old roles and expectations. Each partner has needs that are no longer being satisfied and this leads to rage and hostility.

They fight about everything—the kids, his family, her family, money, household chores; all of it is a potential landmine.

He says disgusting things. "You're a slut." "You're a slob." "You're buying your friends." "You flirted to get that job." She cries, screams, or withdraws and does everything she can to avoid displeasing him, following the familiar pattern of women in verbally or physically abusive relationships.

Her friends, if they are aware of the problem, counsel her to leave him. They tell her that his underlying anxiety and insecurity are what is causing his controlling, abusive, and possessive behavior, and that unless he gets help he won't change.

But it's not always about the guy. Sometimes both parties play out their psychic dramas and needs in putdowns and witty barbs with a very mean subtext, which are deeply embarrassing to the onlookers who are needed for the drama to be satisfying to the players. They are addicted to each other; they get energy from their sparring and anger—this is when they feel most alive, most engaged, have their emotional highs. Often, they have their best sex after one of their many fights. He says, "I only do this because I love you so much." Sometimes she believes him.

Women in Toxic relationships who have children suffer hugely. They wonder, Should they leave? What will happen to the kids? How much and what do the kids know?

Usually, what is required to get her to leave is the very attribute she has lost in the relationship—her self-esteem. And her parents often don't help. "You should stick it out for the kids. Everyone has problems. You'll get over it. It's just a phase and in any case, I'm sure you're just overreacting," they say.

And just when she is at her lowest, he may have an affair and do the leaving. On the other hand, with the burgeoning confidence that sometimes occurs at midlife, she may be one of the growing number of women who leave bad marriages in their forties. She does this with the support of divorced friends and therapy.

"She's the Boss"

Everyone describes him as a nice guy. He's easy, good-natured, affable. She's more intense, "no nonsense." They have kids. She could be any of the mothers we met earlier, but she is most often the good girl Supermom. Her work motivation is usually a Sociability-seeker or Security-seeker. Occasionally she is a Career-builder.

This is the stuff of sitcom relationships. Nincompoop daddy, smart mummy who tolerates in a passive-aggressive way all the dumb things Daddy does and says. Everyone says, "There's no question who wears the pants in that relationship."

When they were younger, they did a lot of fun things as a family. They've visited Disney World twice, and they've been to every Marine Land, Wonder Land, Nature Land, Butterfly Land, Dinosaur Land, and Fun Land within driving distance. They have a lot of couple friends with kids the same age; they have been friends with many of these people since high school.

Ask him to make plans about anything outside work time and he says, "I'll have to ask the wife, she's the boss." When his wife asks him for his views on anything related to the house, kids, or leisure activities, he says, "You're the boss."

Some women in these relationships like this. "He's just like the other kids," she says to her friends, with a slightly exasperated smile. It makes all matters of decision-making related to home and hearth much easier. And it ensures that the idiot on the couch doesn't interfere in her domestic fiefdom.

Some are pissed off. They tell their friends, "He has the initiative of an eraser, does nothing unless I nag him, and unless we're talking about the kids, we have nothing to talk about." At midlife her kids have flown the nest, but she says she still has "another kid around the house to look after."

Most women in "She's the Boss" relationships feel ambivalent. They subscribe to so-called traditional gender stereotypes, and like to be needed and to exercise domestic control. Family is very important to them. They think, he may not be a powerhouse, but he is a good husband and father, a "family man." On the other hand, being married to someone they see as a schlub is not very sexy. Moreover, not only is he passive at home, he's also passive at work and in other aspects of his life. She secretly has fantasies about a Real Man, a Clint Eastwood take-charge type of guy, someone with a personality.

She had an affair once, with a guy she met at a professional conference. She feels very guilty about this but regularly replays the delicious memory. She has told no one, not even her best friend.

Will the marriage last? At midlife, he may decide he is tired of being a dishrag or have his own midlife crisis. The kids are grown up, so he can leave her now. Or she may be bored, and looking for something more meaningful (translation: challenging and therefore interesting) in her life. She also worries about what they'll have to talk about once the kids have left home—they haven't had a real conversation in years. The prospect of his eventual retirement and having him underfoot is even more terrifying. But she also likes the security, not to mention having a deep distaste for the messiness of divorce.

This leads to very interesting conversations with her best friend, who is the only one in the world who knows that she is thinking of leaving him. "Can I spend another twenty years with this boredom?" she asks. But then she thinks about what her other friends would say, how well they work as a couple, how many couple friends they have, not to mention what her kids will think.

It's a tough decision. If she is a Self-Developer, Authenticity-seeker, or Novelty-seeker, there is a fair chance she will leave him. If not, which is more likely, she will conclude that "no marriage is a bowl of cherries" and that the good outweighs the bad. She can get her intellectual stimulation from her friends. They had some good times together. And he does have a toolbox (even though she has to nag him to use it).

The Eggshell

In this relationship it is understood that one partner has special needs; the role of the other person is to support them, make their life easier, and ensure their needs are met, often subordinating their own needs in the process. This may mean walking on eggshells to avoid a fight, making "allowances," or being excessively solicitous of the other person's comfort. In effect, to smooth the way for the other person.

He may, for example, be a temperamental writer, or a gifted but egotistical scientist. Or he may suffer from mental illness. She may suffer from depression, be moody, excessively "needy," or unusual in some other psychological way. She could be anyone from a highly individuated, expressive woman who does not suffer fools gladly (think of the Saint, and the women who don't get to fit in whom we met in Chapter 2 or the Authenticity-seekers we met in Chapter 4), to someone with a borderline personality disorder.

When they entertain, she gets up in the middle of dinner and wanders into another room without explanation. Or she changes her mind at the last minute about going out. Or she has a meltdown or freaks out at a mild comment that she experiences as an egregious insult—think of the Yummy Buddy Moms and the Overly Identified Moms. (The mythology about the relative importance of his needs over hers stems from his work; the opposite—that her high-profile work needs to be supported—is rarely true. But just as women can be attracted to sensitive wounded men, so can men be attracted to sensitive wounded women.)

If he is the one with the special needs, the relationship functions like the Deal. Except instead of getting the fancy house, she gets the opportunity to "save" him or to be associated with him and his work if he is gifted and bask in his reflected glory. At midlife, her own repressed needs and desires may bubble to the surface, leading to a clash of egos.

When she was younger, for example, and she would complain about him to her friends, there was an undertone of boasting when she said with an indulgent smile, "Well, you know what David is like"; now she is just tired and angry. She says, "I have nothing left.

I feel beaten and empty." If she is able to recover her emotional strength, she may leave him. She knows it is next to impossible to renegotiate the roles in this relationship.

What happens to her if she is the one with the "special needs" depends on the nature of her needs. If he has left her, sometimes she discovers that she allowed him to keep her dependent on him; in fact, not only can she cope, she experiences a surge of power and competence. She says to her friends, "All those years that I felt incompetent, needy, how did that happen? Was it me? Was it him? Or was it both of us?" Her friends say, "It takes two to tango" and tell her about the *Cinderella Complex*, a book that their mothers read in the early eighties about women's fears of being independent. They also talk about enabling and codependency.

But sometimes her needs are too great. She has been "damaged" in ways too deep to become fully independent (even with psychotherapy). If he does not leave her, they continue to play out the clearly defined roles in what is often a painful psychodrama. And then again, sometimes her "special needs" are what make her interesting and intellectually attractive. Sure she is moody, but she has a brilliant mind and an unusual take on the world. He finds her very sexy. Making accommodations for her is a small price to pay.

The Blended

According to statistics, by 2010, there will be more stepfamilies in Canada and the United States than any other family configuration. Their challenges are significant.

He wants a mother for his kids; she wants romance. She wants a father for her kids; he wants her to himself. She thinks he should discipline his kids more; he thinks she's too lenient. And the kids, they're angry and resentful about someone muscling in on their biological parent's turf, especially if the relationship started as an affair that hurt that parent. It's a toxic stew.

She read the books about stepparenting and consulted a counselor: "I love him, we can do this," she said. No matter how hard she tried not to be seen as wanting to become "Mother," the kids hated her. Older daughter acted out and had serious psychological difficulties. She's been seeing a shrink for several years. Younger son just ignored her: "You're not my mother, why should I listen to you?"

She asks her husband to talk to them but he says, "You just have to give them time." She suggests family counseling but he bristles. "It's not necessary. I don't have any problems," he says.

They are critical of each other's parenting style, using expressions like "not being held accountable," "no sense of responsibility," and "not imposing limits."

She told her best friend, "Men divorce their wives, and then out of guilt, either over- or underparent their kids. They let themselves be manipulated by their children, especially their daughters. The wives are secondary." She says she could write a book about it and would call it *Divorced Dads Are from Uranus: Why They Can't Move Past Their Shit.*

Her childless friend, whose partner has a twenty-five-year-old, is in a similar situation. "Why can't he just tell his effing son that we want an adult relationship, which means he can't move back in?"

Is it worth it? they wonder amongst themselves. "The men will never get rid of their baggage. They still haven't worked out their shit with their previous wives," they say.

Another friend who has two children of her own says, "I wish I'd known my love for my own children was built in, my love for my stepchildren wasn't. I really like one of them, I'm proud of her, even if it took several years of constant fighting to get here. I can't stand the other; it's mutual."

And then they think about one of their friends. She had two young children when she had an affair with the man who ultimately became her life partner; he had three adolescents at the time. He left his wife and moved in with her. Other than a brief tumultuous period when his daughter lived with them, she had no contact with his kids. She and her partner were Processors (see below): whenever they had a problem, they discussed it, endlessly, almost into the ground. But it worked. Her daughters say how lucky they are—they have both a dad and a stepdad. She has a pleasant but formal relationship with his kids, who are now young adults.

Will the relationships last? If both partners are prepared for the period of constant negotiation and to set expectations for roles and responsibilities they will. But I wouldn't put my money on the childless woman who resents her partner's inability to say to his son: "You can't move back." She ultimately will conclude that he is weak.

The Processor

Processors discuss every detail of their relationship. No ground goes uncharted or is off-limits. She describes herself as "an emotional connection junkie." She wants to be challenged and always growing to a deeper level; she becomes bored and dissatisfied if she is not completely engaged. (In her work she is usually a Self-developer and/or an Authenticity-seeker.) Sometimes he wearies of this never-ending processing, but he has learned to play the game and often enjoys it. They come to this inclination naturally: they both work in humanistic fields such as divinity, counseling, or human resources.

They have had a couple of rough patches, but they rode them out. "We'll talk about this even if we have to stay up all night, and the next night, and the next night until we understand what's going on and we feel comfortable," they say. "The relationship is too important."

People in Processor relationships are not afraid to examine their own feelings, motivations, and what they are projecting onto their partner. When she got very busy at work, he took it as a personal rejection. He thought she cared more about her colleagues than him and that she found them more interesting. He realized he was feeling inadequate because his work was not going as well as hers and that he had felt "threatened."

Or when he flew home across the country to visit his sick parents, she was hurt he didn't invite her to come. She wondered, Didn't he realize by not inviting her, he was basically saying she wasn't supportive of him? After a few all-nighters that got into a lot of "When you do this, I feel that" and "When you say this, what I hear is . . ." she realized she was projecting her bad feelings about herself because she doesn't really care about his parents. It made her feel guilty to realize that she was not as supportive of some aspects of her partner's life as she had thought.

A few times she has considered leaving him. Her friends marvel at the intricacy of her vocabulary for discussing her feelings about him. Sometimes they think, "Just leave him or shut up. Stop taking your emotional temperature. You're becoming boring." But secretly sometimes the friends who are long-married are jealous that her relationship and her feelings are so important that she can discuss and evaluate them in this way. "Am I missing out on something? Have I settled? Am I defensive or just taking the easy way out by not thinking about my relationship?" they wonder.

In contrast, a few of his old friends who have been privy to some of the conversations he has with his partner think, "What kind of a guy are you? Real men don't have these kinds of conversations!"

The worst thing she can personally imagine is *settling*; she needs to be completely honest with herself and dig deep to understand what she is really feeling.

Will the relationship last? At midlife they may renew their vows and deepen their intimacy. They talk about how their relationship has changed—what's worse, what's better. Or they may decide that it is no longer meeting their deep-seated needs for intimacy and meaning, which for them is the ultimate source of fulfillment.

The Shell

Somewhere in the years of working and child-rearing and keeping their show on the road partners in a Shell relationship drifted apart. They were too tired to have sex and in any case, she or he wasn't particularly interested. Occasionally she wondered if her husband was having an affair, but she wasn't too bothered one way or the other.

For many years they have not spent time together. The kids and work always came first. There wasn't much left over in terms of time or energy; and they really did not care what the other person was doing or thinking. They were connected through the kids, not each other.

It wasn't always a loveless relationship. Early in their marriage, when they had started fighting, and she was angry about his lack of communication skills, she had tried to talk about it but it only led to screaming matches. She would say, "You've become so cold, so emotionally unavailable." He would say, "Stop nagging. What do you want from me? This is who I am." When that didn't work, she suggested they go for counseling. When he refused to go back the second time, she told him, quite accurately as it turned out, "One day I won't care enough to have fights with you." She had secretly wondered, but would never bring it up to him, whether he felt threatened by her professional success and that she was his intellectual equal.

She had briefly considered leaving her marriage when the kids were younger, but decided not to for their sake, a decision she does not regret now. She had an affair with a coworker that lasted two years—it ended in much the same way it began, without much fanfare.

At midlife she lives a very independent life. She travels with her girlfriends and has hobbies that she pursues on her own. She says she doesn't need a man to play an important role in her life. They sleep in separate bedrooms.

In some cases Shell relationships are amicable. He occasionally accompanies her to the opera. They entertain their couple friends a few times a year. She thinks of him as her roommate. There is some residual warmth in the relationship—they have a shared history and are both committed to being seen as a family for the sake of the kids, even if they are now grown up. In other cases, relations are strained. She is frosty with him, if she talks to him at all. Years of petty resentments and repressed desires have taken their toll. But there is not enough energy for this to be a Toxic relationship—he's just a person who many years ago was a player in her life.

Sometimes at midlife he leaves her for another woman. More often, she leaves him. They have moved too far apart, the relationship has dissolved into indifference. She cannot tolerate living this way for the rest of her life. Other times she makes a different kind of compromise. When she considers divorce, she decides against it, telling her friends, "Our assets are too intertwined. It would cost a lot of money. Why make a lawyer rich? It's also much cheaper for us to share a roof. I'm not sure I could afford it."

She also says, "I'm not really into having a relationship. If it were to happen, great, but I'm not looking for it. How likely, at my age, is it that I'll find someone?"

She feels good about her life. Her children and her grandchildren, if she has them, make her happy. She has varied interests outside her work—she's active in the community, gardens, paints, and loves doing fun things with her friends. But, heck, if the opportunity for an affair presented itself, she would be ripe for it.

The Companionable

The poster couple for this kind of relationship is the elderly man and woman you see promenading in comfortable silence, holding hands. They may have been together for years, or this may be their second, third, or fourth serious relationship. If they are still on their starter marriage, their relationship may have evolved at midlife into this kind of relationship, but usually the long-time married who are in this type of relationship have always had some elements of this type. The hallmarks of a Companionable relationship are mutual trust, support, and taking pleasure in each other's company. Unlike most of the other relationships, the power is *equitably divided*.

In the child-rearing years, there were times when they drifted apart. If they have chosen to be childless, they have long led a life in which work, hobbies, travel, and each other were the centerpieces of their relationship.

Many men and women in this kind of relationship think of their partner as their best friend, which does not mean they tell each other everything. They may have secrets from each other; they may even have had or are having affairs, which their partner does not know about. They may, especially if they have recently gotten together, have great sex. They may have sex rarely, as they may not find having sex with their best friend very sexy. Regardless, they feel an intimate bond with each other. She describes his brain as the greatest aphrodisiac. When she has an issue at work or with her friends, he is the person with whom she "debriefs." When she has a huge fight with her sibling, he moderates.

The women in Companionable relationships may be living very independent lives, but they feel very differently about their partners than women in roommate relationships—they see their partner as an integral part of their lives. If they meet in the midlife years, they may even choose not to live together. She says, "I don't want him in my space—I designed it for me." Or "I don't want to be in his space, it's ugly," or "I don't want to deal with his kids, and clean the house." Instead they travel together and spend a few days a week at each other's house.

Some midlife women enter what, to the outside world, especially bitchy friends, looks like a Deal kind of relationship. He is older, affluent, and semiretired. He provides security in exchange for companionship. It is a Companionable relationship, however, because he does not expect her to subjugate her needs to his; there is genuine affection, if not love, on both sides.

If she is long-married, there are things about him that used to drive her crazy. When she thinks about them, she can still get irritated, but not in the same way she used to. Over the years they have learned to talk more frankly about issues and hear what the other person is saying without blaming, or attributing each other's behaviors to underlying personality deficiencies. She accepts who he is. When she gets together with her friends, she can bitch about him if forced to, but really she is just going through the motions and playing the game; she doesn't really *feel* bitchy. Over the years they have grown into each other.

It's not all perfect. Sometimes she can still get embarrassed and annoyed when, with their couple friends, he goes on endlessly about something no one cares about. Or he farts and belches. She chides him about this in public, with the indulgent exasperation of a mother reprimanding her child. She can live with his small foibles. She tells her friends, "He's not perfect, but then neither am I." In fact, she feels she has struck a pretty good deal.

Her friends envy her, especially the ones who are experiencing difficulty in their relationships or are single. One single friend said to her, "You and your husband—it's like money in the bank. You don't have to explain, discuss, and negotiate everything. The savings make you relaxed about your life."

She has great friends and interests. She does not depend on him to feel good about herself. She wants and needs him in her life, but not to fulfill her needs for status or to counteract loneliness. He is not her walker.

Relationship Ambivalence

"If I ever get involved in a relationship again, it will be with someone who is either 1) childless or 2) signs an affidavit that the kids are over eighty, live thousands of miles away, and are financially secure."

"I hate being the 'single woman' who shows up at couple events, especially when people start talking about how they met, their kids, etc. But at other times, I appreciate being the total master of my own fate."

"I fear growing old alone. It terrifies me."

"Men are just not as interesting or layered as women. I'd rather spend time with my girlfriends."

"I am single, but not alone. Having a man in my life would be a bonus; it is not a 'need.'"

"Many of my married friends are lonelier than I am."

"Men are lovely, but unreliable. It would take an effortless relationship—which is likely an impossibility—to persuade me to live with someone again."

"I'm comfortable being alone. But the thing about being in a good relationship is you learn more about yourself because that's when you have to deal with your own shit."

"I've been on this one date, and we've exchanged witty e-mails. Before I would have made histrionic declarations of

*eternal love. Now I'm more tentative and proceeding
with caution."*
  —Women discussing how they feel about being single

Of course not everyone at midlife is in a committed relationship.
A few, such as Georgia, worried desperately about being lonely.
Her marriage dissolved when she was forty-five. Seven years later
she says, "I get depressed to the point of suicidal thoughts when I
think of spending the rest of my life alone. I am an only child,
expect my sons to leave me, have no daughters. The statistical
reality is that I may never recouple again, and this will be my life
challenge, being lonely."

But most of the women I interviewed are ambivalent about
their relationships. (For a brilliant, fascinating, and sometimes disturbing analysis of marriage and the role of women today, check
out *The Meaning of Wife* by Anne Kingston, which examines the
inequalities that women still face.) They express sentiments similar
to Kristine who is single now after three relationships that didn't
work out. "It annoys me that some people assume I must be lonely
and then try to fix me up. I miss the cuddling, I wouldn't mind
having sex, but my life doesn't feel compromised, or less full than
the lives of my friends in relationships. If it happens great, but if
not, that's OK too."

Arguably, if you need a man to make you not lonely, then you
are not complete as a person. Loneliness is about feeling dis-
connected from the world and people around you. It's *not* about not
having a guy. Perhaps if you do not like being alone, then you do
not like your thoughts.

As one woman commented, "I felt more alone in my marriage
than I do now. Bless my girlfriends. Between my book club, night
classes, community activities, and just doing things with my friends
I've never felt so connected. I can imagine myself in a relationship,

but I can equally imagine it not happening. I can spend time with myself. Actually I think I'm my own best friend."

Many women expressed this dilemma—they want companionship, but they also want to maintain their independence. Many of my acquaintances who are in relatively new relationships are torn about whether they want to continue in these relationships. As one said, "I guess now we are becoming like the guys, commitment-phobic. When you've created a good life for yourself, do you really want the complication of a guy with his ego needs, mucking it up?"

One widow was undecided, although for different reasons, about how much she wanted to invest in a new relationship with a man she had been friends with for many years. Two years after her husband died, the relationship blossomed into a romance. She feels lonely at times and intensely misses the intimacy and deep friendship she had with her husband whom she describes as "her soul mate." She worries that if she were to make a commitment to the relationship it would be for the wrong reasons—not because she is attracted to him, but because she is trying to fill a void. "That would be very unfair to him," she says. And she also cannot stop herself from making comparisons between this man and her husband, and finding him wanting.

Patricia is similarly torn about whether she wants to "commit" to the man she's been seeing for the past two years. She captured the dilemma poignantly. "I have recently realized that I am strong and can function well on my own, and that his issues are increasingly less interesting to me. So I think, 'Do I really want to be with this guy knowing . . .' Still we have fun together. So he's like having a pal to hang around with and do activities with, with the bonus of physical affection, comfort, and sex, and the physical dimension makes him more interesting than spending time with girlfriends. Also, I haven't yet conquered the human need of wanting someone to be there, to care, to hold me . . . when my dog dies, a tumor grows, my car is stolen, the roof leaks."

What many single women today want in their relationships is much like what they want in their work relationships, namely to *design* the relationship—the right amount of time spent together, balanced by the right amount of independence.

If I had to summarize the underlying sentiments for most of the women I spoke to about being single at midlife it would be as follows: "Men are nice, but they are also high maintenance. It's far more interesting to spend time with female friends because the conversations with women are far more interesting.

"But, well, even if I don't *need* a man in my life, it would be great to have the companionship and intimacy. It would be a bonus, but I'm not prepared to settle for just any man. I am self-sufficient, and I need a man who is self-sufficient, and who is not intimidated by my self-sufficiency. I'm too old to deal with someone else's issues, to look after someone, to submerge my identity to the ego of a man. I've been there, done that, and have the scars to show for it."

And besides, according to single women, finding an interesting, emotionally as well as physically available man at midlife, is like finding Waldo. One woman says that she has turned first dates into a hobby. "They're never interesting enough to go for a second."

A fifty-one-year-old acquaintance says available men fall into predictable categories. She says the "only interesting and available men are married." She believes, and certainly has enough experience to qualify her as an expert, that "all married men are available. But unless you're up to your eyes in *amore*, it's not on." (Another friend, despite the fact she had affairs during her various marriages, says, "No married men. Ever. I wouldn't do that to a sister.")

But I digress. Back to the types of men. "He's either too old and it's like having sex with your father, an attraction for some, but quite disgusting to me, or he's a younger guy, cheap and bitter from previous divorces. He invites you out to dinner. You pay. He always forgets his wallet. Now there are some great younger guys who aren't carrying emotional baggage who I've been with, but I guess I'm not a good cougar, it never lasted.

"Or he's your age but has all these issues. He is 'sensitive New-Age guy' who plots the potential for the relationship on graphs with your birth order and date of birth to determine compatibility. Or he is 'fussy macho guy' who is gun shy and pathologically commitment-phobic. You can't use the word *love* unless you are talking about your cat.

"Or he is impotent or a bad lover who says as he fumbles, 'Oh, if you'd only known me when . . .' Or, and this is the most common type, he's an 'old fart.' Regardless of his age, he talks endlessly about things you couldn't care less about. You could get up and strip, and he wouldn't notice—he's too preoccupied with his old war story."

This last type raises a delicious question: Are older men *boring*?

I have a theory that women age better than men. I will tell you why later. But for now, particularly in the light of the significant number of women, both single and those in relationships, who commented that women are far more interesting than men, and complained that their partners or men they dated were boring, or had no interests, or were pedantic or had no personality, I would say: "There are *far more* boring older men than there are boring older women."

As one woman put it: "I want to discuss interesting things, who he is, who I am, things about life. I want a guy who has a generosity of spirit. But all that the guys want to talk about is their work, sports, something that happened in the news, or their past. They *love* talking about their past. So we're looking for something to connect on which feels good and human and all they want to do is hang out with other guys and compare their toys or their stock options or their company's marketing plans or trade old war stories."

On the other hand, from a man's perspective, we can be pretty boring too. Endless discussions about emotions, not to mention handbags, may not be the average guy's definition of interesting conversation.

He's Not Perfect: Can You Accept It?

"My mother used to say, 'Women get married assuming he'll change. Men get married assuming she won't. And they're both dead wrong.'"

Pam, a fifty-two-year-old with a daughter in university, has been in a relationship off and on for the past five years. During this period I have heard an ongoing litany of complaints about her partner's inadequacies. "He can't stand up to his son." "He's a pushover with his ex." "Everything we do is my idea." "He's boring." She is a major processor, and ideally she would be in a Processor relationship with a processor kind of guy. Unfortunately, he's a "She's the Boss" kind of guy, a nice guy who would rather chew off his arm than discuss their "issues."

By her own description, she is someone who likes giving advice. If there was a psychological scale that measured preference for intervention and belief in ability to influence and change others with advice, she would score very high. She has been trying, unsuccessfully, to give her partner advice about what he should and should not be doing with his son, his ex, and so on but has not been able to influence his behavior. (*Quelle surprise*, you are probably thinking, although there is a high probability that while you recognize the folly in someone else, you have been known to do this yourself, so don't become too self-congratulatory.)

I think all women have a bit of Pygmalion in them. A psychologist, who describes herself as a serious observer of the battle of the sexes, says, "Because women are inclined to be more perfectionist, they set high standards for the guys in their lives. She assumes that he would want to be a better person and that she has the inside track on what that means, so she tries to change him, believing she is actually doing him a favor." (Some men do this to women as well, but the psychological underpinnings—possessiveness, insecurity, and anxiety—and the resulting controlling behavior, and even abusiveness, are different.)

But back to Pam, whose story raises themes in our relationships with men, the first being trying to *fix* the problem. I always say to her: "You're a good example of a slowed-to-a-halt learning curve. At what point are you going to realize you can't change him?" For women, "hope reigns eternal."

And then there is the question of her tactics. She told him he had to show more initiative, challenge her, push back. Not surprisingly, the poor schlep is now completely frozen. He does not have a chance. Nor does she in getting what she wants. In fact it took Pam several sessions with a therapist to conclude that she needed to work on accepting, not educating her partner, or else move on. In the end, she did decide he could never be the "interesting, nuanced, intellectually challenging partner" she wanted.

At midlife, if we are capable of moving forward with grace, we accept who we and others are. Just as we have defined personalities that will not change, so do our partners. And we need to recognize that what we describe as our partners' inadequacies has less to do with them than what we project onto them in terms of our own needs and feelings about ourselves—just as we do with our children.

I often hear women in my workshops say, "My partner just turned into this major jerk." In fact he was probably always a jerk, but he was *their* jerk, and it met their needs. He didn't just wake up one day miraculously transformed. He slowly changed, she slowly changed, there was a gradual shift in perspectives, and an interaction of personalities that led to the shift. Interestingly, psychologists have found that people in healthy relationships have positive illusions about their partners, seeing them through rose-colored glasses. Maybe they are just seeing reality now.

So the question is, as with work, do we decide to enjoy what we have, or are too many needs just not being met? Sometimes you give up one thing in favor of something else. Zara, for example, a widow, is with a man whom she finds conversationally boring. She says, "He doesn't read, his interests are limited, his emotional range is limited. But when we do things together such as travel, play tennis, or have sex (he's a great lover), and I enjoy being with him. He's not perfect, but on balance I'd rather have him in my life than not." They are in a Companionable relationship, usually spending weekends together and living independent lives during the week.

Similarly Louise, who has been married for twenty-seven years, said, "When you're younger you think you are going to have this Prince Charming, major romance, major passion, and this great intellectual connection. The passion, and all the emotional highs are gone. But what I have instead of passion is compassion. And contentment. If I want intellectual stimulation, I look to my friends." Recall that some women said they wanted similar things now from their work—contentment rather than passion.

On the other hand, sometimes the trade-off is simply not worth it.

The Breakup: It May Be the Right Decision, but It's Not Easy

"As boomers, we think of everything in terms of our needs and if it feels good, pleasurable. If it doesn't, everything is disposable. . . ."

"I did the unthinkable. I not only left my marriage when I had three young kids, I left the country. I took a lot of shit for that. But if I hadn't been a stay-at-home mother and put off everything important to me, I don't think I would have felt this overwhelming urge. It was the first time I took a stand—leaving my marriage— and then one thing led to another. Maybe it was a funny kind of empowerment."

"I knew when I was walking down the aisle that I wasn't in love. But it just seemed like the right thing to do at the time."

"I'm proud of myself for ending the marriage . . . asserting my right to feel good about my life and being strong enough to do it."

"Leaving my husband was the most difficult thing I ever did. When you have kids, so much of what you feel is tied to your kids' well-being; they are an extension of you. 'How will they be affected?' is your constant siren song."

"My husband and I were invited to a dinner party at another couple's house. I am very attuned to those wispy, delicate nuances between people. Within fifteen minutes I broke out into the only body rash I have ever had. I took him aside and told him I knew he was having an affair with the woman and then exited the party and our relationship. Looking back I'm pleased with my exit strategy. It was nice for once to not be nice."

"I should have left earlier. My parents' disapproval over my leaving had a traumatic impact on me. My mother kept on saying I should keep on trying. I was terrified of losing their disapproval and love."

"Books and people will tell you that if you leave your marriage, your kids will suffer, but I think staying together for some people is far more destructive. When you are unhappy, you can't see the world properly. I withdrew so much from my husband I actually withdrew from my children as well. I wish I hadn't stayed so long."

"I have tremendous guilt over breaking up the family unit. I worry what this has cost my kids, I worry they will see me as selfish. This is how their father describes me."

"I'm twice divorced, and all my family including my parents are divorced. Do my kids have a chance at a stable relationship?"

"You are never really divorced until the kids have grown up. Fifteen years later, we are still battling."

"Even if we weren't married, we had been together for three years. I had weeks of anguish. He ended it but I instigated it. I worried obsessively . . . did I let the right guy get away or was it the right move, but I feared being alone?"

"After I left I had some great experiences and buckets of loneliness, but I felt strong knowing I could take care of myself. One day, learning my ex had remarried, I lay on the couch and couldn't move."

There are all kinds of trajectories to divorce and relationship dissolution—infidelity, drug or alcohol abuse, boredom, drifting apart, or verbal, emotional, or physical abuse.

Susan's story, for example, is fairly common. She had an affair with a coworker; his wife found out and told Susan's husband. He was furious (although as it turned out he was also having an affair). He called her a slut. He alternated between screaming and crying. He never missed an opportunity to berate her, especially in front of the children. And then he pushed her.

She said, "You ever do this to me again, you're out of here." She moved into the basement. A few days later, she says, "He came down to where I was sleeping. He was hammered, pushed me, and that was it." She left.

"I felt so guilty, leaving the kids with him, and I missed them obsessively. He kept calling and begging me to come home. He promised he would never do it again, and that he would stop drinking. I went home, and basically the story repeated itself."

It is commonly said that men leave marriages for other women while women leave marriages for themselves. A landmark study conducted by American Association of Retired Persons (AARP), an advocacy group for people over fifty, found that in divorces of couples over forty, 66 percent were initiated by women. Often the reasons are not a "push" as in Susan's case, a move away from a toxic marriage, but a "pull" to something better, being alone, an act of self-assertion. Diane, for example, who was in a "She's the Boss" relationship, said that when at age forty-one, she contemplated the idea of spending the rest of her life "with this boring, boring guy, I thought, 'Should I let the suffocating boredom kill me and die a slow boring death, teaspoon by teaspoon, kill myself right now and put myself out of my misery, or just end it?'"

Kate was in a joyless Shell marriage for twenty years. Her husband had many affairs, there was no communication, and he refused to go for counseling. She wanted to leave but was scared of being on her own, so she kept delaying it, telling herself she would need to find the perfect opportunity. Then her mother died.

She says, "It was like someone had thrown a bucket of cold water on me. I realized that I didn't have the time to wait for the perfect opportunity. After that I moved slowly but deliberately toward separation."

Kate's experience of the separation was similar to that of many women who described both the pain and the unleashing of confidence. "The first two years were very tough—but they were also the most rewarding. The freedom I experienced and the sense of accomplishment were exhilarating. I was so proud of how I came through it all."

Although there are different arcs to divorce, the wounds can be deep, especially if the woman was rejected; she is hurt, angry, and often in her heart feels that she is defective, experiencing the rejection as a *repudiation* of her deepest self. As one woman said, "I thought if I was a more lovable person, he would have stayed, that

I was unlovable." It took her three years to move through the anger and pain and start to recover. Five years after he left her, she says, "I'm just starting to date but I'm not sure I would ever surrender myself to love again."

But most women who were in the rejected role, with the help of friends, support groups, and self-help books ultimately do make effective transitions. Take Teresa, for example, whose husband left her for another woman after twenty years of marriage. She says, "I looked at this as a life transition, and I knew from reading books that any kind of transition takes time and support. I sought out women who had experienced divorce and today were living successfully. Their experience offered me hope and optimism for my future. They listened to me, reassured me, encouraged me. I wouldn't have gotten to this great place that I am in my life now without them."

Married, living together, or seriously dating, one feels the pain of the breakup. (That is why, every year, we see a new batch of best sellers on how to move on.) And it takes the same kind of time to digest the issues with the end of a personal relationship as it does when one is moving out of a bad work relationship.

Of course, when there are children in the picture, there are gut-wrenching emotions and guilt involved. Several women who described themselves as leaving marriages from hell still second-guess their decision because they ended up in divorces from hell. One woman put it this way: "I can't begin to tell you how much I hate, pathologically hate, my ex. But for the sake of the kids I wonder if I should have just stuck it through. My ex uses the kids as a pawn, plays these sick games with them. But still I obsess— would they have been better off to have had a father in the picture?"

Her comments were typical. Whether it was an acrimonious or an amicable divorce, many women described their exes as absent. They worried about the impact on their children, and wondered if they should have stayed in the relationship. As one woman said,

"He's remarried and his wife hates me and the kids. Being a weak-willed person, he went along with her and basically cut off most of the relationship with them. I think his absence from their lives has been damaging. I'm not sure what the outcome will be; it scares me. I also blame myself. Maybe I should have stayed with him and just sucked it up. I don't think so, but when I get down on myself, these are thoughts that keep me up at night."

On the other hand, what is the impact of growing up in a toxic environment? As this woman commented, "I made my decision to leave when one of the kids asked, 'Why is Daddy always angry, and why are you always crying?' That was the turning point—I thought, how healthy is this for them? What are they learning about love? How much emotional security are they really getting?"

All the mothers who left their partners feel, on balance, they made the right decision but virtually all of them expressed some occasional nagging doubts. Should they have left earlier? Should they have tried to stick it out? Of course, it seems you can never win because you can never know with absolute certainty that what you did was the right thing. I guess that's called life.

Georgina described the dilemma well. "I knew that a sad or angry or scared mom was not a good mom. But you read all the books about the negative impact of divorce on kids. And you think: How can anyone really know this? How can you compare outcomes of kids whose parents stuck it out versus those who didn't? No two marriages are the same. And no children are the same. But you will never know what would have happened if you had taken a different route. You have to trust your gut and take your own counsel."

When I wrote a column for the *Globe and Mail*, "Is it time to break up with your job?" I received many e-mails from women who said that they substituted the word *job* for *partner*. Obviously the issues for mothers are more complex and painful as they go more to the core of who we are—loss of income vs. hurting our children—but the assessment of the relationship, whether it's with a job or partner is often similar. So are the emotional competencies necessary to make desired moves—the knowledge we can cope and that we deserve to feel good about ourselves.

I agree with the women who said getting separated is not, to paraphrase, "a selfish baby-boomer feel-good indulgence" when the price for staying together is the loss of emotional well-being. I also agree that an "angry, sad, depressed mother" is not a formula for good mothering, and toxic home environments do not provide children with the emotional security they need. No one can really understand the depth or trajectory of someone else's pain. Some women can "stick it out" for the sake of their kids. But others can't— also for the sake of their kids. Divorce is the brave and not the cowardly option.

When It Comes to Sex, There Is No Normal

A fifty-year-old friend who has what she describes as "mad, passionate" sex three times a week says, "I think most women are getting more." When I tell her she is way above the average, she is incredulous. "You mean some people don't even get it once a week?" Everyone wonders, "Am I normal?" and the only thing that is normal is the question they ask themselves.

In *Perfectly Normal: Living and Loving with Low Libido* (2005), Australian clinical psychologist and sex therapist Dr. Sandra Pertot says, "Thirty years as a sex therapist has highlighted for me what should be recognized as a self-evident truth—that people are not the same sexually in the same way that they are not the same with respect to height, weight, intelligence. . . ."

She quotes a study conducted in the United States in which 43 percent of women identified themselves as having one or more sexual problems, and asks if it is possible for such a large percentage of the population to feel inadequate. She concludes they are not dysfunctional at all but are comparing themselves unrealistically to a media-induced ideal.

Numerous factors affect sexual frequency and attitudes at midlife including social class (the higher the class, the lower the frequency), hormones, partner's perceived attractiveness, lifestyle (the more work demands, the lower the frequency), early socialization, and sexual personality (shy, inhibited, adventurous).

But age also plays a role. In a study of two thousand women for *Health Plus*, a magazine targeted at women over forty, 45% said they had a greater sexual appetite than when they were younger, 77% said sex was better in their forties than in their twenties, and 51% said they would rather have an orgasm than a cuddle.

Women on Their Sex Lives

"I still don't like having my breasts touched. After you've breast-fed, you think of them functionally and mechanically."

"We live in such a sexualized society, so we always ask is my frequency normal, which is ridiculous. We all have different needs."

"Our relationship is far bigger than sex. A friend told me if you're not doing it once a week, there's something wrong with the relationship. Studies show that it's about intimacy and having your emotions satisfied . . . that's as important as sex."

"I'm thinking of giving up sex. I have limited time on this planet. And even with toys, sex takes me a verrrrry long time, so it's very time-consuming. Have sex or write a book?"

"Sex? What's that? Oh yeah, I remember now. My husband is impotent and refuses to take Viagra. He says it makes men become blind."

"Our sex life after twenty-two years of marriage is even better than when we were younger. There is nothing off-limits."

"I love my husband on a deeper and deeper level. We have sex about once a month. I usually have an orgasm. I'm often not keen to have sex though, due to fatigue. My kids take a lot of physical energy. Also by the end of the day I've had two thousand cuddles, I really don't need anymore physical affection."

"What sex life?"

"The problem with middle-aged sex is middle-aged guys—not a sexy sight."

"I can do it as long as I can fantasize."

"I love his body. I find gray hair and love handles very sexy."

"I will do anything, and I mean anything, to avoid having sex with him. I think it's because I get no affection from him. A simple hug or kiss. A hand on the shoulder. Choosing to snuggle under a blanket. Nothing. I need this. I need to feel we are emotionally connected and that he still loves me. I have expressed this need numerous times and it falls on deaf ears."

"My ex always had to have sex, and if he didn't get it, he was like a bear with me. I submitted because it was easier. In the end it was like he was raping me. Now I'm with a guy who is

older than me and interested in pleasing me. The sex is fantastic because of the emotional connection."

"I prefer my hand to his penis."

"We don't have sex, but we are very intimate. We hold hands, hug—it's very satisfying."

"I have sex an average of three times a week, twice a night."

"I pulled out of my marriage emotionally many years ago. So this is a 'no-go' area."

"His brain is my aphrodisiac. He's fat and kind of ugly. But his brain still turns me on. We do it usually on vacations."

"We have sex about once a month. It's kind of mercy sex."

"With work and the kids . . . I'm too tired and not interested. I don't think he is either."

"When I went into perimenopause, I just lost interest."

"Sex toys? No, none, we don't need them!!!"

"Sex toys? This is a disgusting question. Please remove me from your list."

"We have seven toys. We give them as birthday presents to each other."

"It is far better to remain technically faithful, that is, faithful with a technically advanced device. The Hitachi Magic Wand is

pretty good—two settings I call Rock and Randy. Sometimes I call them Peter and faster Peter."

"It's hard to get the juices flowing. I have to remind my husband, 'Make sure the oven is warm before you put in the turkey.'"

"My friends said their sex drive went away around menopause. Not mine, oh Lord, not mine."

"Many of my older therapy clients tell me they're just not interested in it anymore. And then they go to a party, their eyes connect to a guy's, and they feel a stirring."

Monogamy Is a Bitch for Some

"I would never jeopardize my relationship for a quick toss in the hay. I both love and respect my partner too much."

"I had an affair for all the reasons all women do it. To break the tedium, to break the rules, to get some attention."

"I almost had an affair once, but I didn't simply because I couldn't take the anxiety . . . but I fantasized a lot. Once I was single it turned out the guy I almost did it with was a drab copy of what I expected."

"I could have an affair since my husband and I are roommates, with nothing in common. But I can't be bothered. I hide myself in my work and my studies."

"It's killing me. There is this guy who I have this amazing magnetic attraction for. We've talked about it. I'm dying to do it,

*but I have all this good-girl detritus which finally won't let me go
through with it. The fantasies occupy a lot of my head space."*

*"I have four coaching clients who are in their late thirties,
early forties having affairs. Two are having them with women.
They say they're not gay, they just find women more interesting."*

*"I practice Marxist (Groucho) monogamy. I wouldn't have an
affair with anyone who would have an affair with me."*

*"Having an affair is something I don't regret. I have these
delicious memories. I don't want to feel there is something
I didn't do."*

*"My affair destroyed my family. If you are thinking of it,
my advice is DON'T DO IT."*

In the previous chapter we saw that the potential faultlines for
midlife affairs are numerous. Women at midlife are prime candidates
for affairs.

We know the reasons. She wants to feel sexy, desired, and young
again. She wants the thrill of doing something illicit with the threat
of discovery. She wants to punish her partner for years of grievances,
including his affairs. She feels he doesn't understand or care about
her problems, and that there are parts of herself that are unrecog-
nized by her partner her lover fulfills. She wants an antidote to the
boredom and tedium of her life.

But often the reason for the affair is not because she is trapped
in a horrible or even unsatisfying relationship, or sees this as a
fleeting feel-good opportunity. Debra, for example, has been married
for seven years; this is her second marriage. From her description it
is a Companionable relationship. She says she cares deeply for her

husband and that although they don't have sex frequently, the sex is good, sometimes great.

Despite this, she is having an affair. This is her second affair in this marriage. The man is her boss. (In her book *NOT "Just Friends": Protect Your Relationship From Infidelity and Heal the Trauma of Betrayal*, psychotherapist Shirley Glass says about half of unfaithful wives in her practice had affairs with someone at work and the number of work affairs has grown significantly.) She also had affairs in her previous marriage. She jokingly describes sex and affairs as her hobby, but says she is not promiscuous.

Her current affair is different. "I always made it a rule that I would love them, but not *fall* in love with them." This time she has broken the rule. "I became like a girl in high school. If he didn't call or e-mail me, I would freak out. I was always feeling needy, wondering, Does he love me?" She came to realize that she wanted to marry him. "I broke affair rule number one and told him this. I hoped either he would leave his wife, or at least it would be liberating for him to know how I felt rather than playing the 'I'm not going to give you too much power over me' game, and for me to know where I stood," she says. He said he would never leave his wife.

A year later she is still having the affair. She says, "Even though he'll never leave his wife, I'm still lucky if happiness is valuing what you have. At least it will never get to 'he farts in bed and throws his dirty underwear on the floor.' I have stability and something special with him. I'm happier having him in my life, even if on a part-time basis, than not. I could not deal with the pain of losing him."

As with all issues related to women, there are many takes on whether it's okay to have an affair. From the "never" to "yes" to "never, but maybe."

The nevers made comments such as this: "The only absolute bottom-line rule in our relationship is exclusivity. I would never compromise my relationship by having an affair. I can see how it happens, I've been in situations where it could have happened, but I would never do that." Or "Never. And I've never allowed myself to be in a situation where it could happen. I can't even imagine it." Or "I would not have an affair, but I flirt a lot. That's OK, I think, in fact it's good for you and your sex life." For these women it is a question of trust and values, and they would not cross that line.

Others, mostly in "Shell," "Toxic" or "She's the boss" relationships, are having affairs or would like to. One said, "There is nothing really left in my marriage. I am having an affair—that's the only thing holding my marriage together, that I'm getting intimacy outside it." Similarly another said, "My marriage is empty. I'm considering it."

And a few found the idea titillating. As one woman put it, "If he had an affair, I think I would kind of like it. It would make him seem sexier. And if there was someone I found, well, I wouldn't say no. I think it can spark things up sexually."

Some women, however, fall into a twilight category of "never, but maybe." For them the "never" is a difficult nut to swallow. They have a lot of angst.

Denise, for example, spent two tortured years longing to have an affair with an old boyfriend she had bumped into. She was wracked with guilt (she describes herself as a churchgoing Pollyanna type) but she was obsessed. She couldn't get him out of her mind. She consulted a medium and two therapists. Her friends were so sick of hearing her angst they said, "Put us all out of our misery. Just do it."

Finally she decided to do it, and they booked a rendezvous. At the last minute she changed her mind. As Kinsey said, if something pleasurable is prohibited, it becomes an obsession. She is still obsessed. She says the jury is out on whether she will do it.

"There is still an outside chance that I could step over the line if my id takes control. But having an affair would mean I would have to become the kind of woman who cheats and lies, and I don't want to be a person who cheats and lies. And I can envisage the consequences. The thought of devastating the people I love most for an afternoon romp in the hay in a hotel room is unconscionable."

She says, "Affairs pose a Hobbesian dilemma—you are tortured regardless. This opportunity might be my last kick at the can. I may never get another offer. Do I want to go through the rest of my life without ever having tasted the delights another man can offer? One of the therapists I consulted gave me an insight when I asked her what purpose this man was meant to have in my life. She said I should regard him as a catalyst for midlife change. So I am using this experience as a launch-pad for renaissance in other sectors of my life. My ego really enjoys the thought that he continues to pine for me, that unless I cave in, he won't get over me. But man, am I tortured."

Indeed, you are tortured. Passion literally means suffering. Most women I know who have had an affair make comments like this woman: "It's like a drug and you become addicted. I couldn't imagine living without him. No one, no one could make me feel this way. But you're always suffering, always in pain."

When her partner discovered she was having an affair, her marriage broke up and her lover ended it. Five years later she is still obsessed with him, even though they have had no contact. "I fantasize about him almost every night," she says. "Would I do it again? That's a tough one. I destroyed my family that I will never get over. But oh, to have had love so intense . . . you only get that once in a lifetime. But no, probably not. The price probably wasn't worth it."

Many women have come very close and struggle with the idea of monogamy. Lauren says, "As good as my marriage is, and there is no greater blessing than a good marriage, I struggle with one issue—monogamy, which in my opinion is a bitch. However based on my experience counseling tormented friends who are having torrid affairs, the alternative to monogamy wreaks havoc on your life, especially if you have a lot of good-girl detritus left in your psyche, as I do."

Her solution? "I stay away from Byronesque men and Chardonnay. He was a most inauthentic, yucky man. The mirror opposite of my husband. My friend said he was my shallow self. On the other hand it's good for the foreplay with my husband. I felt the texture of temptation. I saw it, smelt it, heard it, felt it. But I would have felt so guilty, I couldn't live with myself."

A psychologist friend who has counseled many women who are having affairs says, "Women go at infidelity with much more intensity, and internal conflict, than men. Men can contemplate having an affair, and if it happens, great. But women become obsessed right from the beginning, even if they don't consummate the relationship. The chemistry is so explosive."

Are Some Women More Likely to Have an Affair Because of Their Personality?

Sixty-one-year-old Carole, like Debra, has been very busy. She has been married three times and is now in a new relationship. In response to my question, "Have you ever had an affair?" she said, "Please be specific. Mine or his? In which relationship? With which sex? If I wasn't actually married, just living with someone, does that count? Four affairs—two with women, two with men."

Why do some women cross the line and others do not? Why do some taste the temptation and resist while others don't? Obviously opportunity, values, and the quality of the relationship play a role. But these considerations aside, I think some people may be more inclined because of their personality characteristics. Just as in work we saw that some people are more capable of tolerating a less satisfying work situation, or are constantly restless even when they are in a good work situation, some people are less capable of tolerating a less than satisfying personal relationship, or else need more to feel their lives are complete.

I have heard many women make comments such as this: "I've never had an affair but every one of my friends is or has. I sometimes wonder if there is something *wrong* with me . . . am I boring or too scared or too unadventurous?" They raise an interesting question.

In *Undressing Infidelity*, author of *Why More Wives Are Unfaithful* Diane Shader Smith concluded after interviewing more than 150 women that women who have an affair court risk, intensity, variety, and novelty.

I have a theory. I know directly or through a friend about thirty women who have had affairs; I have enough details about these women to have a sense of who they are. What they have in common is that every one of them has as one of their top motivators "Self-developer" or "Novelty-seeker." In other words, they have a greater appetite for risk and are more easily bored. (Of course, just because they have this motivational style doesn't mean they will have an affair.)

Some people may just be more adventurous. I sent the e-mail from the three-times married, four-times affaired woman to some friends (minus identifying details) and asked them what they thought. None of these women had had affairs (yet), but they had all come close. Their responses could be summarized as follows: "What a gutsy, saucy woman! How does she get the nerve? How does she carry it off?"

In a wildly unscientific survey, I asked five women who had had an affair why they did it. Is there anything about them, in their opinion, that makes them different? This comment from a woman who is having an affair with a coworker was typical: "Obviously, there needs to be the opportunity and the chemistry, but I think I'm restless. In part I like to live on the edge. But I also feel that having just one partner is not enough."

Motherhood and Relationships: Are They Unhappy Bed-fellows?

I mentioned earlier that I did not find the deep wells of misery in mothers that author Judith Warner in *Perfect Madness: Motherhood in the Age of Anxiety* found. Sure many of them were harried—but I didn't see the desperation. And as we have seen, the world of mothering for the working mother has changed significantly over the last ten years.

But I did discover something else: there was a notable difference between how mothers described their relationships with partners, compared to childless women. Overall the childless women described their relationships as more intimate and satisfying. They also had sex more frequently. (Although there is no normal, there is evidence that sexual frequency plays a role in a sense of well-being. According to British researchers at the University of Warwick, based on a survey of sixteen thousand Americans, people who have the most sex are happiest, sex having the greatest impact on happiness for educated people. On the other hand sexual frequency declines with education, so maybe they are more deprived and therefore more appreciative.)

About 80 percent of the married women between the ages of thirty-nine and fifty with kids at home said they were too tired and did not have enough energy or time to have sex more than once or twice a month, if ever. The mothers fell into two camps regarding their feelings about their sex lives. For some, lack of sex is a disappointment. As one forty-two-year-old woman said, "I've just come into my prime. I think of sex regularly, but planning is required, and of course time alone. Sometimes we sneak it in early in the morning before the kids are up. But we don't spontaneously cuddle, which I miss."

But in today's superchild culture, subservience to children in many cases correlated with distance from mates. For many of the women who described themselves as living in "Shell," "She's the boss," or "Toxic" relationships, their only connection to their partner was their children. I became very depressed after reading their responses. Many wondered what their relationship would be like ten years down the road. I think most of us can figure that out.

In contrast most of the childless women described their relationships with their partners as very close. This comment was typical: "He is my second skin, my soul mate. We have a bond I can't describe. Without children we have been able to make each the centerpiece of our lives. We are free to pursue what is important to us as individuals and as a couple."

So many different experiences. So many different views of what is important and what we need to feel good about our lives. But whether we are mothers or not, single or in a relationship, the one thing we all agree on is how important our friends are.

What We Wish Someone Had Told Us

"I've been married for eighteen years. Our relationship is better and deeper than ever before. We feel better about ourselves and are less stressed by trying to combine the work and family thing. We can relax and really experience each other."

"I had let my marriage take my soul. I have worked hard to get myself back, but it is a work in progress."

Although we all have different expectations of our relationships, we agree on the big issues.

Create a life that is not dependent on a partner. Maintain your interests and friendships. Have an identity outside your relationship. Be capable of amusing yourself. Only you can make yourself whole. Don't project your needs onto your partner. If he does something that you find embarrassing, he is embarrassing himself, not you.

Don't allow yourself to be swallowed. Don't subordinate your needs to his. If he makes more money than you, it doesn't mean he is more important. (Ditto, if you make more money than he does.) At any given time, however, you may need to sacrifice your desires in favor of his. Expect reciprocity.

Don't swallow him. If you treat him like a child, he will start to *act* like a child, which is not very sexy; you will ultimately resent each other.

Enjoy and accept him for who he is. Don't try to fix him. Listen to your inner voice if you have doubts about committing. He won't change. Show appreciation for what he does rather than what he doesn't do. Don't compare him to your friends' partners.

Make time for each other. Don't allow your work and/or mothering and/or other commitments to consume all your attention and energy. If your relationship is important, you need to feed it. To this end, many women have a weekly date with their partner.

Recognize and discuss your feelings when they occur. Take ownership of your emotions and thoughts. As one woman said, "I was partially in denial. I knew we had a problem, but it just seemed too much work to talk about it. And I was so busy, and just kept thinking things would get better on their own. So our relationship continued to deteriorate, until eventually there was nothing there. Maybe if I had been willing to articulate the issues, we would still be together."

Be realistic. There is no such thing as a perfect guy or a perfect marriage. All relationships have tough patches.

Monitor your thoughts and your speech when you have a disagreement. Are you blaming him? Are you invoking underlying personality deficiencies? Are you obsessing over what he did wrong?

Know what is important to you. Some women can tolerate a bad marriage for the kids, others cannot. You know what you need. There is no "normal," whether we're talking about our sex lives or our relationships. For some it's passion, for others it's contentment, for others it's being a good parent.

Don't tolerate any kind of abusiveness or behavior that makes you feel belittled. You are far better off on your own if the price you pay for the relationship is your emotional well-being. Take action, whether that means seeking professional help or leaving the relationship *before* you get into a downward spiral of depression and self-doubt.

Take your own counsel when it comes to ending a relationship. Regardless of what the studies show or your parents tell you, no one can understand your pain, and no one can predict what outcomes will occur if you leave or stay in a relationship because of the kids. Most of the divorced women said that they were proud of leaving their bad relationships as it was the ultimate act of believing in themselves. Many also said they wished they hadn't hung on for so long.

Get support through a bad period. Seek professional help. Read books. Talk to others who have weathered similar experiences. Virtually every woman who had left a bad relationship said they couldn't have done it without the support of their friends and professional counseling.

chapter ten

Women Confidential:

Secrets of the Sisterhood

*"When women get together to dish, everything is on the
table from aging to pubic hair configurations to Margaret
Atwood. Often in the same sentence. Our partners may
listen politely, or pretend to listen, to our tortured musings,
then pronounce their diagnosis, prognosis, and proposed
treatment regimen with a dismissive wave of the hand.
But our friends will examine every angle, share their
similar experiences, and the similar experiences of every
person they have ever known, then work together with us
on a solution, or at least a working hypothesis."*

*"I have very little extended family in this country, so my
friends are my surrogate family. I have a core group of
about eight women friends who constitute my inner circle.
They are close confidantes with whom I share secrets,
burdens, anxieties. The relationship is reciprocal. I also*

*have many other friends who are not confidantes but with whom
I have very stimulating relationships."*

*"My friends open up all kinds of interesting possibilities.
I envisage them becoming more important as I get older."*

*"I meet every few months with a group of friends I met twenty-
five years ago in my first job. We have gone through single life,
married life, children, affairs, divorces, remarriage, divorces
again, lots of sex, no sex, bigger jobs, lost jobs, bigger houses,
downsized houses. We talk in excruciating and painful detail.
Sometimes we cry, but usually we laugh hysterically (something
which won't be so funny when we are older and dealing with
incontinence). Those who are married say: 'I would never tell
these things to my husband.'"*

*"Lest it sound as if all my friends and I do is bitch and whine,
let me add that most of our social interaction is really stimulating.
We exchange ideas, tickle each other's brains, and just generally enrich each other intellectually."*

*"When I broke up with my boyfriend, I moaned obsessively for
weeks to my friends, 'Did I let the right guy get away?' I owe
them each four thousand Woman Hours."*
    —Midlife women on the nature of female friendships

When I was a child, my mother sometimes hosted a
women's book club in our home. I loved these get-
togethers. I would crouch at the top of the stairs and
eavesdrop on their conversations. The best part was when their voices
dropped, because I knew they were talking about something especially
tantalizing. Although I couldn't hear what they were saying, I understood there was a special and delicious character to the subtleties of

their language, and an intimacy to their relationships. They inhabited a world I knew would someday be mine, but for now was off-limits.

A body of research supports what we already know: our friends are good for us, and we are good for our friends. A landmark UCLA study on female friendships, for example, shows that these friendships shape who we are, soothe us during tumultuous times, fill emotional gaps in our marriage, and help us remember what we are about. (Interestingly, there is a physiological component too—the release of a hormone in women when they bond with their friends during stressful times.)

In workshops I sometimes ask, "If you were in a lifeboat with your best friend and your partner, and you could save only one, who would it be?" There is embarrassed laughter. "Hmm, I'd have to think about that," women often respond.

As one woman astutely commented: "Women give each other confidence to change our lives from the inside out by changing how we think. Our friends are there for interventions when we are doing dumb things that threaten our well-being. It's like that game played in corporations—stop, start, continue—where an individual subjects themselves to candid feedback. We play it spontaneously.

"Stop e-mailing that man who is not your husband. Start asking yourself why you are doing it. Continue to work on that tape in your head. You are capable of moving on. And do I think you should buy that? Well, no, you look dowdy in brown."

In the last chapter, we saw that many single women said that as long as they have good female friends in their lives, they don't really need a partner. In a relationship or not, most women said they experience other women as more interesting and nuanced than men. They made comments such as "If I have something important to talk about, something where there are layers to be probed—and there always are—my husband doesn't get it. So why waste his time and mine?" (Almost all the women I interviewed said there are things they tell their girlfriends that they would not tell their partners.)

"Men can be amusing. But if you want to have an interesting conversation, talk to a woman."

Of course we don't all see the world in the same way. A small minority commented, "I don't like to work with women or hang out with them. They're bitchy, competitive, and mean." I feel sorry for these women and wonder what has wounded them, because for most of us, friends are a lifeline.

Friends: The Power to Wound (as Well as Heal)

Friends play a critical role in our lives. Because of our deep attachments to them and what they mean to us, our friends also have the capacity to hurt us.

Marilyn, for example, had a friend she particularly valued both for the conversations she had with her, and also because she enjoyed her friend's husband that meant they were also couple friends. Her friend told a story about her in a very public venue that she found humiliating. She mulled it over, and realized that although it would be messy, she had to confront her friend. "She honestly didn't get it. She didn't understand why I was upset. So for me it wasn't so much the betrayal as how she handled it, and what it said about who she is as a person. I could no longer be friends with her because how can you be friends with someone where there is no trust in the other person's basic ability to know what is acceptable and what is hurtful."

When it comes to our friendships, we are all still in high school. Except where once we said "what a bitch," now we say "she has no emotional intelligence." Four years later, Marilyn still reflects upon this lost friendship and why her friend behaved the way she did.

We may not remember the names of guys we had sex with, or in some cases, much about our starter marriages, but we remember every detail of lost friendships.

Every woman has a story to tell about a wounded friendship that she can recount, blow by painful blow, even if it occurred many years earlier. For some, like one woman who was rejected by her best friend as a social inferior when she married a very rich man, there is still unresolved anger and hurt. "Sometimes I still obsess over this and think about telling her how I felt, just to get some closure."

Indeed status issues are often the underlying cause of lost friendships. You are rejected because you aren't of the right social class. Or because your fortunes have been better than hers, and she feels inadequate. Kristin's story was typical. As she started to get acclaim for her work, her best friend became increasingly passive-aggressive. "She would make snide digs like, 'It may come as a surprise to you, but not all of us can take expensive vacations,' or 'It must be nice to be able to afford a monthly pedicure.'"

In looking at the responses to my survey and thinking about why I have fired former friends, I found what was typically a combination of four underlying causes in addition to those related to status. These are feeling betrayed, as in Marilyn's case, feeling "used" (she only calls when she needs something), seeing something in the other person's personality such as cruelty or narcissism that is deeply objectionable, and being the target of excessive, often passive-aggressive neediness. (In terms of work relationships, through her twenty years of research into friendship, sociologist Jan Yager has found that it takes an average of three years to know whether or not someone is a true friend.)

But sometimes we are to blame, and we have a nagging regret because we hurt someone and could not say "sorry." Lauren, for example, did not attend her friend's second wedding. "I didn't think she would care. She married a celebrity, and I thought I wasn't as important as the other celebrity guests, so she wouldn't even notice. I found out later she was deeply hurt. But I just couldn't bring myself to call her up and apologize. I still feel ashamed of this. The thing I'm most ashamed of was that it was my ego that caused me not to go because I didn't think I was as important as the A-list."

Many of the women described things they have done to friends that they are ashamed of. Interestingly, only one woman reported shame for her behavior in a former relationship with a man. Perhaps, because we identify with other women, we can identify with the hurt we inflicted and therefore feel more accountable for our behavior.

Our emotions about our friendships are as complex as we are.

Envy and Competitiveness

"I'm not jealous, but I have to express my inner bitch:
I don't understand why she gets these great contracts
and everyone loves her when she's as neurotic as hell,
not particularly talented, and her work is crap. But honestly
I'm not jealous. I wish her well."

Many women said they are not envious or resentful of the successes of women in their network. "Do I compete with other women? That's so high school and so 1950s. I don't have to compete with anyone," one woman insists. "I regard all women as potential members of my sisterhood."

Perhaps this is true for her, but I think this is just something many women tell themselves; just as we have a complex relationship with the idea of being ambitious, so do we with the concept of competitiveness, one of the expressions of ambition. A more honest statement would be "I am happy for them when they are successful, but, and this is something I don't like about myself, part of me wonders why them and not me." Three of the women, for example, who claimed they don't begrudge friends' or acquaintances' successes subsequently made a comment such as this woman's:

"I'm not really envious. It's just that she has this great house, and these perfect kids, and this great job, and I wonder what makes her so special." I have also seen these competition-deniers play "to win" in the ugly Mommy Wars.

As we saw in Chapter 4, we don't shed all of our earlier life-stage attitudes. At midlife, many of us, especially ambitious, accomplished women, are still competitive. Except that now that we no longer define ourselves purely in terms of our titles, we compete for *engagement* and *passion*.

Elaine talked about her biannual get-togethers with a group of former colleagues, all of whom left or were fired from their senior-management jobs. "The arena has changed, but we continue to do battle. Rather than sparring over resources, titles, spans of control, now we compete over who has the most interesting life. Climbed the most mountains. Raised the most venture capital. Published a bestseller. Joined the most boards. Traveled to the most impossible-to-get-to places. As we share our stories, it is painfully obvious if all you did in the past six months is get your golf score down by a few points, you are going to look like a big-time loser.

"It's storytelling—clever, funny, deeply personal, and usually with a bit of spin. But do we feel the pressure to have a really good story for the next meeting? You better believe it. It's a strange sort of support group, but it works."

Perhaps it is because we still have some competitive desires that we feel uncomfortable about that we want to find environments and friends that will not bring out these behaviors. But reaching midlife doesn't mean we attain sainthood or become a completely different person.

Competitiveness is connected to our desire to achieve. Many women are still striving to achieve, even if in a different arena than in the past. No one wants to devote their later years to becoming a really crappy painter or writer or fund-raiser. But at the same time the competitiveness is different. Instead of thinking, "Your success is my failure" (which is a male form of social comparison), for many it's, "Your success has spurred me to pursue my success. It motivates me, because I compare myself to you, and I want to do as well as you (maybe even better). Otherwise I will feel like I haven't done my best, or that I've walked away from a challenge because I'm frightened of failure."

Rather than denying competitiveness, it is far more honest to recognize it and manage its uglier manifestations.

Looking for More and Different Kinds of Friends

"I want to meet interesting, uncompetitive women who will stimulate me."

"I was at this women's networking event and all these women seemed so smug and self-congratulatory. Like they were saying: 'We are women. Look how we connect with each other.' But there was a huge undertone of loneliness and sadness."

"One day you wake up and realize everyone you know is connected to your work and therefore not an intimate or someone who can stretch you in new ways, or are former friends from when your kids were younger, but now the kids are gone you have nothing in common."

If at midlife our friendships are a critical part of our lives, we are nevertheless looking for something different than when we were younger. Now we care more than ever about who our friends are as human beings. As Marlene put it: "Ten years ago I decided that I would never again sustain a relationship with anyone who is cruel, unkind, or uncaring. This may seem like a no-brainer, but I think that when we're young, we often tolerate behaviors in friends that we don't tolerate in midlife. Life is too short to have friendships in which there is one-upmanship, envy, or malice."

In the process of working and/or child-raising many women did not sustain old relationships or cultivate new ones, and this is now a source of significant regret. This was particularly true of the women who had devoted earlier years to being successful in a corporate environment. As Philippa said, "When I was deep into the ambitious part of my career, I had no time for friends. When I had kids, friends were based on proximity and the age of their kids."

Many midlife women are lonely—especially the more ambitious ones who wore a mask in their corporate careers to fit in and move ahead. They modeled the reserve that characterizes successful men, having felt they would not be seen as serious if they engaged in more feminine bonding behaviors. I have many female friends and clients who confide in me saying, "You are the only one who I am telling this to," and as often as not, proceed with a story that is not particularly revelatory. But when you've spent twenty years being guarded, it's hard to know what is intimate; indeed it's hard to know what you are really feeling.

As one woman said, "I spent my career at a corporation and I parked all my emotions. I never really learned to identify my feelings because feelings were girlie and indulgent." These women would never talk intimately about themselves except to someone they see as a confidante. (Interestingly, I have noticed younger women are more open with each other and are more prepared to discuss deep-seated feelings, even if it makes them look "weak" or confused. They are less inclined to edit themselves for the sake of appearances.)

At midlife many women want to broaden their network—for intellectual and social reasons, as much as professional ones. They join book clubs or women's clubs so that they can meet people outside their normal business milieu and, as one woman put it, "Learn from them. I wanted a safe [read: uncompetitive] environment where I could be introduced to what other women were thinking and reading, and basically just connect. The more interesting women you know, the more you learn about how interesting the world is."

These women actively look to expand their number of friends, whether married or single. For example, after ten years Kimberley's relationship suddenly ended with little explanation or discussion. As she was trying to come to terms with this profound emotional upheaval, she thought, "How can I improve different aspects of my life now that I have to start over? My circle was limited. I had a very close old friend who gave me unconditional emotional support during my grieving period. I also had my professional relationships, but they didn't go beyond a superficial connection. I wanted to develop a closer bond with more women."

On the theory that like attracts like, she invited fifteen friends and acquaintances for a get-together, and asked them to each bring a friend whom she didn't know who they thought she would like. The group now meets monthly, attracting about seventy-five people and is growing.

How they function is representative of how women interact with each other and what they want at midlife. "There is the assumption that people will like each other, as opposed to test each other," Kimberley says. "We ask nothing of them, except bring a friend, which in modern women's lives is unusual. But the other part is that we recognize that the professional and the personal are intertwined. Most of us have a volunteer or community or artistic interest. We want to share these, and if others are interested, solicit their support. It's about meeting genuinely nice people whom I would want to welcome into my home."

Of course one person's meat is another's poison. Many introverted women say they would rather go for dental surgery than attend a women's networking event, even if it wasn't business-related. And if it was business-related, it would be even worse. Joanne, the head of training for a financial institution, attended a "women in business event" because she wanted to meet "interesting new people. But when I arrived I felt like a piece of fresh meat in a pond of piranhas, as if I had stamped over my forehead, *million-dollar budget for consultants.*"

As an introvert, I'm not hugely comfortable at large networking events. Okay, actually I hate them. But as a yenta, I love to introduce interesting women to other interesting women. When I was fifty, I handpicked a group of twelve people whom I knew directly or through friends and clients, and invited them to my house. The women all made a connection; all opened the kimono on their personal lives (three of them had slept with the same man), and there was the normal bitching and laughter that occur when almost good girls get together. There was a no-holds-barred discussion on topics ranging from partners, kids, sex, exes to bosses, clients, and aging. Toward the end of the evening, one woman said, "Wow, this was great. Look how many business cards I've collected." Fortunately she was the first to leave. She missed the point of the get-together, thus providing us with delicious stuff to talk about.

It's Not Gossip, It's Critical Analysis

"The best part of going to people events with my best friend, is the postevent analyses."

"I know this woman who said she doesn't talk with her friends about anything other than events, books, and family activities. I thought 'how emotionally and intellectually impoverished her life must be.'"

Some years ago, I overheard a conversation at a cocktail party that left a lasting impression on me. A woman was telling a story to a friend about a mutual acquaintance whose fortunes had turned very nasty. I could tell by her tone of voice that although she was feigning concern, she was relishing every delicious detail of this poor woman's fate. Touché, I thought when her friend aggressively interrupted her and said, "I'm glad you brought this up. How can we *help* her?"

Margaret Meade supposedly told one of her daughters that she would never make a good anthropologist, because she didn't enjoy gossip. I like this story because it shows what gossip really is—a manifestation of an interest in human nature. I am not a gossip in the sense that I don't talk about the sad or unfortunate or just plain awful things that happen to people. I hate hearing about people being fired, or marriages breaking apart, or people getting sick. In other words, bad things happening to people, which they would not want others to be dishing about. What interests me is the "why" people do things (what many of the women described as the "psychoanalyzing" they love to engage in).

So just as in school you learned how to do a critical analysis of a novel, gossip is how we understand ourselves and our world better. In part it's *social comparison*. One woman, for example, commenting on her monthly get-together with her inner circle said, "We ask each other nosy, obnoxious questions to see if what we are feeling and thinking is normal. Am I the only one who gets pissed or bored with my husband, who fantasizes about affairs, who thinks so-and-so is completely repressed or stupid? I want to deepen my insights and check them against others."

Or as another said, "When we discuss what each other is thinking it's a kind of self-affirmation. It's saying 'Yes, I'm like you and you're like me.' This deepens the bond."

This self-affirmation is a critical component of gossiping. As one woman said, "It's a way of making myself feel better. When I've psychoanalyzed the crap out of someone, then I feel I'm not as stupid or needy as she is, ergo I'm better than she is."

But although most of us do engage in critical analysis, some women are uncomfortable with the idea of gossip. Many of the women surveyed made comments like, "I don't gossip. I think it's mean."

But as Zara said, quite rightly, I believe: "Yes, I gossip, there I said it. But many women pretend they don't and are quite crafty about it. They start with a mild comment about someone, and then, bam, they're off to the races, tearing the poor woman to shreds. I'm just as guilty. Although I like to think I'm just assisting in the understanding of another woman, it really is a way of feeling smugly superior because we're not messing up the way they are. We judge ourselves by our intentions, but everyone else by their behavior."

One woman elegantly summed up another role of gossip. "It offers a relatively harmless and temporary release from the shackles of moral rectitude and political correctness," she said. And in case you think it's wrong to gossip, according to evolutionary psychologists, we are hard-wired to gossip; they describe it as the human equivalent of "social grooming" among primates. Language evolved to allow us to gossip, to fill the time-consuming grooming gap.

So we gossip for many reasons—to understand what is normal, to test our beliefs against that of others ("is it just me, or do you also find . . . ?"), to pump ourselves up, and to express ourselves. One woman plays what she calls the "bed, wed, off with his head game" (who should you have sex with, marry, dispose of?) with her closest friends. She says, "We list three men of common corporate acquaintance. It's a very empowering exercise for women who sense they have been on the receiving end of such an assessment. Men talk about who they want to have sex with in the workplace all the time."

I think of "critical analysis" as a special talent no different from being able to sing. At its best, it shows insight into others, curiosity about people and the world, and an understanding of individual differences. Only a small percentage of women are truly gifted in this.

Six Types of Friends

"There are nuances in my relationships with each of my friends. With one, I'll share anxieties about child-rearing that a childless friend might not be able to help me with. With another, I'll discuss aging parents. Still another will be the right person with whom to discuss my marriage, work, or other concerns."

"I have my A, B, and C lists."

To some extent our personality will determine the nature of our friendships. Introverts, for example, compared to extroverts, have fewer friends, and the friendships will typically be of a closer nature; extroverts will have more friends and will make less distinction between their friends (best friend, next best friend, and so on). But we all have different kinds of friendships that meet varying needs. As you read about these six types, think about your friends—in what categories they fall, and how they would describe you.

The Inner Circle

They are your best, or almost best friends. Some you may have known since high school or university—the shared history provides a special intimacy.

You talk about everything from your sex life (or lack of one), to affairs and partners. No foreplay, no pretenses—you expose the awful, raw truth, and you know they are there to catch you. You couldn't have managed through some pretty nasty experiences without them.

It's almost, but not completely "no-holds-barred." Although everything is put on the table for dissection, not everything is always dissected with complete honesty. Sometimes when they do stupid things like repeat the same pattern in their relationships, you bite your tongue. Once you told one of them the awful bitchy truth and she didn't talk to you for a year. You think, "You can't tell someone something unless they are ready to *hear* it. Why hurt them or risk pissing them off?" But if you think she is doing something really dumb or dangerous, or that she can hear you, you will take the risk.

In any case, you may share the awful bitchy truth to other close friends, what you can't say to her face.

The Outer Circle

You met them through your work, a women's networking event, or later in life when you found yourself single or the kids left home. With some you have shared interests and enjoy doing things with them. With others you talk about work/life issues and your highs and lows at work. You gossip about others in the network when they are not there. You may be mildly competitive with some of them. You complain to mutual friends about some of their personalities. Members of your outer circle do not know the intimate details of your life, and you know about as much as you care to about theirs. Sometimes you worry that some of them would like to be part of your inner circle, but think, "I just can't connect to her in that way."

The Networker

Many of these fair-weather friends only call you when they need something from you, whether an introduction to a client or a recommendation for a dressmaker; otherwise you might as well be dead. At midlife this can get on your nerves. You fire all but the ones who are amusing, as they often can be, or will help you if you need it.

This group also includes the accountants who keep a running ledger in their head of everything they have ever done for you. They see relationships as based on exchange—"I'll scratch your back, you scratch mine." They have a stronger memory of what they've done for you, than what you've done for them. You find their book-keeping approach to friendship silly and irritating (unless you are also an accountant type). Otherwise you think, "I want an emotionally satisfying connection, not a relationship based purely on what will be of instrumental value. I'm too old for this."

The Big Sister

You are one of a lucky few if you have this person in your life. She cares deeply about your welfare. She is one of the only people who will tell you honestly when you have done something stupid, even if it hurts, and you can "hear" her. She has coached you through endless travails with your work, kids, partner, friends, parents, basically any and all issues. You think of her as your life mentor. You feel bad sometimes that she gives you so much more than you give her, but you understand that she gets emotional satisfaction from supporting you. If you have a "little sister," you follow your big sister as a role model.

The Self-absorbed

Many friends fall into this category. What they have in common is that they have made themselves into their own hobby.

She may think she is endlessly interesting, a role model to all, and talk incessantly about herself. Your role as her audience is to allow her to bask in the glow of your imagined approval. This is how she pumps up her ego. She has narcissistic tendencies, suffering from delusions of admiration. She is the star of everything she talks about and tells you about what people say about her. She can also be very boring. Because she is so self-absorbed she assumes you care about everything that she has done and can go on and on about herself without checking to see if you are even vaguely interested.

On the other hand, she may be interesting and amusing when she shares her neurotic obsessions. And she may even be capable of giving back to you when you need her.

Do you fire her? You do a cost-benefit analysis. If she is high-maintenance, has no concern for your feelings, you get nothing out of the relationship, and is boring, yes. But if she is smart, capable of paying attention to you, and occasionally says something interesting, you decide to keep her as part of your inner or outer circle.

The Needy

She also needs you to bolster her ego but in a different way. Rather than looking for applause for her accomplishments, she is looking for sympathy, or advice, or for you to shore up her self-esteem. She can be charming when she talks about her inner child, or she can be a mess, endlessly demanding, easily hurt, prone to anger, interpreting the mildest comment as an insult. Although over the years the outlines of her stories may shift, at the core the issues are the same.

Do you fire her? You consider it, but if you feel you are an important source of support for her or can really help her, you think, "Well, maybe this isn't so much fun, but I can make a difference in her life. She needs me. It would be wrong to walk away."

Dealing with One-Way Relationships

How do you deal with one-way relationships? Many midlife women say they are not interested in maintaining friendships where there is no reciprocity, where their needs are not as important as the others'. Not surprisingly, the women whom I would describe as self-absorbed or "accountants" were particularly likely to make this comment. But you can't expect all your friendships to be balanced. Personally I have many satisfying relationships where others' emotional and intellectual needs are met much more than mine. This doesn't bother me, as long as I find them amusing or can help them. The only expectation I have is that they don't hurt me. I don't feel that all my relationships should meet my needs as well as theirs, just as my "big sister's" needs will not be met as much as mine. And of course they are meeting some needs, if only to feel good about myself for being helpful. It is only with my inner circle, a very small number, that I expect or even want, reciprocity. So who at midlife do you fire or edit from your life? You be the judge in terms of what you want and need from your friends.

Why We Age Better than Men in the Ways That Count

"You'd think by the number of books on menopause that the most interesting thing about us is what happens to our hormones."

"Women become more curious and exploratory as they get older, men become less."

"I do not know one fifty-five-year-old guy whom I would describe as enthusiastic or bursting with a sense of possibility. I can describe most of my friends this way."

I have not talked about *physical* aging in this book, but I think I can summarize how we all feel. Even if we love the liberating psychological aspects of not caring about how others see us, when it comes to the physical, well, it can be a bitch. (ATTENTION GUYS: Please show sensitivity and skip the rest of this paragraph.) There is not a woman I know over forty years old, including the least vain among us, who has not at some point looked at herself in the mirror and pulled up her jowls to see how much has fallen or what she would look like if she had a face-lift. Every woman has at least one part of her body that she is unhappy about, whether it's teacher's arm (tricep flapping), bra back (skin flopping over the bra), waist roll (think about it), cottage-cheese thighs, or elephant-skin knees. But at least it gives us something to complain about with our friends. (One consolation: Our pores get smaller.)

And here's some irritating news: men's faces age better than ours. They've been exfoliating and massaging their skin daily since they started shaving, have more collagen, have not been burying their faces in makeup for decades, and have thicker skin. It's not fair, they don't appreciate it, but there you have it. More galling, some are now upping this unfair advantage by using antiaging creams. But we age better where it really counts—in terms of our personalities, socially and emotionally. We also live longer, of course.

As I was wrapping up this book I said to my husband, "Maybe we could do a husband/wife thing, kind of like that woman Cathi Hanauer who edited *The Bitch in the House*, which was followed by her husband's book *The Bastard on the Couch*. Except, instead of calling it *Women Confidential*, you could call it *Guys, Nothing Confidential*."

"No, that would be impossible," he replied (thoughtfully and sensitively overlooking the insult). "Your book is based on women telling the truth, but men don't want to tell the truth, they may not even *know* what it is."

Women don't always *tell* the truth either, but we are far more likely to *know* it. Why? Because we have spent our lives paying attention to and caring about manymore things in our environment than men have and because we have had to respond to manymore needs. As a result of our social comparison tendencies and differences from men in our relational style, we also *know* more about people and emotions.

We are more interpersonally sensitive, adept at reading nonverbal cues, intellectually curious, less concerned about presenting "well," and have a wider range of behaviors in our repertoire, all characteristics of psychological wellness. As Dr. Merrijoy Kellner,

Professor Emerita of The Institute for Life Course and Aging at the University of Toronto said "At midlife woman are engaged in more aspects of the world, more prepared to take risks, more open to and looking for new experiences, more interpersonally flexible, and have a greater tolerance for ambiguity; this is why they age more successfully."

In part I think we can thank that pesky approval-seeking we engaged in when we were younger, constantly modifying our behavior to solicit acceptance. Men, having less pressure on them to please others and therefore being less attuned to and molded by their environment, are more fully baked by the time they are in their twenties (and as one friend said, "crispy fried by the time they are fifty"). I think well-known feminist artist Judy Chicago, the producer of *The Dinner Party* amusingly captured this when she said at a talk, "There are three faces to men: pleasant, jocular, and angry."

I did my PhD on the psychological underpinnings of the Type-A behavior pattern (the hard-driving competitive behavior linked to coronary heart disease). Men's sense of self has traditionally been primarily tied to their work accomplishments. (Gen Y men seem to have a broader source of self-definition.) Women, in contrast, derive their sense of self from more areas of life—their children, friends, partners, nonwork involvements, and so on. So at midlife these women have manymore opportunities to be engaged in the world because of their more diffuse sources of self-fulfillment.

This is why men and women tend to react differently to job loss at midlife. When faced with age discrimination and the frequent need to downscale work desires to lower "status" work, the men often behave as described in the New Deal relationships. It is a huge blow to their identity and many become depressed. The women, in contrast, often see this as an opportunity to do something different and interesting with their work lives. They look at their income needs in practical terms, not as a marker for status.

When exploring new opportunities, they say things like, "Well, I still need to pay off my mortgage which is $X. Although this is less than what I was making before, it will be wonderful to do something new. I can manage."

My present research also suggests that men and women are looking for different things from their work at this life stage. In a study with 330 employed managers and professionals between the ages of forty and forty-nine on motivational preferences based on motivational types, the top motivation for women was "Self-developer," for men "Autonomy-seeking," with men scoring significantly lower on Self-developer than did women. In other words, midlife women want to grow, develop themselves, and take professional risks while men want to be left alone to do their own thing.

This restlessness is consistent with women's responses to my survey question, "Are you in transition?" to which about 80 percent said "yes." (Most of them were responding metaphorically as nearly all of them were employed.) Many made comments like this one. "Always in transition. Even more so now. Questioning myself. Wanting to learn more and test myself. Wondering what more I can do, experience."

And here is some more good news for women on the work front. Sussannah Kelly, Managing Director of Boyden Global Executive Search has interviewed hundreds of people in her search practice as well as in her former senior human resource roles. She says, "Whether we are talking scientists, accountants, CEOs, people who work for government, NGOs, or corporations, women see more colors, while men are more monochromatic. Because women are more layered, curious, are constantly learning and wanting to grow, and have less ego baggage, they are better adapted to the challenges of the contemporary workplace. And in general, whether we are talking about work or not, are more interesting."

But of course you already knew that.

Summary Dish: Fourteen Secrets of Success for Work and Life from Women for Women

What does it mean to have a life worth living? This is the distilled wisdom of what interesting midlife women have learned about creating a life they feel good about which honors their most important values, needs, and glorious complexities.

- **Know and act on what is really important to you.** Don't put up with a bad situation in any significant area of your life. Things don't get better without conscious awareness, choice, and action. Ask yourself on a weekly basis: Am I happy? Which of my important needs are being met, and which are being neglected? What do I need to do for greater life satisfaction? Your life is not a dress rehearsal.
- **Understand what you are really good at.** Know and be able to articulate your core skills and the environments in which you are happiest and most productive. Express your talents by finding or designing your work to reflect your strengths and who you are. Your unique talents are gifts that you need to use.
- **Be authentic.** Refuse to compromise your personality or repress important parts of yourself. Be honest about expressing your feelings and values when the cost of not doing so will be a violation of your own moral code. Do what you know is the *right* thing. Quite simply, if the cost of doing something is that you will feel that you have sold your soul, don't do it.
- **Define yourself independently of your roles—as mother, daughter, worker, leader, friend, partner.** Don't make any one role the centerpiece of your identity. Your life is rich and offers huge opportunity for meaning and satisfaction through many channels. Have diverse interests and seek fulfillment through all of them.

- **Make your own decisions.** Take your own counsel: throw away the people-pleasing scripts. Maintain an independent stance in regard to received wisdom. Create a life that works for you independent of others' views and expectations.

- **Pay attention to the niggling voice that says, "I'm not happy."** It's telling you something important. Welcome rather than repress it. Identify the issues. Understand that change takes time and courage—there is no bromide for dealing with significant life issues. Get support from people who care about you. Seek professional counseling if you need it.

- **Think in terms of life chapters.** You can have it all, but not all at once. Devote each chapter to satisfying one need fully rather than living in a gray zone where all your needs are compromised. Think about what you are getting, not what you are giving up. Be mindful and in the moment.

- **Cherish and grow your friendships.** Your friends are your lifeline. Do not allow your busyness to interfere with maintaining significant relationships. Enrich your life by cultivating interesting new people for your network beyond your normal affiliations. Find a "big sister," and be a "big sister." Don't think of your friendships with an accountant's mentality—I scratch your back, you scratch mine. Don't keep score of who has done more for whom. Be there for your friends in the bad times.

- **Give back to individuals and the community.** Be a mentor and role model to younger women. Care about people and the environment. Many women cite giving back to others as one of their chief sources of fulfillment.

- **Invest in yourself and stretch yourself.** Be bold and take risks knowing you can deal with uncertainty. Keep on learning. Try something new. Involve yourself in previously neglected life arenas. Finish your unfinished business. Reconnect to earlier career themes. If it doesn't feel a bit scary, chances are it's not very interesting.

- **Accept others for who they are.** Be respectful of individual differences whether in your children, partners, or staff. Do not try to change them. Appreciate who they *are*, rather than bemoaning who they are not. If you get angry with someone because they are not behaving the way you would like them to, ask yourself: What gives me the right to demand or expect them to conform to my standards? Which needs of mine am I projecting on them?

- **Edit out the stuff that doesn't add value to your life.** Get rid of commitments that drain you emotionally. For every commitment ask yourself: How does this make my life fuller? What would be the price of not doing this? How will I feel about that? Look at all areas of your life. For everything you own, ask yourself: Does the cost of maintaining this (whether dusting it or paying for it) enrich who I am and how I feel?

- **Have a healthy relationship to money.** Start saving when you are young. Make wise financial decisions. Distinguish between what you want and need. Be financially literate. Don't define yourself by your stuff, salary, or bank balance. Living within your means buys you freedom. If you downsize financial commitments that own you, you upsize your life. Don't use purchases as a way of satisfying/meeting unexpressed emotional needs, or money as a measure of self-worth.

- **Be kind to yourself and others.** Look after your body. Be emotionally and spiritually healthy. Be generous with your praise both in celebrating your own accomplishments and those of others. Think of the legacy you would like to leave behind. Live a life you would be proud for your children and others to emulate.

This is perhaps the most important secret of all.

ACKNOWLEDGMENTS

I am privileged to have in my life so many wise, interesting, and funny women. All of you were a key source of intelligence as you passed on not only your own stories, but also those of your friends.

Thank you to my insightful sounding boards and dear friends Tamara Weir-Bryan, Jane Hutcheson, and Lynn Moses who throughout the writing process helped me build and refine my ideas, and were always there to analyze the subjects in depth. I am also indebted to Lynne Everatt for her comments on the manuscript, not to mention her wry take on the issues.

I am very grateful to *Globe and Mail* editors Terry Brodie and Joan Ramsay, and CareerJournal.com managing editor Laura Lorber for providing a forum to test some of the ideas in *Women Confidential*.

This book could not have been written without the hundreds of women who told me their stories and shared their observations with such candor and generosity. Whether through surveys, follow-up interviews, or simply chance meetings, you were devastatingly honest. I owe a particular debt of gratitude to the life mentors, many of whom spent a month completing the "nosy questionnaire" to ensure it best captured their feelings and experiences so that *Women Confidential* could make a difference in other women's lives. Thank you for your insights; they provide the backbone of *Women Confidential*. I wish I could mention all of your names, and thank you personally.

Thank you to associate publisher (nonfiction) Susan Renouf, copy editor Jenny Bradshaw, art director Kong Njo, and agent Robert Mackwood for enabling this project to come to fruition.

And finally thank you to the most important contributor to this book's success, my husband, Andrew Weiner, for debating with me on all the delicious issues, and as always for being the best editor in the world.

APPENDIX

DISCUSSION GUIDE:
Questions for you to think about or discuss with your friends or reading group

Chapter One
Almost Good Girls:
Meeting Expectations during the Approval-seeking Years

What kind of messages did you get about being "nice," and how did they impact you?

Were you a good, almost good, or bad girl?

What were your earliest images of work?

Did you know what you wanted to do professionally?

What were your formative career experiences?

What were your experiences of working and mothering?

Chapter Two
The Awful Truth about Corporate Life:
Organizations Are Built by Men for Men

Can you be authentic in organizations?

How important is being authentic to you? What does it mean to you?

Are the rhythms of organizations unfriendly to women? What have your experiences been?

Who do you identify with in the archetypes of women who populate organizations? Why?

Do/did you ever feel "different"? Are you someone who feels comfortable with or alienated by corporate life? Why and how?

Which of the stories and comments do you identify with most?

Chapter Three
Besieged and Restless:
The Emotional Mathematics of Contemporary Career Maladies

Are you suffering from career malaise?

Which of the contemporary types of career distress described are you dealing with?

Which of the stories and comments do you identify with most?

Chapter Four
Moving Forward with Grace:
Who You Are and What You Need in This Life Chapter

Are you in transition from earlier to later work or other desires?

Have your values changed?

What did you used to want? What do you want now?

Which of the eight motivational types do you identify with most? What conflicts between top motivators are you grappling with? How can you solve these challenges?

Which of the stories and comments do you identify with most?

Chapter Five
Facing the Inner Demons:
The Anatomy of Moving On

Do you have any regrets about your work choices?

Are you dealing with any of the emotional challenges, such as dealing with uncertainty and overcoming fear, described in this chapter?

Are there moves you would like to make but are having difficulty with? What is holding you back?

How can you overcome these challenges? Who can help you?

Do you have a healthy relationship to money? Why or why not?

Which of your needs do you want to satisfy in this life chapter?

Which of the stories and comments do you identify with most?

Chapter Six
Women in Motion:
The Paths to Midlife Renewal

Do you agree that you can't really reinvent yourself?

What are your core strengths, attributes, and values?

How can you reconfigure your underlying strengths?

Which of the paths described represent a viable and desirable option for you?

Which of the stories and comments do you identify with most?

Which piece of advice from the women resonates the most for you?

What advice would you like to act on?

Chapter Seven
Motherhood:
What We Know and Wish We Had Known

Do you agree that mothers compete with each other or "spin" the truth?

Have you ever experienced what I called the Mommy Wars? Do you participate?

Which of the six contemporary mother archetypes do you identify with?

How would you describe your parenting style?

Do you think one can be proud of one's child or do you think that mothers take too much credit or blame for what their children are like? Why or why not? What are you proud of?

Are you experiencing or have you experienced guilt in terms of work/life choices that you have made?

Do you have any regrets about your behavior as a mother? What would you do differently if you could do it over again?

Which of the stories and comments do you identify with most?

Which piece of advice from the women resonates the most for you?

What advice would you like to act on?

Chapter Eight
Childlessness:
It's a Complicated Story

If you are childless: Was it choice or chance?

Do you think women should be advised to have their children when they are younger?

Do you feel there are underlying stigmas against childless women?

Which of the stories and comments do you identify with most?

Chapter Nine
Relationships:
What We Want, Know, or Should Know by Now

Which of the nine contemporary relationship archetypes do you identify with most in terms of your present and/or past relationships? Why?

If you are divorced, what was the trajectory? How did you cope? How do you feel about decisions you made?

What advice would you give to someone considering divorce?

If you are single, how do you feel about that? Are you "looking" for someone? Do you have "relationship ambivalence"?

Your sex life and affairs: you decide what you want to discuss.

Do you agree that some women, by virtue of their personality, may be more likely to have affairs?

Which of the stories and comments do you identify with most?

Which piece of advice from the women resonates the most for you?

What advice would you like to act on?

Chapter Ten
Women Confidential:
Secrets of the Sisterhood

Have you ever been deeply hurt by a friend? What happened and how do you feel about it now? What would you have done differently? (It's never too late . . . what can you do to change the situation?)

How important are your female friendships to you? What do you look for in your friendships? Do you agree that the character of female friendships is different than that with a male partner?

In which of the six types of friends do yours fall?

How would your friends "type" you?

Have you ever fired or are you considering firing a friend? Why?

Do you agree that women age better than men in terms of their personal interests and desires? Why?

Which of the stories and comments do you identify with most?

Which of the fourteen secrets resonates the most for you?

What advice would you like to act on?

If you had one piece of advice to pass on to a younger woman, what would it be?

THE NOSY QUESTIONNAIRE

[Author's note: Here is the survey the life mentors completed.]

All responses will be treated with extreme delicacy. There will be no details that could possibly identify you.

Your story and the insights you have gained are important to women of all ages. Please answer as many of the following questions as you want, or use these questions as a guideline to tell me your story.

Thinking back over your work-life and career . . .

Are you satisfied with what you have achieved? Why or why not?

What are sources of disappointment or regret?

What are sources of pride? What were your most significant accomplishments in terms of personal satisfaction?

What was your most spectacular failure? What if anything would you do differently? Why?

Are you satisfied with the "status" you attained in your career?

Are you satisfied with your financial status/savings? Would you save/spend differently if you were doing it over again?

What challenges did you deal with as a woman?

Did you ever feel "different"?

On authenticity: What does it mean to you? Can you be authentic and be successful? Is the corporate world friendly to women and their style/needs? Does working in an organization require you to sell your soul? Why?

Have you made significant career moves? Why?

Do you have any unfinished business? What?

What would you want a young woman to know about work and career/life decisions if she was starting out?

Looking to the future, and thinking about work . . .

What are you excited about?

What are you worried about?

Do you have plans for next chapters after this work chapter? What? What are you looking for at this life juncture? When did you start to think about "what next?"

Do you think about retirement? What does it mean to you? What are your plans for later career professional engagement?

How would you like to contribute?

What kinds of financial concerns, if any, do you have?

Now let's talk about your feelings about your children. And your feelings if you didn't have any children.

If you have children . . .

How old are they?

Are you happy with how they turned out? Why?

Are you disappointed in any way?

What, if anything, would you do differently in terms of how you raised your children?

What issues are you grappling with or did you grapple with vis à vis your changing role as a mother of older children?

Are you comfortable with the amount of time you spent with them?

Did your career interfere with time spent or activities with your kids?

Did you make any sacrifices in terms of your work or your kids? If so, what were they? Are you happy with those decisions?

What are your concerns about your children?

Do you worry about them, and if so, what do you worry about?

Are you confident about their future employability?

Are you happy with your relationship with your children? What is the biggest source of pleasure/disappointment?

What would you want a young woman to know about parenting?

If you didn't have children . . .

Do you regret this?

Was this something you planned?

What interfered?

Has not having children had an impact on your life, and if so, how?

On parents . . .

Are they alive? If not, how did/are you dealing with their death? Do you think about them? Do you wish you could have done things differently?

Do/did you have any unfinished business with your parents? What would you wish had been different? What would you do differently?

Do your parents occupy a significant time investment? Can you fulfill your responsibilities comfortably?

Do/did you behave with your parents as you would wish your children to behave toward you?

On partners . . . (Please forgive my nosiness—answer what you want)

Anything you can tell me regarding the nature of your attachments: Married for many years and still in love/bored/happy to have a companion . . . single and lonely/worried about being alone when you are older/loving your independence/somewhere in between . . . recently divorced and worried about your age/attractiveness/feeling great . . . reflecting on perfect, passionate love . . . looking for intimacy . . . sex toys? . . . affairs? . . . feelings about monogamy?

If you have been married for a long time, have you redefined your relationship?

Have you dealt with any tragedies? How are you coping?

What are you happy/excited or sad/regretful about?

Any advice for young women? Lessons learned?

Nonwork engagements—volunteer, spiritual, creative, travel, recreation, mentoring . . .

What have you been involved in?

What are you satisfied with? What needs did it fulfill?
How important were these nonwork engagements to you?

What, if anything, do you wish you had done more of?
What interfered?

What regrets do you have?

Looking to the future . . .

What kinds of involvements do you see? What needs will they fulfill?

How important are these nonwork engagements to you?

Do you see any potential obstacles or challenges?

On friendships

Looking back . . .

How important were your friendships?

Did you nurture them? Did you lose any important relationships? Why?

What would you do differently?

Any tragedies associated with your friends? What did you learn?

Advice for young women?

In general . . .

How important are friendships to you?

What do you talk about with your friends? (Work, kids, people/things that piss you off/excite you?)

Do you gossip? Why? About what? What is the role of gossip?

What are you looking for?

Will you do anything to secure or deepen friendships?

On psychological issues

What emotional/psychological challenges have you dealt with?

To what personality traits and emotional characteristics do you attribute your success? Your failures?

Wrapping Up

If you had to distill the most important thing you are regretful about, what would it be?

If you had to distill the most important thing you are proud of, what would it be?

What are the most interesting things you have done in the past five years that gave you a deep sense of satisfaction/pride/renewal?

Overall how do you feel about your future? What are you most optimistic about?

What are you looking for?

If you had to distill the most important thing you are looking for, what would it be?

If you had one piece of advice for a young woman, what would it be?

NOTES

Chapter One

20   Gilbert, N., "What do Women Want?" *The Public Interest* (Winter 2005).

Chapter Two

40   Pfeffer, J.; Sutton, R.I., *The Knowing-Doing Gap: How Smart Companies Turn Knowledge into Action* (Boston: Harvard Business School Press, 2000), p.199.

41   Elder, S., "The Emperor's New Woes," *Psychology Today* (March/April 2005).

42   Committee of 200, *The C200 Business Leadership Index* (Chicago: Northern Trust, 2005).

43   Catalyst Information Center, *Statistical Overview of Women in the Workplace* (Toronto: Catalyst Information Center, 2005).

43   Heilman, M., "Penalties for Success: Reactions to Women Who Succeed at Male Gender-Typed Tasks," *Journal of Applied Psychology* (June 2004).

47   "You'll have to get up early to get one past dear old granny," *National Post* (April 26, 2005).

47   Catalyst, *Women in U.S. Corporate Leadership: 2003* (New York: Catalyst Information Center, 2003).

60   McMurdy, D., "You can't buy a life," *National Post* (November 13, 2004).

60   Families and Work Institute, *Leaders in a Global Economy:*
     A Study of Executive Women and Men (New York: Families
     and Work Institute, May 2003).
60   Levey, L. (New York: Catalyst Information Center) n.t.
62   Steinhauer, Dr. P., "Children and Youth in the 90's:
     The Needy Generation and How to Address their Needs,"
     Address on behalf of the Toronto Board of Health
     (November 21, 1995).

Chapter Three
76   *Globe and Mail* (March 18, 2005) n.a., n.d.
76   Hewlitt, S. A.; Buck Luce, C., "Off-Ramps and On-Ramps:
     Keeping Talented Women on the Road to Success,"
     Harvard Business Review (March 2005).
84   Opten, D., Personal Communication, n.d.
84   Teather, D., "Old, Ugly and Fired," *Salon Magazine*
     (April 8, 2005).

Chapter Four
97   Cited by Bridges, W., *The Way of Transitions: Embracing Life's*
     Most Difficult Moments (Cambridge: Da Capo Press, 2004).
101 Moses, B., *What Next? Find the Work That's Right for You*
     (Dorling Kindersley Ltd., 2006).

Chapter Five
112 Jeffries, S., *Embracing Uncertainty: Breakthrough Methods*
     for Achieving Peace of Mind When Facing the Unknown
     (New York: St. Martin's Press, 2003).

Chapter Six
143 Right Management Consultants, *The Right Stuff* (August 2005).
154 Handy, C., *The Age of Unreason* (Boston: Harvard Business
     School Press, 1989).

Chapter Seven
174 Hewlett, S. A., *Harvard Business Review*, n.d., n.t.
195 Krakovsky, M., "Why One Kid May Be Enough," *Psychology*
     Today (January/February 2005).

196 Owen, M., "Household sterotypes still resilient, studies say," *National Post* (June 25).

Chapter Nine

241 Kingston, A., *The Meaning of Wife* (Toronto: Harper Collins, 2006).

246 "The Illusion of Rejection," *Psychology Today* (January/February 2005).

250 Montenegro, X., "The Divorce Experience: A Study of Divorce at Midlife and Beyond," *AARP Magazine* (May 2004).

254 "Health Plus Magazine Study," *DailyRecord.co.uk* (September 7, 2005).

264 Flora, C., "Sex: The New Leading Indicator," *Psychology Today* (November/December 2004).

Chapter Ten

271 Tayor, S., et. al., "Female Responses to Stress: Tend and Befriend, Not Fight or Flight," *Psychology Review*, 107 (3): 41-429.

273 Yager, J., *Who's That Sitting at My Desk? Workship, Friendship or Foe?* (Stamford, CT: Hannacroix Creek Books, 2004).

281 Dunbar, R., *Grooming, Gossip and the Evolution of Language* (London: Faber and Faber, 1996).

287 Tannen, D., *Talking From 9 to 5: Women and Men at Work* (Whitby: Quill, 1995).

287 Heatherington, L., et. al., "How did you do on that test?: The effects of gender on self-presentation of achievement to vulnerable men," *Sex Roles: A Journal of Research* (August 2001).

288 Chicago, J., Presentation (Toronto: Verity Women's Club, 2005).

289 Career Advisor. BBM Human Resource Consultants Inc. 2005.

289 Kelly, S. of Boyden Global Executive Search, Personal Communication, n.d.